The Negro Population

of Chicago

Otis Dudley Duncan
and Beverly Duncan

The Negro Population

of Chicago

A Study of Residential Succession

THE UNIVERSITY OF CHICAGO PRESS

Library of Congress Catalog Number: 57-5271

THE UNIVERSITY OF CHICAGO PRESS, CHICAGO 37
Cambridge University Press, London, N.W. 1, England
The University of Toronto Press, Toronto 5, Canada

This monograph serves a twofold purpose. First, it is a significant addition to the fund of knowledge in sociology; second, it provides a factual foundation for dealing with aspects of one of the more acute problems of the day in the urban United States—the accommodation of the in-migrant Negro to the city. As a volume in the monograph series of the Chicago Community Inventory of the University of Chicago, this work of the Duncans was designed primarily to report the results of a sociological research project. The findings, however, in addition to their contribution to social research, have a direct relevance to the problems created by the great migration of Negroes to cities of the North and West during the forties—a migration which gives every evidence of continuing for some time to come. In consequence, this volume will have as much interest to urban "social engineers"—those interested in policy formation and the administration of programs designed to ameliorate the problems of urban living—as to social scientists.

As a research monograph, this work contributes to three subfields of sociology: urban sociology, human ecology, and race relations. In the field of urban sociology this is a piece of empirical research that describes important aspects of urban growth and the accommodation of an in-migrant population. In the closely related field of human ecology this volume constitutes a longitudinal case study of succession in population type and land use. To the field of race or intergroup relations this investigation contributes a quantitative and ecological frame for investigating the personal and cultural dimensions of the accommodation and assimilation of an in-migrant minority group. In its treatment of available data the monograph will be found to meet high standards of technique and objectivity with a minimum of speculation. The findings are presented for the reader to make his own policy interpretations.

As a contribution to the social engineer for social planning and action programs, this study has several significant facets. Perhaps most immediately evident are its implications for city planning, for public housing, and for programs of urban renewal. The authors' description of the stages of "consolidation" and "piling up" point, in fact, to the basic contributing factors in the formation of the urban slum—the exploitative land use which threatens entire metropolitan communities with blight. The economic and social obstacles which prevent the in-migrant Negro from occupying residential areas in accordance with standards of the white population in respect of room density and living facilities produce the patterns of occupancy which are described. Policy-makers and administrators concerned with the eradication or prevention of the slum and with urban renewal will find in the processes of "invasion" and "succession" depicted by the Duncans the critical points at which intervention is necessary if these goals are to be achieved.

In fact, the process of "piling up" which is described may be regarded as the consequence of the disparity between Negro income and housing costs, on the one hand, and the social and attitudinal factors which tend to create a Negro ghetto, on the other. Until a way is found to deal with these basic economic and social factors, the processes described in this volume will possibly produce urban slums more rapidly than present agencies and programs can clear them.

City planners, urban renewal authorities, and housing agencies by no means represent the only planning and administrative groups who will be interested in this volume. Private and public welfare and health agencies; persons and institutions concerned with intergroup relations; educators, public and private; civic and governmental agencies; and labor, business, and industrial groups will also find much of value. For in analyzing the most important change in the composition of the population of Chicago in our generation, the Duncans have provided an accumulation of facts that cannot be ignored by any person or agency responsible for planning or administering an action program in Chicago or, for that matter, in any large city faced with a similar situation.

This monograph has been prepared as one of the projects of co-operative research between the Chicago Community Inventory of the University of Chicago, the Office of the Housing and Redevelopment Coordinator, and the Chicago Plan Commission. It represents a further example of what it is hoped will be a demonstration of the mutual advantages of the close co-operation between university research workers and planning and administrative personnel. Through such co-operation the techniques of research can be used to illuminate the difficult problems which confront the administrator and to lay a factual foundation to facilitate, and to provide a sound basis for, policy formation.

PHILIP M. HAUSER, Director
Chicago Community Inventory
University of Chicago

This study was carried out with two distinct, though related, purposes in mind. First, it attempts to meet, in part, the demand for factual information concerning trends in the characteristics and distribution of the Negro population in Chicago. The extent of this demand is indicated by the large number of inquiries on this subject directed to the Chicago Community Inventory by civic leaders, businessmen, planning officials, race-relations workers, and others. Although many of the data in the study are available in published sources, their collation and accurate interpretation are tasks that often involve greater resources of time and analytical skill than the citizen or official has at his disposal. The data are scattered in several publications, they are presented in a variety of forms, and their interpretation requires a knowledge of many technical statistical definitions. Moreover, much of the available statistical information is not published or is published in such a form that extensive calculations must be performed to secure useful summary figures. The tables and charts in this monograph give answers to many of the frequently asked questions about Chicago's Negro population, though many other questions cannot be answered with these or any other extant statistics.

The second purpose of the monograph is to advance the scientific understanding of the structure and development of the contemporary urban community. Viewed in this light, The Negro Population of Chicago is an ecological "case study." The case is not necessarily considered to be a "typical" one; indeed, there are grounds for believing that it approaches an "extreme type" in many respects. There is no doubt that many of the processes observed in Chicago have counterparts in other large cities which have likewise experienced a rapid growth in Negro population and the development of a segregated residential pattern. But any useful generalization about how these processes work in most cities can be derived only from the comparative study of an adequate sample of cities. Meanwhile, the Chicago study provides a number of suggestive hypotheses and develops some analytical techniques that may prove useful elsewhere. It is hoped that further research will refine the hypotheses and improve the techniques.

The combination of the "practical" and "scientific" objectives in one monograph has, perhaps, stylistic disadvantages. The data are presented in a more extended form than would be necessary for an audience of technical experts, whereas the attempt to test somewhat complex hypotheses entails some exposition of technicalities having no great interest to the non-specialist. To help overcome these problems, a considerable amount of material has been placed in appendixes, and results have been described with no more than the necessary minimum of technical language. The first chapter provides a quick overview of the main conclusions and should serve to guide the reader to those sections of the study which interest him most.

While accepting full responsibility for all conclusions and interpretations and for the accuracy of computations and factual statements, the authors wish to express their thanks to the persons and agencies whose co-operation made possible the study's completion.

The statistical compilation and analysis were supported, in part, by the Office of the Housing and Redevelopment Coordinator of the City of Chicago and the Chicago Plan Commission on the basis of their arrangement for co-operative research with the Chicago Community Inventory. The other major source of support was a grant from the Social Science Research Committee of the Division of the Social Sciences, University of Chicago. Important parts of the analysis were made possible by the co-operation of the United States Bureau of the Census and the Illinois Department of Public Health in furnishing unpublished statistical tabulations.

The statistical computations were carried out under the supervision of Richard W. Redick and Gerald S. Newman, research assistants at the Chicago Community Inventory. Clerical assistance was given by Charles Barnes, Alexander Broel-Plateris, David Lane, and Roger Nathan. Maps and charts were prepared by Richard W. Redick and W. Richard Scott. The manuscript was typed by Mella Kessler and Mrs. Clayton Williams. Problems of the design and execution of the study were the subject of a graduate seminar on "Research Methods in Human Ecology" in the Department of Sociology, University of Chicago, in the autumn quarter of 1954; members of the seminar—Levy Cruz, Jacob Feldman, Surinder Mehta, Donnell Pappenfort, and Emerson Seim—made useful suggestions which were incorporated in the study. For valuable advice, criticism, and co-operation, the authors are indebted to their colleagues on the staff of the Chicago Community Inventory, Donald J. Bogue, Philip M. Hauser, and Evelyn M. Kitagawa.

OTIS DUDLEY DUNCAN
BEVERLY DUNCAN

List of Illustrations

Page

Page

Page

Page

Chapter I

Introduction and Summary of Main Findings

A generation or two ago social scientists studying city life were likely
to devote a good deal of attention to problems of assimilation and accul-
turation of the immigrants who composed a large part of America's
growing metropolitan population. This scientific interest mirrored a
popular concern with "Americanization" and issues of immigration con-
trol. At the risk of oversimplification, one can say that the old "im-
migrant problem" has given way to the new "race problem" in public
consciousness and academic inquiry. The "race problem" is not
"new," of course, but events and trends have pushed it more and more
into the focus of attention.

Consider the following illustrative facts. Between 1940 and 1950
the non-white population more than doubled in thirty of the metropolitan areas of the United States, all but one of these being in the North
or West rather than the South, the historical region of Negro concentration. In many instances these large proportional increases in non-
white population involved rather small absolute numbers, but this
was by no means uniformly true. The Detroit metropolitan area, with
173,000 non-whites in 1940, experienced an increase of 109.5 per
cent, to 362,000 in 1950. The Chicago metropolitan area showed a
non-white increase of 80.8 per cent, from 335,000 to 605,000 during
the decade. Smaller, but still large, percentage increases were involved in the growth of the non-white population from 669,000 to
1,046,000 in the New York metropolitan area; from 337,000 to 485,-
000 in the Philadelphia metropolitan area; and from 151,000 to 216,-
000 in the St. Louis metropolitan area. In all these instances of
rapid growth of non-white population, the corresponding increases
of white population were only moderate.

The bare facts of rapid population growth, by themselves, are not especially meaningful. But, examined in a context of other relevant facts, they provide a good part of the explanation for the current exigency of the "race problem." In most of the large metropolitan areas of the North, Negroes made up a very small proportion of the population forty years ago. The northward migration of Negroes in the World War I period brought thousands of migrants into communities hitherto lacking experience in the assimilation of a sizable racial minority. As the flow of migration continued into the prosperous 1920's, competition between whites and Negroes for living space intensified and, on occasion, led to racial violence. White groups organized to resist the movement of Negroes into previously all-white neighborhoods, working both openly and covertly and employing both legal and illegal measures. Prior to the great waves of migration, Negroes had lived in more or less segregated areas, but often in mixed neighborhoods. Economic differentials alone or in combination with ties of kinship and acquaintance would have been sufficient to produce a considerable degree of segregation. When to these factors was added the mobilization of forces to "contain" the Negro population, the outcome was usually a "Negro ghetto," as described in Weaver's book by that title, published in 1948. Incidentally, the development of the "ghetto" was nowhere more evident than in Chicago. Although a considerable degree of arbitrariness attaches to any effort to compare cities, all statistical tests yet proposed by social scientists agree in showing that Negroes are as highly segregated in Chicago as in any metropolitan center in the country.

The influx of Negro population to the great cities of the North was retarded somewhat by the depression of the 1930's but was resumed during the World War II period of labor shortage and the postwar period of prosperity. The Negro migrants of this period had little alternative to seeking out homes in the already overcrowded ghettos. With disproportionately small expansion of the area of the ghetto, the additional numbers resulted in ever greater crowding and congestion, posing a major obstacle to the satisfactory adjustment of the migrants to the community, over and above the difficulties that any newcomers might expect to face. It is small wonder, then, that city officials, police, social workers, public health officers, and the like usually find the "race problem" inextricably involved in their attempts to cope with problems of housing, health, safety, and welfare.

Although the facts of residential segregation and rapid increase of Negro population are widely known, it is doubtful that even generally well-informed citizens and responsible officials are abreast of the changes that have occurred in the dimensions and configuration of the "race problem" in metropolitan areas in recent years. Many of the relevant facts, though not unavailable, cannot be obtained without considerable expenditures of time and energy. It appears, then, that the research worker can make a contribution to the efforts of those who deal with the problematic aspects of Negro life in metropolitan centers by providing in convenient form a compilation and interpretation of the obtainable facts. The assumption is, of course, that ameliorative measures planned on the basis of systematic knowledge have a better chance to succeed than those guided by hunches or limited personal impressions.

At the same time, research on this subject holds much interest for the academic student of the metropolis. When it is observed, for example, that for two consecutive decades the white population of Chicago has decreased while the Negro population has grown, it becomes plain that an understanding of trends in metropolitan community structure requires knowledge about the racial aspects of population increase, social stratification, and residential adjustment.

The present monograph is but the latest in a series of major studies of Negro life in Chicago that have examined the subject from various points of view. The starting point for much of the research of the last third of a century has been the now classic report of the Chicago Commission on Race Relations, The Negro in Chicago (1922),[1] which grew out of a study of the 1919 race riot and the conditions that produced it. Another important early study is Frazier's The Negro Family in Chicago (1932), a monograph which combined statistical analysis of Negro population characteristics in an ecological frame-

---

1. Works mentioned in this chapter, along with other pertinent studies, are listed in full in the Bibliography at the end of the volume.

work with presentation of historical and documentary materials. During the 1930's extensive compilations of data were undertaken under WPA auspices, eventuating in such sourcebooks as Ogden's The Chicago Negro Community: A Statistical Description (1939) and Scott's Occupational Changes among Negroes in Chicago (1939). The WPA studies, along with other materials, served as a basis for Drake and Cayton's Black Metropolis (1945), which was, however, an anthropological synthesis presented in semipopular style rather than an analytical research report. To conclude a list which could be greatly extended by including studies of smaller scope, mention should be made of Wallace's "Residential Concentration of Negroes in Chicago" (1953). This study, although as yet unpublished, has become known to research workers and race relations experts as a penetrating analysis of racial segregation and its implications for public housing and city planning in Chicago.

Unlike some of the monographs just mentioned, The Negro Population of Chicago is limited to demographic and ecological analyses. Several circumstances suggested the advisability of such a limitation: the accumulation of data from two censuses not yet fully exploited; the desirability of making both broad comparisons and detailed analyses of relationships; and the authors' interest in methodological experimentation. Moreover, it seemed best to leave to other hands or to another occasion the task of drawing pragmatic inferences from the findings. The existence of a rich literature on problems of Negro life in Chicago guarantees that the reader seeking a "balanced interpretation" need not terminate his quest here.

By limiting its scope while essaying a thorough treatment of the data falling within its purview, the study seeks to avoid fallacies of the "illustrative method" that mar many discussions of Negro problems. Amid the complex and diversified changes occurring in a large community, one can readily find individual instances that appear to support one or another theory of the causation or consequences of the expansion of the Negro population. But, as it will appear, it is much more difficult to reach simple, broad generalizations on the basis of an analysis of all cases conforming to a stated criterion. At least in the field of population analysis, the fund of data at the disposal of the

investigator permits him to observe the canons of a genuine comparative method. These are illustrated here by meticulous intra-
community comparisons; their extension to comparisons among communities is an urgent directive for social research.

A terminological note is necessary before proceeding to substantive matters. In statistical materials, as well as in the exposition,
reference will be made to both the "Negro" and the "non-white" population. These are not strictly equivalent terms. In accordance with
the usage of the United States Bureau of the Census, the "non-white"
population includes, besides Negroes, persons who, by birth or ances-
try, are Japanese, Chinese, American Indians, or of other non-white
(principally Asiatic) stock. The "racial" classification of the Census
Bureau is based on popular concepts rather than on clear-cut biologi-
cal criteria; therefore, persons of mixed white and Negro parentage
or mixed Indian and Negro parentage are classed as Negroes, unless
recognized in their community of residence as belonging to another
race. Unfortunately, many census tabulations are available only for
the twofold color classification, white versus non-white. Figures for
"non-whites," therefore, are only approximately descriptive of Negroes. In the city of Chicago as a whole, the approximation is ordinarily a good one, because Negroes constituted 96.5 per cent of the
non-white population in 1950. However, in analyses of small areas
within the city this proportion may be quite different. In this study,
where the focus of interest is on the Negro population, data on the
non-white population are employed where there is reason to believe
that they represent the Negro population adequately. In any technical
context the term "non-white" is used to refer to data where both Negroes and other non-whites are included, and the term "Negro" is re-
served for situations where separate data by race are actually available. However, in the phrasing of general conclusions and interpretations, reference may be made to "Negroes," even though the statements are supported only by data for non-whites, if it has been determined that differences between Negroes and other non-whites can
have only a negligible effect on the results. At a few points it is possible to compare Negroes with other non-whites to supplement the
Negro-white comparisons. In Chicago in 1950, not quite two-thirds of

the "other non-whites" were Japanese, nearly one-fifth were Chinese, and about one-sixth were of other non-white races.

The remainder of this chapter consists of a summary of the major procedures and conclusions of the monograph. The summary follows the chapter outline of the volume, to permit the reader to determine readily which parts of the study contain information of most interest to him.

Chapter ii traces the growth of Chicago's Negro population during the twentieth century from 30,000 persons in 1900 to 492,000 in 1950, or from 1.8 to 13.6 per cent of the city's total population. Curiously, the rate of increase in the Negro population over the 1940-50 decade, 77 per cent, was almost identical with the average rate per decade over the entire fifty-year period. However, the growth rates in earlier decades varied sharply from this average, revealing a cyclical pattern of Negro population growth. The most rapid growth occurred in the decade of World War I, but the growth rate continued to be high in the succeeding ten-year period. The depression decade, 1930-40, witnessed the lowest percentage increase, although the Negro population in 1940 was 19 per cent larger than in 1930. The decade of World War II brought a resumption of high growth rates. In absolute terms the increase in numbers of Negroes between 1940 and 1950 was greater than that of any preceding decade; but, because the Negro population was already sizable in 1940, the relative growth rate was below that of 1910-20 or 1920-30.

Two conclusions stand out from the analysis of population growth during the first half of the twentieth century. First, it is evident that the growth of the Negro population has come to substitute for the growth of foreign-born population, which formerly was a major factor in the over-all increase in the city's numerical size. Moreover, given the decline in numbers of the white population during 1930-50, the city would not have increased at all except for the influx of Negroes. Second, the increase in Negro population responds strongly to such contingent factors as war-induced labor shortages and the full-employment conditions of business prosperity. It seems clear that the "pull" of opportunities in the city is a more important factor in causing variation in Negro population growth rates than is the "push" of conditions in the areas from which Negro migrants come to Chicago.

It is evident that the high growth rates of the Negro population in recent decades could have been produced only by a heavy migration of Negroes. Chapter iii presents estimates of net migration which show that the relative importance of migration in the increase of Negro population has varied over the forty-year period, 1910-50. The net in-migration between 1910 and 1920 accounted for 94 per cent of the increase of that decade, whereas net migration accounted for only 72 per cent of the increase of the decade 1940-50. As the base population grows, natural increase will gain in importance relative to net migration, and an increasing proportion of Negroes will be natives of the city. At any rate, this has been the historical trend.

Negro migrants to Chicago have been predominantly young adults, many of them doubtless single persons. However, shifts in the age distribution of migrants, observed in comparing 1940-50 with earlier decades, suggest that the recent migration involved a larger proportion of family units than was true in the earlier periods.

Little reliable information is available on the social characteristics of Negro migrants to Chicago, but chapter iii summarizes such statistics as exist. The bulk of these migrants originate, as one would guess, in the South, particularly in Mississippi, Arkansas, Tennessee, Alabama, and Missouri. However, the proportionate contribution of the South to the migrant stream may well be smaller in the future than in the recent past. There is evidence that the migrant population is inferior to the native population or older residents in educational attainment, as would be expected from their geographic origin. Absorption of large numbers of such migrants retards the rise in educational level of the Negro population of the city as a whole.

Chapter iv compares the Negro with the white population on a number of social and economic characteristics. A special effort is made to detect changes in the relative status of the two populations, for such changes may be indicative of progress in the assimilation of the Negro population into the social and economic life of the city. A convergence of the two groups in their population characteristics may be supposed to represent assimilation. The meaning of a divergence, however, is not equally clear, because it is possible that the assimilation of natives of the city and of migrants of earlier periods is obscured in the statistics by the effect of recent migration. As noted in the preceding paragraph, this can be shown to be true of educational status; but for other characteristics the component of change due to migration cannot be separated out analytically.

Perhaps the most striking and significant changes observed between 1940 and 1950 were in the industrial pursuits and occupational status of Negroes. In 1940, two-thirds of the employed non-white females were in personal services, as compared with only one-third in 1950. Correlatively, non-white females entered manufacturing jobs in sufficient numbers almost to equate the non-white proportion in manufacturing with the white. Non-white males likewise achieved proportional representation in manufacturing, with a decline in the relative frequency of employment in personal services and retail trade. Accompanying these industrial shifts was a rise in occupational status, relative to the white population. This brought non-whites, for the first time, into more than proportional representation in the occupation group of operatives and kindred workers (roughly equivalent to "semiskilled" workers), whereas such representation had previously been confined to the manual-labor and service occupations. Important gains were made, as well, in clerical occupations, particularly by non-white females; the same cannot be said, however, of other white-collar jobs. As an over-all summary of the occupational changes, a convenient figure is the "index of dissimilarity" or percentage of non-overlapping of the white and non-white occupation distributions. This index decreased from 37.1 to 35.4 per cent for males between 1940 and 1950 and from 46.1 to 43.1 per cent for females. Despite the significant change, therefore, the Negro occupation distribution continued to contrast rather sharply with that of the white employed labor force.

No doubt an important explanation for the Negro's economic gains was the marked improvement in general employment conditions between 1930-40 and 1940-50. Both white and non-white unemployment rates were diminished by roughly two-thirds, comparing 1950 with 1940. However, even in a period of approximately full employment, there remained a pronounced difference in unemployment rates on a relative basis.

Comparison of changes in Negro and white family characteristics is beset with a number of technicalities which make it difficult to offer a brief summary. Although on some characteristics there was a slight convergence of white and non-white distributions, the opposite was true of others. From a study of the statistics, the major impression one gets is of the persistence of tendencies toward much greater incidence of family disorganization among non-whites than among whites, as indicated by their higher proportions of persons with broken marriages, families headed by females, residents of quasi-households, and unrelated individuals in households. An adequate explanation of these phenomena would involve a complex analysis of such factors, among others, as housing congestion and unfavorable living conditions, disruptions attendant upon migration and the difficulties of migrants in adjusting to a new type of community, and the social heritage of family instability traceable to the Negro's condition under slavery.

Differences between whites and non-whites in housing characteristics are usually in the direction that could be predicted from knowing that Negroes have lower average incomes. But, in addition to purely economic effects, the color differentials seemingly reflect (1) a competitive disadvantage of the Negro on the housing market and (2) unfavorable conditions resulting from a rapid growth of population not balanced by a proportional expansion of the housing supply. The operation of the first factor is inferred from the finding that Negroes pay higher rents for a given quality of housing than whites; the second is evident in a deterioration of non-white housing conditions over the decade 1940-50 with respect to standards of room occupancy. The analysis of differential changes in housing characteristics, carried out on a city-wide basis in chapter iv, is elaborated in subsequent chapters dealing with small areas of the city.

As an over-all indication of relative social and economic advantages, there are probably no more significant data than those pertaining to the chances of life and death. An illuminating finding, then, is that the gap between white and non-white longevity in Chicago was reduced by approximately half between 1930 and 1950, as measured by the life-expectancy at birth. Further reduction of the differential can perhaps be accomplished by a mobilization of the city's public health resources, irrespective of other changes that may occur. But it is probable that as long as Negroes remain a partially assimilated, disadvantaged, "minority group," their subordinate status will be reflected in statistics of differential mortality.

Following the city-wide summaries and comparisons of chapters ii-iv, the monograph turns to an intensive study of the territorial expansion of the Negro population in Chicago, the changes in residential characteristics accompanying racial succession, and the patterns of differentiation of Negro residential areas as related to succession. Chapters v-viii comprise a more detailed statistical analysis of the process of residential succession than has heretofore been made for a large American city. Because the analytical approach is unfamiliar and, in part, lacks precedent, it is necessary to give considerable attention to methodological matters and to set forth the findings in some detail.

Chapter v deals descriptively with the spatial counterpart of the Negro population increase between 1920 and 1950. The major findings are apparent on inspection of the series of maps, Figures 5-8. Despite a lack of detailed area statistics for 1910, it seems that the major outline of the Negro community, as it appeared in 1920 (after the heavy in-migration associated with World War I), was largely determined by the pre-existing pattern of Negro settlement. The newcomers were absorbed into areas in which Negroes already resided, replacing the white population formerly inhabiting these areas. In the three decades following 1920, there was a further consolidation of the South Side "Black Belt," the core of which was to become an almost exclusively Negro residential area. As the Negro population continued to increase, there was an areal expansion of the "Black Belt" and, to a lesser extent, of certain other Negro residential areas, notably on the Near West Side, which, like the Black Belt, had contained nuclei of Negro settlement at least as early as 1910. However, areal expansion never quite kept pace with population growth. Hence Negro residential areas, as they were consolidated, also became more densely populated.

Examination of changes in racial composition on a census-tract basis over the thirty-year period discloses considerable variation in the rate of consolidation of Negro residential areas; no adequate explanation of this variation was found in the study. Nonetheless, one important uniformity in the process stands out. Areas inhabited by substantial proportions of Negroes tended to increase their Negro proportions, whether rapidly or slowly, whereas a decrease seldom occurred, once an area had reached a proportion of, say, 10 per cent Negroes. There are, then, no major parts of the city which once contained substantial Negro settlements that are now inhabited solely by whites. In fact, there are only isolated instances of tracts with mixed white and Negro populations in which the Negro proportion failed to increase. Finally, most of the areas in which Negro residence developed after 1920 were contiguous to the main "Black Belt" or to other areas of historical concentration of Negro population. The more important exceptions to this rule were produced by publicly financed housing projects.

A theoretical and methodological discussion of the concept of succession forms the subject matter of chapter vi. Recognizing a variety of possible meanings of the term "succession," this study focuses solely on succession as the change in racial composition of a residential area. Specifically, racial succession takes place when one racial category of the population replaces another as residents of an area. Succession occurs over time, and it is convenient to think of it as a process involving a sequence of stages. Referring to the replacement of white by Negro population in a specified area, succession begins with the penetration by Negroes of an area hitherto inhabited exclusively by whites. When the number and proportion of Negroes in the area become significantly great, invasion has occurred. Further increases in Negro population, accompanied by decreases in the white population, amount to a consolidation of the area for Negro residence. Consolidation is completed when the area has become exclusively Negro, or virtually so. A final stage, piling up, is recognized if, after complete occupation of an area by Negroes, the Negro population continues to increase, entailing an increase in gross and net population density.

Manifestly, this sequence, as described, is an abstract conception

which may or may not be useful for descriptive or analytical purposes.
There is no implication that the sequence, once begun, <u>necessarily</u>
continues to completion. Logically, consolidation presupposes invasion,
which, in turn, cannot occur before penetration. On the other hand, a
piling-up effect may well become evident before consolidation is complete. As a matter of definition, there is nothing to preclude the halting,
or even reversal, of a cycle of succession. However, the use of the
stage scheme would be hard to justify except on the hypothesis that
this is unlikely to occur.

Empirical application of the hypothetical stages inevitably involves
arbitrary decisions. Three <u>ad hoc</u> limitations on the present study conditioned these decisions to a considerable degree. First, an analysis
of succession was undertaken only for the 1940-50 decade. This per-
mitted the classification of census tracts according to the stage they
entered after the 1940 Census and avoided complications certain to
arise, had the classification attempted to utilize observations from
three or more points in time. Second, no effort was made to study the
initial stage—penetration—in view of the lack of relevant census data.
However, it was found advisable to divide the consolidation stage into
three substages: early consolidation, consolidation, and late consolidation. Finally, given the study's interest in examining changes in population composition and housing characteristics accompanying succession, it was necessary to frame the classification in terms of the
availability of census-tract data showing a breakdown by color on
these characteristics. Without going into details here, it may be stated
that a good deal of experimentation resulted in the classification of
154 census tracts according to their stages of succession in 1940-50.
Approximately equal numbers of tracts were allocated to the five
stages, invasion, early consolidation, consolidation, late consolidation, and piling up. The spatial locations of tracts in each group are
shown on a map, Figure 12. Treating each group of tracts as an aggregate, the proportion of Negroes in the invasion tracts increased from
0.5 per cent in 1940 to 28.6 per cent in 1950. Similarly, for the other
groups, there was an increase from 4.9 to 39.5 per cent in the early-
consolidation tracts; from 26.2 to 62.1 per cent in the consolidation
tracts; from 91.5 to 97.8 per cent in the late-consolidation tracts;

and from 99.0 to 99.3 per cent in the piling-up tracts. At each stage
there was also an increase in total population, i.e., an increase in
gross population density.

From rough estimates of net population movement and fragmentary statistics on residential mobility it was possible to derive some
plausible conclusions about the role of mobility in succession. Net
residential movement accounted for roughly 60 per cent of the increase in Negro population in the piling-up tracts, 65 per cent in the
late-consolidation tracts, and 75 per cent in the aggregate of the remaining stages. Apparently, this movement involved disproportionate
numbers of in-migrants from outside the city in the piling-up and late-
consolidation tracts. These, then, might be said to comprise a "port
of entry" for the migrant population. Correlatively, disproportionate
numbers of Negroes moving to the invasion tracts were drawn from
other parts of the city. The evidence, though indirect, supports the
proposition that the early stages of succession are led by Negroes
who already have some experience with life in Chicago rather than
by newcomers to the city—a proposition which, of course, holds only
in the sense of a statistical preponderance admitting many exceptions.

The classification of census tracts by stage of succession in
chapter vi is employed as the framework for an analysis of the changes
accompanying succession in chapter vii. For each of the five groups
of tracts there is a comparison of the 1940 with the 1950 values of
the following characteristics: population density, room crowding of
dwelling units, educational attainment, unemployment, employment in
white-collar occupations, homeownership, rent, and percentage of
dwelling units with central heating and mechanical refrigeration.
Where the data permit, comparisons are made for the white and non-
white populations separately, as well as for the total population. The
study design encompasses not only changes in the mean census-tract
values of these characteristics but also an analysis of the relationships between the 1950 and 1940 values on a tract-by-tract basis.
Computation of the regression equation permits a more complete
statement of the average change than could be made from inspection
of the mean shifts alone, while the correlation coefficient provides a
measure of the relative stability of census-tract characteristics over

a ten-year period. The matter of stability is of some importance, on the hypothesis that succession is accompanied by orderly selective changes in population and housing characteristics rather than a disruption of the major patterns of urban residential structure.

No attempt is made to catalogue here the plethora of specific findings in chapter vii, which presents these findings in extended form, for whatever interest they may hold for readers concerned with particular areas of the city and to serve as a basis for the summary comparisons in chapter viii. It should be noted that the analysis is most informative with respect to the first and last of the five stages of succession. Hence it is possible to offer some significant summary propositions about the concomitants of invasion and of piling up.

Each of the invasion tracts had a non-white population amounting to less than 2 per cent of its total population in 1940; by 1950 the non-white proportions in these tracts ranged from 4.5 to 98.4 per cent, and each tract contained at least 250 non-white inhabitants. Thus, the rate of succession in these tracts varied considerably. It is probable, too, that some of them were invaded early in the 1940-50 decade, leaving enough time for consolidation to be well advanced by 1950, whereas others were doubtless invaded only toward the close of the decade. Unfortunately, census data do not permit one to ascertain these variations in timing of invasion. A comparison of characteristics of the non-white population in 1950 with those of the total population in 1940 permits rough inferences as to the selectivity involved in the replacement of the initial population by the incoming population. A comparison of the 1950 white population with the 1940 total population permits statements about the relative status of the initial population and that portion of the initial population remaining in an area undergoing invasion (as modified, of course, by any turnover that may have occurred within the white population of invaded areas).

Correlations between characteristics of the 1950 non-white and those of the 1940 white population were around 0.8 for room crowding and homeownership; 0.7 for median monthly contract rent; and 0.6 for white-collar employment, educational attainment, and unemployment. These results support the very important conclusion that succession is highly selective with respect to the social characteristics of the in-moving population. In the sense of a relative comparison among areas, there is a strong resemblance between the characteristics of the invading population and those of the population displaced. This does not gainsay the likelihood that the invading population will differ from the initial population in the over-all average level of certain social characteristics. However, comparisons designed to reveal such average differences are confounded by the fact that changes occur in the average socioeconomic levels of the white and Negro population of the city over a decade, more or less independently of the residential succession process. Thus, if one were to attempt a prediction of the changes which the characteristics of a residential area would undergo during a decade in which invasion occurred, he could be seriously misled by relying solely on a knowledge of Negro-white differentials. It was found, for example, that the 1950 non-white population of the invasion tracts, as compared with the 1940 total (essentially white) population, had higher levels of educational attainment, homeownership, and rent and lower unemployment rates. In these same tracts the 1950 non-white population, as compared with the 1950 white population, had the lower levels of educational attainment and the higher levels of unemployment, as would be expected on the basis of a knowledge of city-wide Negro-white differentials. But the 1950 white-non-white comparisons in the invasion tracts showed non-whites having the higher levels of homeownership and paying higher rents. The complex pattern of differences found in the temporal and racial comparisons forces a recognition of the simultaneous operation of several sets of forces or selective factors: those producing differences between whites and Negroes at any given period of time; those involved in the selectivity of the invading population as compared with the initial population; those involved in the selectivity of the displaced population as compared with the white population remaining in an area after invasion; and those producing (possibly differential) changes in the white and Negro population of the community at large.

The data suggest an important inference about the nature of the invasion process. It appears that, because of restrictions on the housing market and intensification of competition for living space, the invading population must pay higher rents in any given area than would have prevailed there in the absence of invasion. Moreover, the in-movers are likely to purchase property with great frequency, perhaps because they find it easier to acquire housing in this fashion than to rely on the rental market. Such, at least, is a plausible explanation of the findings on rent and homeownership mentioned in the preceding paragraph.

The data on the piling-up tracts are significant in suggesting that changes occurring in tracts already fully consolidated for Negro resi-dence may be as important as those occurring in areas undergoing transition from white to Negro occupancy. Gross population density in the piling-up tracts, already as high as 46,700 persons per square mile in 1940, increased to 54,000 persons per square mile in 1950. Similarly, the proportion of crowded households increased from the already high figure of 25.3 per cent in 1940 to 31.1 per cent in 1950. The designation of such changes as "piling up" seems warranted, on the supposition that they reflect, in large part, the difficulty experi-enced by the Negro population in expanding its residential area under the pressure of increasing numbers. If succession took place without friction or resistance, all areas of the city would receive a propor-tional increment of Negro population. Instead, there was a concentra-tion of the increase in already congested areas of almost exclusively Negro occupancy. Interestingly enough, despite the increase in con-gestion in the piling-up tracts and the undoubted deterioration of living conditions in many respects, there was no decline in the levels of several characteristics indicative of socioeconomic status or stand-ard of living, e.g., educational attainment, white-collar employment, homeownership, and dwelling units with central heating and mechani-cal refrigeration.

It must be noted that the "piling-up" effect was observed at each stage of succession during the decade 1940-50, i.e., increases in density and crowding and failure of the supply of dwelling units to ex-pand as rapidly as the population. Metaphorically, one might say that the end of the decade found a large flow of Negro population "dammed up" at each stage of succession.

Whereas chapter vii treats each stage of succession as a separate unit of analysis, chapter viii involves comparisons among stages. The first salient result of these comparisons is that the same kinds of changes in population and housing characteristics occurred at each stage of succession over the decade 1940-50. Comparison of 1950 with 1940 values of these characteristics for the total population (i.e., white and non-white combined) shows that at each stage and in most individual tracts there were increases in gross population density, room crowding, educational level, homeownership, and proportion of dwelling units with central heating and mechanical refrigeration and decreases in unemployment and in white-collar employment. Two of these changes (density and crowding) represent the "piling-up" effect. Only one of the others (decrease in white-collar employment) was in the direction one would expect from a knowledge of Negro-white differences in the city as a whole in either 1940 or 1950. Thus any inference about the effects or concomitants of succession must be qualified by the recognition that these effects may easily be masked by general trends in the socioeconomic milieu of the areas undergoing succession.

In other words, to infer effects of succession as such, one must take into account changes produced by forces essentially unrelated to succession. Moreover, to infer effects of succession from a comparison of stages of succession at any given point in time, one must allow for factors producing areal differentiation other than racial succession itself. As explained in chapter viii, the 1950 averages of census-tract characteristics by stage of succession may be "adjusted" for differences in the corresponding 1940 averages. A study of the 1950 adjusted averages or of the adjusted changes between 1940 and 1950 leads to the following conclusions: Although population density increased during invasion, the increase was less than at the subsequent stages of succession. The increase in crowding was apparently most severe at the intermediate stages of succession. A substantial increase in homeownership distinguished the invasion stage, though small increases occurred at the other stages. Rent increases (adjusted) were greatest at the invasion stage and least at the piling-up stage, with a relatively smooth gradient over the intermediate stages.

As has been implied, it is dangerous to infer consequences of succession from a cross-sectional (i.e., at one point in time) comparison of sets of tracts classified by stage of succession. This is true because forces other than succession as such produce some of the differences that will be observed. For example, it is shown in chapter viii that differences among tracts by zonal distance from the center of the city are partly related to, but partly independent of, stage of succession. Only in a quite general sense has succession in Chicago followed a pattern of radial expansion of the Negro community outward from the center of the city. Moreover, fragmentary data are available to show that at least some socioeconomic differences among areas now in various stages of succession existed before any of them began to undergo succession.

Reference was made earlier to the notion of stability of area characteristics and its importance as an aspect of the succession process. A summary analysis, in chapter viii, of the numerous correlations computed between 1950 and 1940 characteristics of tracts undergoing succession shows that the typical finding is that of moderate to high correlation, despite the lapse of ten years, the considerable turnover of population, and the occurrence of many large-scale social changes in an era of business recovery, war, and postwar prosperity. One practical implication of this finding may be ventured: Areas in which one or another kind of social problem is localized at a given time are likely to retain such a problematic character for a period of years, even if, in the meantime, the population in these areas has undergone considerable turnover. Or, to state the point in the language of theory, the residential structure of an urban community is in good part independent of the racial makeup of the community's inhabitants.

Additional evidence on this point derives from a study of the correlations between the characteristics of the white and the non-white populations of areas of mixed racial occupancy. This study, carried out for twelve population and housing characteristics, revealed quite high correlations for statistics reflecting the physical characteristics of an area and its residential structures, correlations of moderate magnitude for socioeconomic characteristics of the population, and low or unstable correlations for characteristics reflecting family structure and household composition. Evidently, the residential adjustments of white and Negro populations are conditioned by many common factors. The failure of correlated patterns of areal differentiation to appear on family characteristics has various possible, but necessarily speculative, interpretations. It is suspected that the family traditions of the Negro differ somewhat from those of the white population, as a historical consequence of slavery and the economic organization of agriculture in the rural South. But there is another line of argument. It appears reasonable to assume that the predicament of the Negro family seeking housing differs somewhat from that of the average white family, irrespective even of economic differentials. To compete more effectively with whites in a restricted housing market, Negro families are led to improvise irregular living arrangements—doubling up of families, keeping of lodgers, pooling of incomes of relatives to meet high rents of dwelling units too large for a single family, and so on. The differential incidence of these factors by areas in the city for Negroes need not, therefore, parallel the factors producing differences in family life among whites. Whatever the explanation of the findings of this study, there can be no doubt about the urgency of a need for research on the effects of residential segregation on Negro family life and the probable consequences thereof for social and personal disorganization.

The final section of chapter viii sets forth, primarily in cartographic form (Figs. 23-34), the study's findings on the differentiation of residential areas within the Negro community. Whereas the summary white-non-white comparisons of chapter iv might give a misleading impression of the degree of social and economic homogeneity of the Negro population, these maps highlight the considerable range of variation among different sectors of the Negro population, as classified by area of residence. It is shown, moreover, that this variation, in large part, takes the form of zonal variation, i.e., gradients of intensity according to distance from the center of the city. Thus Frazier's findings for 1920 are confirmed and extended.

A special analysis of residential distribution of occupation groups among Negroes discloses that within the Negro community, as in the city as a whole, spatial distance, or separation, of occupation groups parallels their social distance or relative socioeconomic ranking.

Some minor differences between the patterns for Negroes and whites suggest that the significance of broad occupational classifications for the social stratification of Negroes is not quite the same as for whites —a clue that might be followed up in future studies of social stratification and its residential aspects.

In concluding the summary of the content of this volume, reference may be made to the several appendixes, which include supplementary data for the use of those who may wish to check or extend the study's findings. Likewise included in the appendixes are some methodological discussions, elaborating problems referred to at various points in the text. Though not conceived as a methodological exercise, the project reported here involved some minor innovations and encountered some unresolved problems of method. It is hoped that these, as well as the substantive conclusions, may be provocative of further research.

Chapter II

Growth of the Negro Population

Negroes have lived in Chicago since the founding of the city. The first census reports for Chicago—those of 1840—show that the 53 Negroes in the city then constituted 1.2 per cent of the city's enumerated population of 4,470. Throughout the last half of the nineteenth century the Negro population expanded rapidly, but only rapidly enough to maintain a practically constant proportion of the total population, which was likewise increasing rapidly.[1] At no census prior to 1900 did Negroes constitute more than 1.3 per cent of the city's population. The proportion increased to 1.8 per cent by 1900 and 2.0 per cent by 1910. The latter year marks the beginning of a period of greatly accelerated growth of the Negro population.

The large increase between 1900 and 1950 in the number of Negroes, in both relative and absolute terms, is evident in the data shown in Figure 1. (The chart is plotted with a logarithmic scale, so that lines with equal slopes represent equal rates of change.) At the beginning of the century there were 30,000 Negroes in the city. The number increased to 44,000 by 1910. In each of the subsequent periods —the decade of World War I and the post-World War I decade—the Negro population more than doubled. The 1920 Census enumerated 109,000 Negroes, and the 1930 Census 234,000. The rate of increase was greatly slowed down by the depression of the 1930's. Nonetheless, an increase of 44,000 brought the Negro population to a total of 278,000 in 1940. The 1940-50 decade witnessed a resumption of the rapid

---

1. For census statistics on race and nativity prior to 1900 see Local Community Fact Book for Chicago 1950, ed. Philip M. Hauser and Evelyn M. Kitagawa (Chicago: Chicago Community Inventory, 1953), Table D.

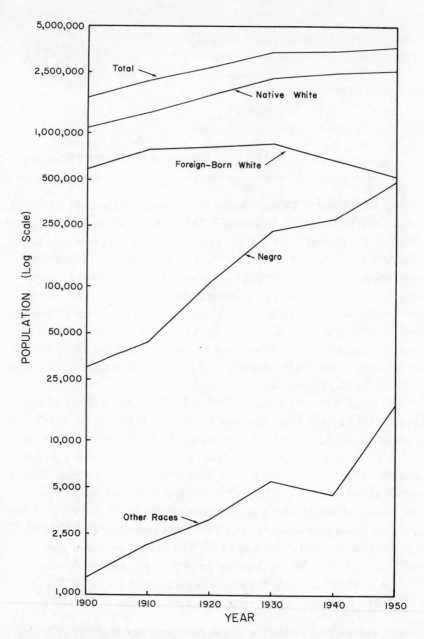

Fig. 1.—Population Growth, by Race and Nativity, for the City of Chicago, 1900-1950.

growth of the Negro population, bringing the figure to 492,000, more than twice the 1930 figure and an increase of 77 per cent over 1940.

In brief, Chicago's Negro population in 1950 was sixteen times as large as in 1900 and four and a half times as large as in 1920. With around a half-million inhabitants, the Negro community of Chicago is a metropolis in itself, exceeding in size all but eighteen of the cities of the United States. Of all the cities in the United States—and, probably, in the world—only New York, with three-quarters of a million, has a larger Negro population than Chicago. One out of every 30 Negroes in the United States lives in Chicago.

It is significant that these high rates of growth in Negro population occurred in a city whose rate of growth in total population was past its peak. Thus in each decade since 1900 the Negro population grew more rapidly than either the total population, the native white population, or the foreign-born white population. Table 1 shows the growth rates of the four race-nativity groups for each of the five decades. The fundamental change in the sources of the city's growth which occurred at the outbreak of World War I is evident from these figures. Between 1900 and 1910 the growth rate of the foreign-born white, though below that of the Negro population, was somewhat greater than the native white growth rate. In the succeeding decade, 1910-20, there was a precipitous decline in the foreign-born white growth rate, concomitant with the upsurge of the Negro growth rate. The foreign-born white growth rate remained low between 1920 and 1930 and became negative in the two following decades; there was a decline of about one-fifth in the foreign-born white population both between 1930 and 1940 and from 1940 to 1950. By contrast, the Negro growth rate has remained relatively high since 1920, though fluctuating, as did total growth, in response to the depression.

As a result of these growth trends, the Negro population by 1950 was almost as large as the foreign-born white population. It seems evident that an important factor in the increase of the Negro population over the last forty years was the abrupt and drastic limitation on immigration occasioned by World War I and the national-quota legislation of the 1920's. In-migration of Negroes has, in effect, substituted for foreign immigration as a major source of the city's growth.

Table 1.—Decennial Percentage Increase in Population, by Race and Nativity, for the Chicago Standard Metropolitan Area, 1900-1950

(Minus Sign Denotes Decrease)

Area and Period	Total Popu- lation	Race and Nativity			
		Native White	Foreign- born White	Negro	Other Races
Standard metro- politan area:					
1940-50....	13.9	15.5	-18.6	77.9	262.7
1930-40*...	3.2	9.9	-20.9	19.2	-15.1
1920-30*...	32.8	37.5	10.1	121.7	79.8
1910-20....	27.9	36.0	6.1	152.8	43.7
1900-1910 ..	31.5	28.7	36.4	45.7	68.2
City of Chicago:					
1940-50....	6.6	5.9	-21.8	77.2	280.5
1930-40*...	0.6	7.0	-21.4	18.7	-17.1
1920-30*...	24.9	27.9	6.2	113.7	76.8
1910-20....	23.6	31.4	3.1	148.2	45.0
1900-1910 ..	28.7	25.5	33.4	46.3	65.2
Outside Chicago:					
1940-50....	31.2	35.2	- 7.4	82.9	134.5
1930-40*...	9.9	16.4	19.0	21.3	2.3
1920-30*...	58.5	65.2	26.4	176.0	111.8
1910-20....	44.5	51.6	20.8	188.9	31.4
1900-1910 ..	43.9	40.6	53.4	41.6	103.7

*1930 figures revised to classify Mexicans as white, in conformity with procedures for other censuses.

Like the Negro population, the population of other races (non-whites, except Negroes) has grown rapidly during the last five decades, and especially between 1940 and 1950. The recent increase in numbers in this group is largely attributable to the resettlement of Japanese from the West Coast at the end of World War II. Even in 1950, however, the population of other races was numerically small—17,000—and constituted only 0.5 per cent of the city's total population and 3.4 per cent of the non-white population.

Table 2, showing the race-nativity distribution of the population

Table 2.—Percentage Distribution of the Population, by Race and Nativity, for the Chicago Standard Metropolitan Area, 1900-1950

Area and Year	Total Population		Native White	Foreign-born White	Negro	Other Races
	Number	Per Cent				
Standard metropolitan area:						
1950	5,495,364	100.0	76.2	12.8	10.7	0.3
1940	4,825,527	100.0	75.2	17.9	6.8	.1
1930*	4,675,877	100.0	70.5	23.4	6.0	.1
1920	3,521,789	100.0	68.1	28.2	3.6	.1
1910	2,752,820	100.0	64.0	34.1	1.8	.1
1900	2,092,883	100.0	65.5	32.8	1.6	.1
City of Chicago:						
1950	3,620,962	100.0	71.4	14.5	13.6	.5
1940	3,396,808	100.0	71.9	19.8	8.2	.1
1930*	3,376,438	100.0	67.6	25.3	6.9	.2
1920	2,701,705	100.0	66.0	29.8	4.1	.1
1910	2,185,283	100.0	62.2	35.7	2.0	.1
1900	1,698,575	100.0	63.6	34.5	1.8	.1
Outside Chicago:						
1950	1,874,402	100.0	85.4	9.5	5.0	.1
1940	1,428,719	100.0	82.9	13.5	3.6	.0
1930*	1,299,439	100.0	78.3	18.3	3.4	.0
1920	820,084	100.0	75.0	23.0	2.0	.0
1910	567,537	100.0	71.5	27.5	1.0	.0
1900	394,308	100.0	73.2	25.8	1.0	0.0

*1930 figures revised to classify Mexicans as white, in conformity with procedures for other censuses.

at each census, 1900-1950, indicates the changes in composition of population produced by differential growth rates. The proportion of Negroes increased regularly, from 1.8 per cent of the population in 1900 to 13.6 per cent in 1950. Over the same period the proportion of foreign-born whites dropped from 34.5 to 14.5 per cent, while the proportion of native whites increased from 63.6 to 71.4 per cent. Thus, in 1950, out of every seven residents of Chicago, five were native whites, one was foreign-born white, and one was non-white.

The growth rates and percentage distributions described for

Chicago are supplemented in Tables 1 and 2 by the same information for the entire Chicago Standard Metropolitan Area[2] and for the portion of that area outside the city of Chicago. The principal trends already described appear as well for the Standard Metropolitan Area as a whole and for the portion outside Chicago: high growth rates for the Negro population, declining rates for the foreign-born white population, and increasing proportions of Negro and native white population with decreasing proportions of foreign-born white population. Actually, the rate of increase in Negro population in the Standard Metropolitan Area outside Chicago has been somewhat greater than in Chicago during each decade since 1910. Nevertheless, the proportion of Negroes in the population has remained substantially smaller than in the city. By 1950, only 5.0 per cent of the population in the Standard Metropolitan Area outside Chicago were Negroes, as compared with 13.6 per cent in the city. The proportions of foreign-born white population and of other races also have remained consistently higher in the city than in the remainder of the area. Significantly, the non-white population in the Standard Metropolitan Area outside Chicago is concentrated toward the city rather than being evenly distributed throughout the six counties. In 1950, when 14.1 per cent of the city's population was non-white, 6.3 per cent of the population was non-white in the Metropolitan District[3] outside Chicago, but only 2.2 per cent in the Standard Metropolitan Area outside the Metropolitan District. In 1940 the corresponding figures were 8.3, 4.4, and 1.8 per cent.

The great variation in the growth rate of the Negro population from decade to decade in the past strongly suggests that it will be difficult to anticipate accurately its future growth. It is a curiosity that the percentage increase in Negro population from 1940 to 1950 was almost identical with the average rate per decade over the entire

---

2. The Chicago Standard Metropolitan Area includes the counties of Cook, DuPage, Kane, Lake, and Will in Illinois and Lake County, Indiana.

3. The Chicago Metropolitan District includes incorporated places and townships located in five of the six counties which make up the Standard Metropolitan Area. Its boundaries inclose a land area of 1,184 square miles, out of a total of 3,617 in the Standard Metropolitan Area.

period 1900-1950—75 per cent. But each other decade varied sharply from this average, seemingly in response to war and economic conditions, which are notoriously unpredictable. On the one hand, it seems unlikely that the recent high growth rate can be maintained for any great length of time; but, on the other, there is no apparent reason to expect an abrupt cessation of growth. In a situation which is necessarily so uncertain, even the most careful calculations of future population must be regarded only as illustrative of more or less reasonable possibilities for the future in the light of trends observed in the past.

If accurate data were available, it would probably be possible to show that the growth of the Negro population varies considerably from year to year. Even the census data, on a decennial basis, make it clear that war and prosperity have been favorable to the growth of the Negro population, while depression has inhibited it. The following very rough estimates indicate that the growth of the non-white population of the city was not evenly distributed over the 1940-50 decade:[4]

(In Thousands)

1940 (census) . . 282		1946 366	
1941 292		1947 400	
1942 297		1948 438	
1943 303		1949 487	
1944 324		1950 (census) . . 509	
1945 347			

These estimates indicate that the growth of the non-white population (including Negroes and other races) was most rapid between 1946 and 1949 and next most rapid between 1943 and 1946. The latter period includes the time of the Japanese relocation; hence the growth of the

4.   These estimates were prepared by Mr. Emerson Seim, research assistant in the Laboratory for Social Science Research at the University of Chicago. They are based on the "vital rates technique" of estimation, which involves inflating the observed numbers of births and deaths by assumed birth and death rates, to yield estimated population. The birth and death rates employed were interpolated from the known rates for 1940 and 1950 and assumed to fluctuate from year to year in accordance with the known national rates. The technique, though subject to considerable error, which cannot be measured, is believed to be more accurate for intercensal than for postcensal estimation.

Negro population may not have been quite so great at that time as the figures suggest. In any case, it appears that, although there was an increase in non-white population each year, the immediate postwar years were those of the greatest growth. If the figures can be trusted, 1949-50 was a year of slackened growth; it was also a year of mild economic recession.

The general picture afforded by these estimates gains some credence from a comparison with an independent estimate of the non-white population of the Chicago Metropolitan District. The enumerated non-white population of the Metropolitan District was 329,000 in 1940 and 596,000 in 1950. A 1947 sample estimate by the United States Census Bureau[5] gave a figure of 447,000, with a sampling error such that the chances were 19 out of 20 that a complete census count would have given a figure between 401,000 and 494,000. If the non-white population of the Metropolitan District had grown by equal amounts each year of the decade, the 1947 figure would have been 516,000, i.e., well above the upper limit of the range of probable sampling variability. Hence these data, like the foregoing estimates, lead to the conclusion that non-white population growth was somewhat concentrated in the last half of the decade.

The apparent slackening of the growth rate during 1949-50 may have been only a temporary response to economic fluctuations, but it may indicate also that the high postwar rates of growth were a temporary phenomenon. Postcensal estimates of Chicago's non-white population, prepared by the Chicago Community Inventory, University of Chicago,[6] suggest that, on the average, the annual growth rates for

---

5. Current Population Reports (Ser. P-21, No. 29 [August 23, 1947]).

6. For more detailed discussion of the estimates and the estimating technique see Otis Dudley Duncan and Beverly Duncan, Chicago's Negro Population: Characteristics and Trends (a report by the Chicago Community Inventory, University of Chicago, to the Office of the Housing and Redevelopment Coordinator and the Chicago Plan Commission) (1956), and Donald J. Bogue and Beverly Duncan, "A Composite Method for Estimating Postcensal Populations of Small Areas by Age, Sex, and Color" (hectographed document, Population Research and Training Center, University of Chicago, 1956).

Chicago's non-white population since 1950 have been slightly higher
than the 1949-50 rate but substantially lower than the annual growth
rates in the immediate postwar period.

The postcensal estimates of non-white population shown below
are subject to error, of course; but they probably give a fairly reliable indication of the changes that have occurred since 1950:

Date	Population (In Thousands)
April, 1950 (census)	509
July, 1951 (estimate)	537
July, 1952 (estimate)	566
July, 1953 (estimate)	596
July, 1954 (estimate)	630
July, 1955 (preliminary estimate)	665

Looking over both the intercensal and the postcensal estimates,
the general picture seems to be that the annual rates of increase
in non-white population between 1940 and 1943 fluctuated around 2-4
per cent; between 1943 and 1946, around 6 or 7 per cent; and between
1946 and 1949, around 9-11 per cent. There was apparently an annual
rate of increase of about 4.5 per cent for both 1949-50 and 1950-51,
and there were annual rates of increase of 5 or 6 per cent between
1951 and 1955. If these estimates of non-white population in Chicago
are reliable, it appears that the growth of non-white population during
the period 1949-51 slackened markedly from the postwar influx; since
1951 there is some suggestion of an acceleration of non-white population growth in Chicago, but the growth rates remain far lower than
those observed in the immediate postwar period. The growth rates
observed during the early 1950's are, on the average, no higher, and
perhaps slightly lower, than the average annual rate for the whole
decade 1940-50.

The excess of in-migrants over out-migrants in Chicago's non-
white population has been an important component of the postcensal
growth, accounting for roughly 56 per cent of the total growth between
1950 and 1955; but the excess of births over deaths is probably accounting for a relatively larger share of the non-white population growth at
present than has been the case in the past. The sheer increase in the
size of Chicago's non-white population, coupled with its age composi-

tion, which is favorable to a high rate of natural increase, suggests that natural increase will continue to play an important role in the growth of this population for the next several years.

Looking further ahead, a 1960 non-white population of 760,000-830,000 in Chicago can be expected if the pattern of population change between 1950 and 1955 is roughly indicative of the changes which will occur in the 1955-60 period. The growth of Chicago's non-white population, and particularly the migration component of this growth, appears to respond strongly to economic fluctuations; consequently, the 1960 projections of non-white population can be regarded only as reasonable possibilities.

Both the 1955 estimate and the rough 1960 projection cited here are higher than the projected figures previously issued for the corresponding years.[7] The discrepancies are due to the fact that both the rate of net in-migration and the rate of natural increase from 1950 to 1955 appear to be slightly higher than those assumed in the previous projection. Projection of the 1950-55 experience would then call for some upward revision of the previously published 1965 projection; but the estimates do not furnish a sufficient basis for such revision at this time.

To place the facts about the growth of the Negro population in Chicago in perspective, it is helpful to review certain national and regional trends. Actually, the local growth of the Negro population is but one manifestation of a general process of population redistribution.

Throughout most of the nation's history, the Negro population has grown less rapidly than the white. The augmentation of the white population through immigration and the higher mortality rates of Negroes combined to reduce the proportion of Negroes in the population from 18.9 per cent in 1800 to 15.7 per cent in 1850 and 11.6 per cent in 1900. This downward trend continued until 1930, when Negroes con-

7.   Donald J. Bogue, An Estimate of Metropolitan Chicago's Future Population, 1955 to 1965 (a report to the Chicago Plan Commission and the Office of the Housing and Redevelopment Coordinator, February 2, 1955) (Chicago: Published jointly by the Chicago Community Inventory and Scripps Foundation for Research in Population Problems).

stituted only 9.7 per cent of the national total. Since 1930 the Negro
population has grown slightly faster than the white, with the result
that the proportion of Negroes increased to 9.8 per cent in 1940 and
10.0 per cent in 1950. There is some question about the reliability
of the small changes revealed by these figures, because the Negro
population is believed to be less accurately enumerated than the white,
and the enumeration error may have changed from census to census.
However, it is clear that the proportion of Negroes in the population
has been relatively constant at about 10 per cent for the last thirty
years. This means, of course, that the disproportionate growth of
Negro population in any given locality represents a redistribution of
population within the nation rather than reflecting a national growth
differential.

The Negro population of the country has always been concentrated
in the South. Before the Civil War about 92 per cent of the Negroes
in the United States lived in that region, and, despite some redistribution of population in the decades following the Civil War, in 1910
the proportion of Negroes living in the South was still as high as 89.0
per cent. The period following 1910, described previously as one of
rapid growth of Negro population in Chicago, was one in which the
proportion of Negroes living in the South decreased markedly to 85.1
per cent in 1920, 78.8 per cent in 1930, 77.0 per cent in 1940, and
68.0 per cent in 1950. Thus the most recent decade, 1940-50, was the
one which witnessed the most rapid redistribution of Negro population.

Without going into details, one should note several facts about
the redistribution of the Negro population since 1910. Both inter-
regional and rural-urban shifts are involved. The North has drawn
the bulk of the Negro movement out of the South. However, during
the 1940-50 decade there was a substantial movement to the West.
In 1950, 3.8 per cent of the Negroes lived in the West, as compared
with 1.3 per cent ten years earlier. Both the northward and westward
movements of Negroes have typically terminated in urban areas. Negroes have also been shifting toward urban areas within the South.
Between 1940 and 1950 the non-white population of all Standard Metropolitan Areas in the United States increased by 44.3 per cent, as com-

pared with an increase of only 20.0 per cent for the white population. In the North non-whites in Standard Metropolitan Areas increased by 58.2 per cent and whites by 11.1 per cent; in the West the increases were 127.6 per cent for non-whites and 48.9 per cent for the whites; while in the South non-whites in Standard Metropolitan Areas increased by 23.6 per cent and whites by 38.5 per cent.[8] In 1950, 9.8 per cent of all persons living in Standard Metropolitan Areas were non-whites, as compared with 8.3 per cent in 1940.

One further regional comparison serves to indicate the position of Chicago as a center of Negro population. In 1950, 14.1 per cent of Chicago's population was classified as non-white. Of the 106 cities in the United States having populations of 100,000 or more, 38 had non-white proportions as high as, or higher than, that of Chicago. By region, 24 of the 32 cities in the South, 9 of the 28 cities of the North Central region, 3 of the 31 cities of the Northeast, and 2 of the 15 cities of the West had non-white proportions of 14.1 per cent or more. Thus Chicago not only has a large Negro population in absolute terms but also ranks high among large non-southern cities in its proportion of Negroes. Yet it is by no means unique or extreme in its proportion of Negroes in comparison with the other large cities of the United States.

---

8. U.S. Bureau of the Census, 1950 Census of Population, Advance Reports (Ser. PC-14, No. 1 [December 16, 1951]).

Chapter III

Migration of Negroes to Chicago

Population growth can take place only by one process or a combination of the two: an excess of births over deaths or an excess of in-migration over out-migration (disregarding apparent growth due to changes in political boundaries and the like). Both natural increase and net in-migration are involved in the rapid increase in the Negro population in Chicago; but the latter is clearly the more important factor from a quantitative standpoint.

To measure net migration over a period of several decades, one must resort to indirect methods. Such methods necessarily yield only approximate information, and in some cases the error may be substantial. However, it is thought that the technique used here[1] is accurate enough to indicate roughly the variation from decade to decade in the amount of net migration and to reveal the broad outline of the age pattern of net migration.

Table 3 gives an estimated breakdown of the decade rates of population growth of whites and Negroes into net migration and natural increase components (see Appendix Table A-3 for the data used in these computations). In these estimates the natural increases (births minus deaths) of migrants and non-migrants are not distinguished, i.e., births occurring to migrant parents are counted in natural increase, whether they occurred prior or subsequent to migration to Chicago.

The data show the overwhelming importance of net migration as a source of Negro population growth throughout the period 1910-50,

---

1. See Appendix B for a brief account of the "survival ratio" technique used to prepare the estimates shown in this chapter.

Table 3.—Estimated Components of Population Growth, by Race, for the City of Chicago, by Decade, 1910-50

(Minus Sign Denotes Decrease)

Race and Decade	Per Cent Increase in Population	Per Cent Increase Due to	
		Natural Increase*	Net Migration
White:			
1940-50....	- 0.1	7.0	-7.1
1930-40....	- 0.7	3.5	-4.2
1920-30....	21.2	11.6	9.6
1910-20....	21.0	12.8	8.2
Negro:			
1940-50....	77	22	55
1930-40....	19	3	16
1920-30....	114	19	95
1910-20....	148	8	140

*Includes births to migrants during decade, either before or after migration.

although the proportion of the total growth accounted for by net migration declined somewhat during this time. The net in-migration of 61,000 Negroes to Chicago between 1910 and 1920 accounted for 94 per cent of the growth in Negro population over the decade. The net in-migration of 104,000 and 37,000 in the two following decades accounted, respectively, for 83 and 85 per cent of the total Negro increase from 1920 to 1930 and from 1930 to 1940. In the most recent decade, 1940-50, the net in-migration of 154,000 Negroes accounted for but 72 per cent of the decade increase in Negro population.

It seems clear that the relative importance of migration as a source of growth is likely to decline as the Negro population increases. While natural increase is roughly proportional to the size of the population—the larger the population, the more births—a given volume of net migration adds proportionately less to a large than to a small population.

Table 3 shows that both net migration and natural increase were slowed down by the depression of the 1930's. The Negro population increased by only 3 per cent from natural increase and 16 per cent from net migration from 1930 to 1940, as compared to 22 and 55 per cent, respectively, from 1940 to 1950. The low rate of natural increase from 1910 to 1920 (8 per cent) is not readily explained but may be due in part to the high rates of mortality then prevailing. It is likely, moreover, that the bulk of the migration came late in this decade and hence that there was only a short period during which new migrants were contributing to the natural increase.

In contrast to the growth pattern of the Negro population, the white population grew more from natural increase than from net migration during each of the four decades, 1910-50. Indeed, in the last two decades there were net losses from migration greater than the gains from natural increase, so that the white population declined slightly both from 1930 to 1940 and from 1940 to 1950. The shift from a net gain to a net loss through migration occurred simultaneously with a considerable decline in the rate of natural increase.

An age breakdown of the net migration of Negroes and whites appears in Figure 2. The data are shown in the form of net migration rates per 100 survivors of the population living in the city at the beginning of each decade. The curves reflect the well-known tendency for migration to be concentrated in the young adult ages. However, there have been some significant shifts in the age pattern of net migration. In each of the four decades the peak rate of Negro net migration occurred for the group of persons aged fifteen to nineteen at the beginning of the decade and twenty-five to twenty-nine at the end of the decade. Throughout the three decades 1910-40, the second highest rate was for the next younger age group (ten to fourteen at the beginning, or twenty to twenty-four at the end, of the decade). However, from 1940 to 1950 a somewhat higher rate occurred for the next older age group (twenty to twenty-four at the beginning, or thirty to thirty-four at the end, of the decade). This shift in age pattern was accompanied by a relative increase in the migration rate for the youngest age group (zero to four at the beginning, or ten to fourteen at the end, of the decade). Whereas their rate was lower than that for the population five to nine (at the beginning of the decade) throughout the period 1910-40, it was slightly higher from 1940 to 1950. The coinci-

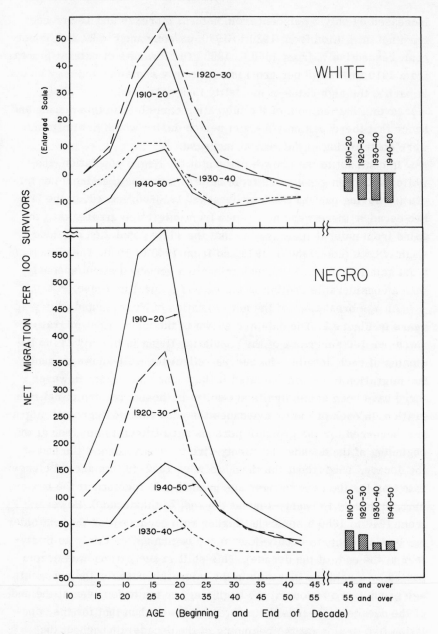

Fig. 2.—Decade Net Migration Rates, by Age and Race, for the City of Chicago, 1910-50.

dence of these two shifts suggests, though it by no means proves, that the migration from 1940 to 1950 involved family units to a great-er extent than in the earlier decades. It is assumed that the migration of young children is largely determined by the migration of their parents or other relatives.

The net migration rates by age for the white population in Figure 2 are shown on a different scale from those of the Negro population, since the level of migration is so different for the two populations. Therefore, caution must be exercised in comparing the two charts. There was a pronounced shift in the migration pattern of the white population between the first two and the last two decades of the forty-year period 1910-50. In the earlier decades, positive rates, repre-senting net in-migration, occurred over the age range five to thirty (at the beginning of the decade) and negative rates for the older adults. In the last two decades net in-migration occurred only between the ages of ten and nineteen at the beginning, or twenty and twenty-nine at the end, of the decade; negative rates, representing net out-migra-tion, appeared for all other age groups. Thus, although net in-migra-tion of teen-age and young adult persons continued during 1930-50, it was insufficient to offset the net out-migration of older adults and their children.

Table 4 shows the Negro net migration rates, 1940-50, by age, with a breakdown by sex. Although the total estimated net in-migra-tion of females somewhat exceeded that of males in absolute numbers —80,000 as compared to 74,000—the male rate of net in-migration per 100 survivors of the 1940 population was slightly higher, 64 as compared to 60 migrants per 100 survivors. The differentiation by sex shows that the male rate was higher than the female for the age group fifteen to forty-four in 1940 (twenty-five to fifty-four in 1950), and the female rate was higher in the remaining groups. The pattern of differences suggests that Negro females migrated to the city at a somewhat earlier age than did the Negro males. The peak rate of mi-gration occurred for the same age group for males and females (fifteen to nineteen in 1940; twenty-five to twenty-nine in 1950). But for fe-males the rates for both adjacent age groups were substantially lower than the peak rate, while for males the rate for the next older group

(twenty to twenty-four in 1940; thirty to thirty-four in 1950) was nearly as high as the peak rate.

Table 4.—Estimated Net Migration per 100 Survivors, for the Negro
Population, by Age and Sex, for the City of Chicago, 1940-50

Age (Years)		Both Sexes	Male	Female
1940	1950			
All ages . . .	10 and over	62	64	60
0-4	10-14	54	51	58
5-9	15-19	52	47	57
10-14 . . .	20-24	119	107	130
15-19 . . .	25-29	163	166	160
20-24 . . .	30-34	137	163	119
25-29 . . .	35-39	75	89	64
30-34 . . .	40-44	43	56	33
35-39 . . .	45-49	26	33	21
40-44 . . .	50-54	19	25	12
45 and over	55 and over	17	14	19

Despite the heavy in-migration of Negroes from 1940 to 1950, a
larger proportion of the Negroes living in Chicago at the end of the
decade were natives of the state of Illinois than at the beginning of
the decade. It can be assumed that a large majority of the Illinois-
born Negroes were, in fact, born in Chicago. In 1940, 27 per cent of
the Negroes in Chicago were natives of the state. A sample estimate
of 33 per cent was obtained for 1949. Even with an allowance for
probable sampling error, this figure indicates that the change over
the decade was in line with a trend maintained since 1920 (see Table
5). The high net in-migration rate during 1910-20 diminished the percentage of Chicago Negroes who were natives of the state from 19 to
15; but thereafter the proportion increased, despite continuing in-
migration.

In comparing the Negro with the white trend in the proportion of
Chicago residents born in Illinois, it must be remembered that foreign-born whites comprised about a third of the city's total population

Table 5.—Per Cent of the Population Born in Illinois, by Race, for the City of Chicago, 1910-49

Year	Total White Population	White Population Born in the United States	Negro Population
1949*	63.1	74.8	32.8†
1940	61.1	77.9	27.1†
1930	54.0†	74.3†	17.8
1920	53.0	76.9	14.9
1910	47.2	74.3	19.3

*Statistics based on sample survey (see Chicago Community Inventory, Chicago Sample Survey, Release CSS-No. 6, December 29, 1949).

†Includes non-white population of races other than Negro.

at the beginning of the century. With the decline in the proportion of foreign-born, noted previously, the percentage of the total white population native to the state has naturally gone up—from 47 per cent in 1910 to an estimated 63 per cent in 1949. However, if attention is confined to the white population born in the United States, the proportion of Chicago residents born in Illinois has fluctuated around 75 per cent and was no higher in 1949 than in 1930 or 1910. The prospect for the future would seem to be for a convergence in the white and Negro proportions of Illinois natives living in the city. The white proportion will probably continue to increase, with the foreign-born population dying out. The Negro proportion should increase, as well, as recent Negro migrants continue to have children and as the older migrants are diminished in numbers by mortality. But if the experience of the three most recent decades is indicative of the future, the Negro proportion will increase faster than the white. Though it will doubtless require two generations or more to equalize the proportions of the two races, it is significant that the future Negro population of the city is likely to include much larger proportions of persons born and reared in the city than was true in the past.

It is a well-known fact that the bulk of the Negro migration to

Chicago originates in the South. Since a large proportion of Chicago's Negro population is not native to the state of Illinois, it follows that a large proportion is southern-born. In 1930, 72 per cent of the Negroes born in the United States and living in Chicago were natives of southern states; in 1940, 64 per cent of the non-white population of Chicago born in the United States reported a southern state of birth; and a sample estimate for 1949 indicated that 59 per cent of the Chicago non-whites born in the United States were natives of the South. There is, therefore, some evidence that the proportion of southern-born Negroes living in the city has been declining.

More direct information on the source of migration is available only for one period. There were nearly 15,000 non-whites reported in the 1940 Census as having lived outside the city in 1935.[2] Not quite

---

2. There is some reason to believe that this figure is substantially below the true number of non-white in-migrants from 1935 to 1940 who were still living in the city in 1940. The reported number of in-migrants (14,739) was nearly equaled by the number (13,124) of non-whites living elsewhere in the United States in 1940 who reported having resided in Chicago in 1935. Thus, on the basis of reports to the census migration question, there was a net in-migration of only 1,615 non-whites over the 1935-40 period. The estimated net in-migration of Negroes from 1930 to 1940 was given above as 37,000. There are several possibilities: (a) The in-migration of Negroes was almost entirely concentrated in the first half of the decade. This seems unlikely, since 1930-34 was a period of generally declining economic conditions, whereas 1935-39 was a period of generally improving conditions. Moreover, the 1934 Census of Chicago reported only 2,400 more Negroes than did the 1930 Census, whereas the total increase for the entire decade was nearly 44,000. (b) The estimate of net migration for 1930-40 is exaggerated. It is possible that the estimate contains a considerable error. But even if the actual net migration were only half as great as the estimate, one would still have to assume that a very large part of it was concentrated in the first half of the decade. (c) The census report of net migration, 1935-40, was a serious understatement of the amount of net in-migration that actually occurred. This alternative seems to be the most plausible one. If one keeps in mind how difficult it is for some people to recall their whereabouts on a date five years in the past and the likelihood that many reports on previous residence were made to the census enumerators by persons other than those to whom the information applied, it is easy to see how there are possibilities for substantial errors of reporting.

If the 1935-40 migration statistics for non-whites are as greatly in error as has been suggested, then one must interpret them with caution. Only relative comparisons of patterns and characteristics can be made, and even these may contain substantial biases.

three-fourths (71 per cent) of these migrants were residents of southern states in 1935. A sample estimate for 1949 indicated that, of the
non-whites who arrived in the city during the preceding year, 56 per
cent originated in the South. This figure, however, has such a large
sampling error that it is by no means certain that a decrease actually occurred in the percentage of non-white migrants originating in
the South between 1935-40 and 1948-49.

Not only does the South send the bulk of Chicago's Negro migrants,
but actually only a small number of southern states provide the majority of the migrants. There were five states—Mississippi, Arkansas,
Tennessee, Alabama, and Missouri—for which 1,000 or more non-
white migrants to Chicago were reported for the 1935-40 period.
These states accounted for 58 per cent of the total of 15,000 migrants,
and Mississippi alone for over one-fifth of the total.

The most apparent explanation of this concentration is that these
states are closer to Chicago than the other southern states and more
directly connected with the city by transportation routes. Negroes mi-
grating from the other southern states find it more convenient to go
to cities which are closer to them than Chicago is. It can be shown
that distance is a significant factor in Chicago's "pull" for non-white
migrants. If the states are classified roughly into broad zones according to distance from Chicago and if the reported number of migrants
to Chicago in 1935-40 is related to the 1940 non-white population in
each zone, the following results are obtained. The non-white rate of
out-migration to Chicago for states whose geographic centers are
within 400 miles of Chicago was 2.6 per 1,000 population; the rate
for states 400-600 miles away was half as large, 1.3 per 1,000; the
rate then dropped to 0.9 per 1,000 for states 600-800 miles away, 0.4
per 1,000 for states 800-1,200 miles away, and 0.5 per 1,000 for states
more than 1,200 miles away. Thus the "pull" of Chicago is less in the
southern states than in the nearby states of the North Central region.
But, because this pull is exerted on a much larger non-white population, the majority of non-white migrants, in absolute numbers, originate in the South.

One could extrapolate from these findings and reason as follows:
Since the Negro population is redistributing itself from a high con-

centration in the South to a more even distribution over the nation and since Chicago's "pull" is greater in the northern states, a smaller proportion of future Negro migrants to Chicago will come from the South than was true in the past. This is particularly likely to hold true if, as southern cities industrialize, they attract larger numbers of southern Negroes than they have been doing.

Direct information on the characteristics of non-white migrants to Chicago is somewhat scanty and probably not highly reliable. It seems probable that the census questions on migration in 1940 and 1950 failed to elicit reports from a considerable number of in-migrants (see n. 2). Those not reporting may well differ in their characteristics from those reporting. The following summary figures, then, must be interpreted with caution.

Of the 14,739 non-white in-migrants to Chicago reported in the 1940 Census, 35 per cent gave their 1935 residence as a city of 100,-000 or more (as of 1930), 36 per cent reported other urban residences, 13 per cent reported rural-non-farm residences, and 14 per cent reported rural-farm residences, while 2 per cent made incomplete reports. The proportion of non-white migrants coming from urban areas is considerably higher than one would expect on the basis of the high proportion of migrants from the South and the concentration of southern non-whites in rural areas. While there may be a bias in the figures, they can probably be trusted far enough to warrant the conclusion that a significant proportion of Negro migrants in recent decades have already had some experience with urban modes of living before coming to Chicago.

There was a concentration of persons in the young adult age groups among non-white persons reporting out-migration from Chicago, as well as among those reporting in-migration to Chicago between 1935 and 1940. However, the out-migrants, with a median age of thirty-two and a half years, were considerably older than the in-migrants, whose median age was twenty-six and a half years. The proportion of in-migrants in each age group below thirty was higher than the proportion of out-migrants; and the proportion of in-migrants was the smaller in each age group above thirty. Thirty-seven per cent of the in-migrants were twenty to twenty-nine years old in 1940, as compared to only 25 per cent of the out-migrants. These findings are consistent with the estimates given earlier of net migration by age, which likewise showed a concentration of net in-migrants in the younger age groups. It seems likely that a good part of the out-migration represents a backflow of relatively recent migrants to the city; but the age comparison merely suggests this conclusion without proving it.

Statistics on characteristics of migrants for the 1949-50 period are available only for movement between Illinois State Economic Area "C" (the five Illinois counties of the Chicago Standard Metropolitan Area) and other state economic areas. The comparisons given here concern non-white in-migrants living in urban parts of State Economic Area "C" and non-white out-migrants from State Economic Area "C" who, in 1949, lived in non-farm residences in the area. Again the data indicate a surprisingly low number of in-migrants. The total estimated numbers of migrants reporting, in the two categories described, were 9,695 in-migrants and 12,030 out-migrants. This indicates a net out-migration for the one-year period. While it is possible that the net balance of migration was in the direction of out-movement for that year, this condition certainly was not typical of most of the years in the decade. Hence the statistics, even if reliable, cannot be taken to represent the more general experience of recent years. Moreover, since the data were secured from a 20 per cent sample rather than a complete enumeration, the comparisons are subject to sampling variability as well as possible errors in reporting.

As in the 1935-40 migration statistics, the out-migrants of the 1949-50 period were somewhat older than the in-migrants, the respective median ages being 25.8 and 24.4 years.[3] The proportion of married persons among male migrants was about the same, regardless of direction of movement: 56 per cent of the in-migrants and 54 per cent of the out-migrants 14 years old and over were married. The corresponding figures for females show a somewhat higher pro-

---

3.   These figures must not be interpreted as showing a decline in the median age of migrants between 1935-40 and 1949-50. The statistics for the former period are based on persons five years old and over; those for the latter period on persons one year old and over.

portion married among the out-migrants: 57 per cent of the in-migrants, but 65 per cent of the out-migrants, were married.

The net balance of the movements was unfavorable to the educational status of the non-white population: the median number of school years completed was 9.3 for out-migrants and 9.1 for in-migrants. This difference, though small, agrees with the finding in chapter iv that the 1940-50 net migration of non-whites to Chicago tended to lower the level of educational attainment of the city's population.

The median income in 1949 of out-migrating families was $1,940, compared to $1,630 for in-migrating families. This suggests that the net balance of the movement was in the direction of lowering the economic status of the population. However, it must be remembered that at least a part of the 1949 income of out-migrants was earned in Chicago, and a part of the in-migrants' income in the places of origin, which probably, on the whole, have somewhat lower income levels than Chicago.

No reliable difference is found between in-migrants and out-migrants of either sex in the rate of participation in the labor force, as of the date of census enumeration in 1950. Nor is there any difference in the rate of unemployment among members of the labor force. However, the rate of unemployment was high for both in- and out-migrants, as compared with the resident population.

Differences in occupational distribution among in-migrants and out-migrants reflect, in part, the fact that the data are secured at the end of the migration period when the migrant is at his point of destination. Thus farm occupations are scarcely represented among the in-migrants, but 11 per cent of the employed out-migrants were working in farm occupations in 1950. Correlatively, 25 per cent of the in-migrants, but only 16 per cent of the out-migrants, had jobs as operatives and kindred workers. Other differences are of doubtful significance, because of sampling variability. However, the sample data show slightly higher proportions of sales and clerical workers and slightly lower proportions of professional and managerial workers among in-migrants than among out-migrants. No doubt the occupational differences reflect employment opportunities in the communities of destination and, therefore, do not afford a safe basis for generalizing about any socioeconomic selectivity in the net balance of the migration.[4]

---

4. For additional discussion of characteristics of migrants see the report, Chicago's Negro Population (cited in n. 6, p. 28).

Chapter IV

Non-white Population Composition,
1950 and 1940

The social and economic changes associated with business recovery and World War II produced rather considerable changes in the composition of Chicago's population from 1940 to 1950. The absorption of a large number of non-white in-migrants is likewise reflected in changes in non-white population composition.

There is considerable interest in determining whether the white and non-white populations resembled each other more closely at the end than at the beginning of the decade. A convergence of population characteristics would suggest that the Negro is becoming assimilated into the community's social and economic life. Actually, the picture is mixed. There is no question about Negroes having made economic gains over the decade, relative to whites. But with respect to several social characteristics, whites and non-whites in Chicago were less similar at the end of the decade than at the beginning.

Age and Sex Composition

The composition of the white and non-white population by age and sex is depicted graphically in Figure 3. The population pyramids reveal significant differences by color for both 1950 and 1940, as well as changes in the pattern of differences between whites and non-whites.

In both 1950 and 1940, females outnumbered males. The female preponderance was greater among non-whites than among whites in both years, but the difference between the two sex ratios lessened somewhat over the decade. The following are the numbers of males

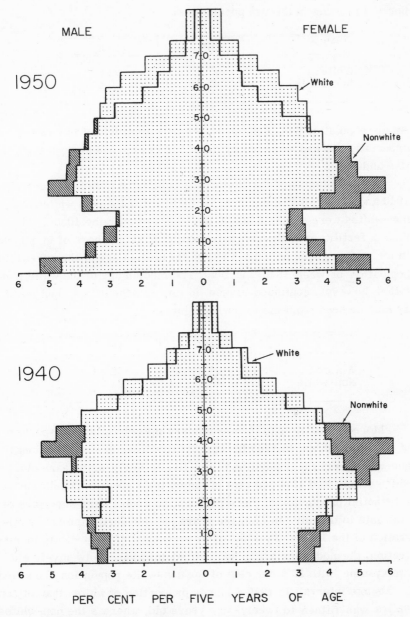

MALE FEMALE

1950

White

Nonwhite

1940

White

Nonwhite

PER CENT PER FIVE YEARS OF AGE

Fig. 3.—Population Pyramids for the White and Non-white Population of Chicago, 1950 and 1940.

per 100 females in the two populations:

	1950	1940
White.	97.1	98.8
Non-white.	92.4	90.6

As the population pyramids show, the predominance of females is especially marked in the young adult age groups and at ages sixty-five and over.

The broadening of the base of the population pyramids between 1940 and 1950 reflects the fact that birth rates for both whites and non-whites were much higher in the 1940's than in the 1930's. The rise in fertility plus the concentration of large numbers of in-migrants in the younger ages actually lowered the median age of the non-white population between 1940 and 1950. The median age of the white population, however, continued to rise, in line with the established trend, as may be seen from the following figures:

	1950	1940
White.	34.3	32.0
Non-white.	29.6	31.9

More revealing than these summary measures is an inspection of the age profiles. In 1940 the largest five-year age group among non-whites was the population thirty-five to thirty-nine years old, which constituted 11.4 per cent of the entire non-white population. A substantial proportion of these persons, no doubt, were survivors of migrants to the city ten or more years earlier during the heavy migration of the 1920's. By 1950, after a renewal of large-scale in-migration, the modal age group had shifted downward to twenty-five to twenty-nine, with 10.9 per cent of the non-white population classified in this age interval. In 1940 a larger proportion of whites than of non-whites was fifteen to twenty-nine years old, whereas the non-whites had the heavier proportion below age fifteen and between thirty and forty-four. In 1950, by contrast, the proportion of non-whites in each

age group below forty-five was higher than the corresponding proportion of whites. In both years the proportions of whites in the upper age groups were substantially greater than the proportions of
non-whites. But differences were much greater in 1950 than in 1940.
Thus the percentages of the population sixty-five years old and over
were as follows:

	1950	1940
White	8.0	5.9
Non-white	4.3	3.9

Because the white population contained proportionately more old
people but proportionately fewer children, the percentage of persons
in the central, productive ages was about the same for the whites as
for the non-whites in both years, although the percentage for both
color classifications decreased during the decade. The following are
the percentages of the population aged twenty to sixty-four years:

	1950	1940
White	65.2	66.5
Non-white	64.8	66.6

Roughly speaking, there were about two persons in the productive
ages for each person in the ages of greatest dependency in both years.

Marital Status and Household Relationship

As a general rule, indicators of disruptions of "normal" family
life were higher for non-whites than for whites in both 1950 and 1940.
To be more specific than this about white-non-white differences, one
must examine the available statistics in some detail.

Table 6 shows the distributions of the white and non-white populations by marital status. Since marital status changes with age and
since whites and non-whites have rather different age distributions,
it is well to supplement the gross comparisons of marital status with

Table 6.—Observed and Age-standardized Percentage Distribution of the Population Fourteen Years Old and Over, by Marital Status, by Sex and Color, for the City of Chicago, 1950 and 1940

Year, Sex, and Color	Observed Distribution					Age-standardized Distribution*				
	Total	Single	Married	Widowed	Divorced	Total	Single	Married	Widowed	Divorced
1950:										
Male										
White.....	100.0	26.8	66.1	4.6	2.5	100.0	27.1	66.1	4.4	2.4
Non-white..	100.0	23.2	68.4	5.3	3.1	100.0	21.5	68.2	7.2	3.1
Female										
White.....	100.0	21.5	63.0	12.4	3.1	100.0	21.9	63.2	11.8	3.1
Non-white..	100.0	15.8	64.7	14.7	4.8	100.0	13.9	61.5	19.9	4.7
1940:										
Male										
White.....	100.0	35.5	59.0	4.0	1.5	100.0	31.8	61.8	4.9	1.5
Non-white..	100.0	31.7	60.0	6.8	1.5	100.0	29.7	60.5	8.4	1.4
Female										
White.....	100.0	29.6	57.4	10.9	2.1	100.0	25.7	59.0	13.1	2.2
Non-white..	100.0	21.4	57.3	19.0	2.3	100.0	19.4	56.8	21.8	2.0

*Standardized by the direct method, using as the standard population the total population of each sex, respectively, in 1950. Since each sex was standardized separately, comparisons between the male and female standardized distributions are not meaningful.

comparisons adjusted for age. In 1950, white-non-white differences were considerably larger on an age-adjusted basis than on a gross basis.

In both 1950 and 1940 the proportion of the population ever married (i.e., married, widowed, or divorced) was higher among non-whites than among whites, and, correlatively, whites had the larger proportions of single persons. For whites and non-whites of both sexes there was an increase in the proportion of ever married persons over the decade. On a gross basis there was a smaller difference between the white and non-white proportions ever married in 1950 than in 1940; but just the reverse was true on the basis of the age-standardized distributions by marital status.

In both 1950 and 1940 a considerably higher proportion of non-whites than of whites were widows and widowers. The difference was much less at the end of the decade than at the beginning, on a gross basis, and slightly less on an age-standardized basis. In 1940 there was little difference between whites and non-whites in the proportion of divorced persons; but in 1950 the proportion of divorced persons was substantially higher among non-whites than among whites, for both males and females, on either a gross or an age-standardized basis.

The following are the indexes of dissimilarity between the white and non-white marital-status distributions:[1]

	Observed	Standardized
1950:		
Male	3.6	5.6
Female	5.7	9.7
1940:		
Male	3.8	3.5
Female	8.3	8.7

1. The index of dissimilarity is a simple measure of the difference between two frequency distributions. Since this index is used frequently in the monograph, a brief statement on its computation and interpretation is inserted here. Consider the observed percentage

The apparent convergence of the white and non-white distributions over the ten-year period is seen to be a happenstance of the shifts in age distribution. When standardized for age, the marital-status distribution of non-whites was less like that of whites in 1950 than in 1940.

Table 7 shows the proportion of married persons who reported that their spouses were not residents of the households in which they were living. The category "spouse absent" includes both persons who are permanently separated and those temporarily residing elsewhere for business reasons, in military service, and the like. In both 1940 and 1950 this form of family disruption was reported about four times as often by non-white married males as by white married males, and about five or six times as often by non-white married females as by white married females. The difference cannot be explained by age, because the age-standardized comparisons give about the same result. There was some decrease between 1940 and 1950 in the frequency of reporting "spouse absent" for non-white males and females

distributions of males by marital status in 1950 (taken from Table 6):

Marital Status	White Males	Non-white Males	White minus Non-white Per Cent	Sum of Differences
Single. . . .	26.8	23.2	3.6	
Married . .	66.1	68.4	-2.3	3.6
Widowed. .	4.6	5.3	-0.7	-3.6
Divorced .	2.5	3.1	-0.6	
Total . .	100.0	100.0	. . .	0.0

In this example the index of dissimilarity is 3.6 per cent, or the sum of the positive differences between the white and non-white distributions (or the sum of the negative differences, disregarding sign, which must equal the sum of the positive differences). Operationally, the index of dissimilarity is the percentage of "non-overlapping" of the two distributions. It is helpful to think of it as a measure of displacement; i.e., if the non-white distribution were made to match the white distribution, 3.6 per cent of the non-whites would have to change their marital status. Indexes of dissimilarity may be computed for percentage distributions according to any characteristic, for example, occupation, industry classification, area of residence, etc. If, instead of comparing two groups (such as whites versus non-whites or males versus females), one compares the distributions of the same group at two points in time, the index of dissimilarity serves as a measure of the net redistribution over the time period between the two dates.

and white females, but not for white males. It is perhaps significant that such a decrease occurred for non-whites during a decade of heavy in-migration, because migration is sometimes disruptive of family life.

Table 8 shows the proportions of the population living in house-

Table 7.—Observed and Age-standardized Percentage of Married Persons Fifteen Years Old and Over Reporting Spouse Absent, by Sex and Color, for the City of Chicago, 1950 and 1940

Sex and Color	Observed		Age-standardized*	
	1950	1940	1950	1940
Male:				
White	4.5	4.3	4.5	4.4
Non-white	18.4	19.7	18.1	19.1
Female:				
White	3.8	4.3	3.8	4.4
Non-white	23.1	26.0	22.6	24.8

*Standardized by the direct method, using as the standard population the total married population fifteen years old and over of each sex, respectively, in 1950. Since each sex was standardized separately, comparisons between the male and female standardized percentages are not meaningful.

Table 8.—Observed and Age-standardized Percentage of the Population Living in Households, by Sex and Color, for the City of Chicago, 1950 and 1940

(See Text on Comparability of 1950 and 1940 Data)

Sex and Color	Observed		Age-standardized*	
	1950	1940	1950	1940
Male:				
White	95.3	96.6	95.3	96.6
Non-white	90.5	97.8	90.5	97.8
Female:				
White	97.0	97.5	97.1	97.6
Non-white	91.8	98.9	92.0	98.9

*Standardized by the direct method, using as the standard population the total population of each sex, respectively, in 1950. Since each sex was standardized separately, comparisons between the male and female standardized percentages are not meaningful.

holds in 1950 and 1940, by sex and color. Only a minority of the population lives in quasi-households, i.e., institutions, lodging houses, hotels, military barracks, and the like. Apparently, a somewhat larger proportion of non-whites than of whites in 1940, but a considerably smaller proportion in 1950, lived in households. One cannot be sure, however, that the statistics reflect a genuine change. In the 1940 Census only lodging houses with 11 or more lodgers were classed as quasi-households, whereas in the 1950 Census lodging houses with as few as 5 lodgers were classed as quasi-households. If it were true that non-whites were disproportionately represented in lodging houses with 5 to 10 lodgers, then the apparent change could be explained as merely a result of altering the classification procedures. Whatever the explanation of the change, it is clear that under the 1950 definitions the proportion of non-whites living in households is about five percentage points lower than that of whites; the difference is not affected by standardizing for age.

Table 9 presents percentage distributions by household relationship for the population living in households. The comparability of the data for 1950 and 1940 is somewhat impaired for the reason already noted: an unknown proportion of persons classified as non-relatives of household head in 1940 would be classified as residents of quasi-households in 1950 and hence excluded from the distribution by household relationship. However, comparisons can be made between whites and non-whites in either year.

Among males, in both years, whites had the higher proportions of household heads and children of household heads, while non-whites had the higher proportions of other relatives of household heads and non-relatives of household heads. The comparison is not greatly affected by age-standardization. Among females, it is striking that a much higher proportion of non-whites than of whites are heads of households. As is true for males, larger proportions of non-whites than of whites were other relatives and non-relatives of household heads. White females had the higher proportions of wives and children of household heads.

The 1950 data indicate a considerably greater similarity between whites and non-whites with respect to their distributions by house-

Table 9.—Observed and Age-standardized Percentage Distribution of the Population Living in Households by Household Relationship, by Sex and Color, for the City of Chicago, 1950 and 1940

(See Text on Comparability of 1950 and 1940 Data)

Type of Comparison and Household Relationship	Male								Female							
	1950		1940						1950		1940					
	White	Non-white	White	Non-white					White	Non-white	White	Non-white				
Observed distribution:																
Total population in households	100.0	100.0	100.0	100.0					100.0	100.0	100.0	100.0				
Household head or primary individual	54.2	45.0	49.4	39.4					10.4	15.9	9.1	16.0				
Wife of head									46.6	32.6	43.1	27.3				
Child of head	35.2	29.5	39.2	28.6					31.5	26.6	35.8	25.7				
Other relative of head	7.4	12.8	7.0	9.3					9.0	15.2	8.5	11.2				
Non-relative of head	3.2	12.7	4.4	22.7					2.5	9.7	3.5	19.8				
Age-standardized distribution:*																
Total population in households	100.0	100.0	100.0	100.0					100.0	100.0	100.0	100.0				
Household head or primary individual	54.5	48.6	50.9	41.0					10.2	17.6	9.9	17.0				
Wife of head									46.5	32.9	43.5	26.8				
Child of head	34.9	26.1	37.3	26.9					32.0	23.5	34.1	23.8				
Other relative of head	7.4	12.3	7.3	9.4					8.9	16.0	9.0	12.7				
Non-relative of head	3.2	13.0	4.5	22.7					2.4	10.0	3.5	19.7				

*Standardized by the direct method, using as the standard population of each sex, respectively, in 1950. Since each sex was standardized separately, comparisons between the male and female standardized percentages are not meaningful.

hold relationship than do the 1940 data. However, in view of the alter-
ation in procedures of classifying lodgers, it is by no means certain
that there was actually a change in this direction.

In summary, the statistical analysis discloses several indicators
of greater disruption of family living or greater variation from conventional patterns of family life among non-whites in Chicago than
among whites. These include higher proportions widowed and, in 1950,
divorced; higher proportions of married persons not living with their
spouses; higher proportions living in quasi-households; higher proportions of the residents of households not related to the household
head or related more distantly than spouse or child; and higher proportions of households headed by females. Most of these differences
seemingly represent persistent patterns, and few clearly interpret-
able trends toward their disappearance are in evidence for the 1940-
50 decade.

Educational Attainment

The level of educational attainment of the population twenty-five
years old and over in Chicago was higher in 1950 than in 1940 for
both whites and non-whites. The median number of school years
completed by whites of this age was 8.7 in 1940 and 10.2 in 1950, a
gain of 1.5 years. The medians for non-whites were 8.3 in 1940 and
8.8 in 1950, a gain of only 0.5 year. Thus, whereas the white exceeded
the non-white median by only 0.4 year in 1940, the difference increased to 1.4 years in 1950.

The comparison between white and non-white educational attainment should be refined to take account of age. Whites and non-whites
have rather different age distributions, and in both the white and the
non-white population educational attainment varies considerably by age.
Figure 4 shows educational attainment, by detailed age groups, for
whites and non-whites in 1940 and 1950. Looking first at panel A of
Figure 4, it appears that the improvement in educational attainment
between 1940 and 1950 for whites was largely concentrated in the
younger adult ages, whereas for non-whites significant gains were
registered at all ages. Thus the median number of school years completed by whites aged twenty-five to forty-four in 1940 was 9.9, and

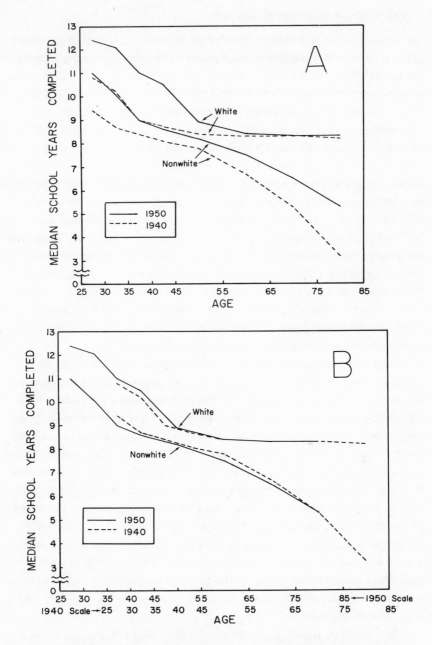

Fig. 4.—Median Number of School Years Completed, for the Population Twenty-five Years Old and Over, by Age and Color, for the City of Chicago, 1950 and 1940.

for whites of the same ages in 1950 the median was 12.0. This represents a gain of 2.1 median school years. The corresponding figures
for non-whites were 8.6 in 1940 and 9.8 in 1950, a gain of 1.2 median
school years. For whites forty-five years old and over in 1940 the
median number of school years completed was 8.4, compared with
8.6 median school years completed by whites aged forty-five and over
in 1950. This gain of but 0.2 median school year contrasts with a
gain of 0.8 median school year for non-whites, the medians for non-
whites aged forty-five and over being 7.0 in 1940 and 7.8 in 1950. It
is significant that the median for non-whites twenty-five to forty-
four years old in 1950 (9.8) was practically the same as that for
whites of the same ages in 1940 (9.9 median school years). Thus, for
the younger adults one could say that the non-white population presently lags about a decade behind the white population in improving
its educational qualifications. To keep this time lag from becoming
greater or to reduce it, the non-white population of school age in
1950 and subsequent years must have considerably more schooling
than comparable age groups have had in the past.

Figure 4 makes it evident that one should expect further improvements in the educational status of both the white and the non-
white populations. The attrition of the older cohorts through mortality will remove a disproportionate number of persons from the population who have low educational attainment, while the entry into the
adult population of the younger cohorts, with their relatively high educational attainment, will raise the general average. The former process will make for a convergence of white and non-white educational
status, since the disadvantage of the non-whites is more pronounced
at the older ages than in the middle range of adult ages. However,
even if educational attainment of the non-white cohorts now in school
should be as high as that of whites, the discrepancy between white and
non-white educational status in the total adult population of the city
could not be eliminated in less than two generations, barring a highly
selective migration.

In Figure 4, panel B, the data just reviewed are portrayed in a
slightly different way, in order to bring out a relationship not immediately evident in panel A of the figure. Here attention is called to

the fact that persons aged, e.g., fifty-five to sixty-four in 1950 are
the survivors of persons aged forty-five to fifty-four in 1940. Having
data from the two censuses, therefore, permits a "cohort" comparison. Among non-whites, for the cohort just mentioned (persons forty-
five to fifty-four years old in 1940 and fifty-five to sixty-four years
old in 1950), there was an apparent change in the median number of
school years completed, from 7.8 to 7.5. Such a change, if real, could
be explained only by either one or a combination of two factors: differential mortality and migration. In general, differential mortality
is expected to improve, rather than lower, the educational status of
a cohort as it ages, since mortality is generally higher among the
socially and economically disadvantaged sectors of the population. Migration to and from a city could change the educational status either
positively or negatively, depending on the type of selectivity involved.
There is, however, a variety of possible errors in the data which affect the cohort comparison. The question on educational attainment
in the 1950 Census was asked in a somewhat more detailed way than
in the 1940 Census, in an effort to minimize exaggeration of the number of school years completed. Both censuses were subject to errors
in the reporting of the population by age. There may be some tendency for persons to remember their educational attainment less accurately as they get older. Finally, the 1950 Census figures are based
on a sample of 20 per cent of the population rather than a complete
enumeration.

Though the cohort comparisons are doubtless affected by errors
from all these sources, there is no particular reason to suppose that
their effects would run consistently in different directions for whites
and non-whites. Thus it may be significant that the white age cohorts
appear to increase slightly in educational attainment between 1940
and 1950, while the non-white cohorts appear to decrease. Furthermore, this contrast in direction of change is not observed in the
United States as a whole, where, at least for the younger cohorts,
positive changes were observed for both whites and non-whites between 1940 and 1950. The data, therefore, suggest that improvement
in the educational status of Chicago's non-white population between
1940 and 1950 was retarded by the absorption of migrants to the city

whose educational attainment was less than that of the population living in the city in 1940. Some analysis of this point is presented below.

Because statistics on school years completed, by age, are available for the non-white population in both 1940 and 1950, it is possible to estimate the educational differential between net migrants and non-migrants. Census survival ratios, specific for age, sex, and number of school years completed, were applied to the enumerated 1940 population, to obtain an estimate of the number of survivors by educational attainment in 1950. The discrepancy between the estimated survivors and the 1950 enumerated population is the estimated net migration (see Appendix B for an explanation of this technique of estimation). Most of the age-sex-educational attainment subgroups experienced a net in-migration over the decade, the few exceptions being mostly in the older age groups.

Of the non-white population twenty years old and over enumerated in Chicago in 1940, 35.0 per cent had completed 1 year of high school or more, and the median number of school years completed was 8.4. The corresponding figures for their estimated survivors in 1950 are 41.6 per cent with 1 year of high school or more and a median of 8.6 school years completed. The improvement in educational status over the decade—assuming it to be real and not a mere error of estimation—could be explained readily as being due to some additional school attendance on the part of younger persons and differential mortality in favor of the more highly educated. Regardless of this point, the estimated survivors had a somewhat higher educational status than the non-white population thirty years old and over actually enumerated in 1950 (see Table 10). Hence the estimated net migrants had a considerably lower educational status than the enumerated population. The median number of school years completed was only 7.3 for the estimated net migrants, as compared to 8.4 for the actual population and 8.6 for the estimated survivors of the 1940 population. Similarly, only 30.9 per cent of the estimated net migrants had completed 1 year of high school or more, as compared to 38.5 per cent of the actual population and 41.6 per cent of the estimated survivors.

The educational selectivity of the 1940-50 net migration is illustrated further in the migration rates shown in Table 11. For the total non-white population thirty years old and over, there was an

Table 10.—Educational Attainment of the Non-white Population Thirty Years Old and Over, by 1940-50 Migration Status, for the City of Chicago, 1950

Migration Status	Median Number of School Years Completed	Per Cent Completed One Year of High School or More
Total enumerated population, 1950. . .	8.4	38.5
Estimated survivors from 1940 population	8.6	41.6
Estimated net migrants, 1940-50. . . .	7.3	30.9

Table 11.—Estimated Net Migration, 1940-50, per 100 Survivors of the 1940 Population, for the Non-white Population in the City of Chicago, by Age and Number of School Years Completed

Number of School Years Completed	Total Thirty Years Old and Over	Age in 1950 (Years)				
		30-34	35-39	40-44	45-54	55 and Over
Total*. . .	44	118	66	40	24	22
None	42	281†	141†	113†	44†	22
Elementary:						
1 to 4 . . .	85	621†	245	127	71	44
5 and 6 . .	54	328†	142	70	29	16
7 and 8 . .	31	154	58	26	9	6
High school:						
1 to 3 . . .	26	63	33	13	8	6
4	34	77	37	20	8	17
College:						
1 to 3 . . .	37	78	56	32	15	7
4 or more	25	100†	25†	30†	4	4

*Rates in this row are not comparable with those shown in Table 4.

†Rate based on fewer than 1,000 estimated survivors.

estimated net in-migration of 44 persons per 100 survivors of the 1940 population twenty years old and over. But the rate was 85 per 100 survivors for persons with only 1 to 4 years of elementary-school education and 54 per 100 survivors for persons with 5 and 6 years of elementary schooling. When the migration rates are broken down by age, the highest rate observed for each age group occurs among persons with but 1 to 4 school years completed, and the second highest rate either among persons with 5 and 6 school years completed or persons with no school years completed. While the individual migration rates in Table 11—particularly those based on small numbers—may be quite unreliable, the consistency of the pattern of selectivity argues that the selection in favor of poorly educated persons is real and not a happenstance of the errors of estimation.

Since a large proportion of non-white migrants originate in the South, where the educational status of non-whites is very low, it is not surprising that their educational attainment should be less than that of the non-white population of Chicago. The median of 7.3 school years completed for the estimated net migrants to Chicago is somewhat higher than the median for the comparable age group of all non-whites in the South in 1950. Hence the migrants are probably a favorably selected group, in terms of the population from which they are drawn. However, this conclusion can be only tentative without more detailed study of the problem.

School Enrolment

Table 12 summarizes the available statistics on school enrolment of whites and non-whites in 1950 and 1940. Unfortunately, there are a number of limitations on the comparability of the data; hence the conclusions which one may draw from them must be carefully qualified.

The non-white population appeared to have a higher rate of school enrolment for persons five and six years old in both 1950 and 1940, although the proportion of this age group in school seemingly declined for both whites and non-whites over the ten-year period.

Table 12.—Per Cent of Persons Five to Twenty-four Years Old Enrolled in School, by Age, Color, and Sex, for the City of Chicago,
1950 and 1940

Sex and Age	1950*		1940	
	White	Non-white	White	Non-white
Male:				
5 and 6 years† . . .	45.8	48.0	55.4	60.4
7-13 years.	96.3	96.6	97.7	97.2
14-17 years	90.6	86.0	88.4	87.6
18 and 19 years‡. .	39.6	31.8	34.0	37.5
20-24 years†	22.6	12.4	10.0	6.7
Female:				
5 and 6 years† . . .	47.0	49.2	56.4	63.5
7-13 years.	96.3	97.0	97.8	97.5
14-17 years	89.0	84.2	85.7	86.6
18 and 19 years‡. .	26.1	23.9	23.8	30.6
20-24 years†	8.3	5.3	4.9	4.7

*Statistics based on 20 per cent sample.

†Comparability of 1950 and 1940 figures affected by change in
reporting of kindergarten enrolment.

‡Comparability of 1950 and 1940 figures affected by change in
reporting of residence of college students.

Two factors help to explain these somewhat surprising findings: first,
in the 1950 Census, kindergarten enrolment was enumerated separately from school enrolment. It is suspected that prior to 1950 some
persons enrolled in kindergarten were erroneously reported as enrolled in school; with the elimination of such erroneous reports, the
apparent rate of school enrolment would decline. Second, the procedures for editing the census schedules provide, in general, that if no
report is given on the enrolment status of persons five to seventeen
years old, they are considered to be in school; whereas, for ages
eighteen and over, persons not reporting are considered not to be in
school. If it is true of school enrolment, as of other questions, that
the non-response rate in the census tends to be higher for non-whites
than for whites, then the editing rule might tend to inflate the non-
white enrolment rate for an age group for which the true rate is not
high. In sum, it is difficult to interpret the recorded white-non-white
difference in enrolment rates at ages five and six.

The differences between whites and non-whites in the proportions attending school for persons seven to thirteen years old are very small. For both groups, school enrolment at these ages is virtually universal. However, it appears that a shift occurred between 1940 and 1950. The non-white enrolment rate was slightly below the white in 1940 and slightly above it in 1950; the shift occurred for both males and females. Inspection of data by single years of age shows that, for females, the non-white enrolment rate was higher than the white in 1950 at each single year of age but one. For males the non-white rate was higher than the white only at ages seven and eight. In view of the small size of the differences, sampling variation in the 1950 statistics, and possible variation by color in completeness of reporting, it is difficult to attach much significance to the apparent changes.

At ages fourteen to seventeen the white enrolment rate was higher than the non-white in both 1940 and 1950. Furthermore, the difference increased over the decade as a result of an increase in the white enrolment rate and a decrease in the non-white rate. In 1950 the white enrolment rate was nearly 5 percentage points higher than the non-white. The difference was less than this at ages fourteen and fifteen and greater at ages sixteen and seventeen.

The comparability of 1950 and 1940 enrolment rates at ages eighteen and over is impaired by the change in census procedures with respect to reporting residence of college students. In 1940, college students were considered to be residents of the places in which their parental homes were located, whereas, in 1950, they were enumerated as residents of the places in which they were living while attending college. It is not known whether Chicago "exports" more college students than it "imports" or whether the net balance of "exports" and "imports" is similar for whites and non-whites, or was in the same direction in 1940 as in 1950. Consequently, there is considerable doubt about the interpretation of the shift in relative positions of the white and non-white enrolment rates at ages eighteen and nineteen.

Perhaps the only conclusion in which one can have full confidence is that non-whites, on the average, terminate their school attendance at an earlier age than whites. Moreover, the difference between whites and non-whites in average age of leaving school probably widened between 1940 and 1950, but it is not possible to state precisely the extent of the change, owing to difficulties in interpreting the statistics.

Labor-Force Characteristics

The decade of the 1940's, under the impact of World War II and economic recovery, witnessed sizable changes in the composition of the labor force. One general effect of these changes was to give the Negro a somewhat more favorable relative position in Chicago's labor force in 1950 than in 1940. Nevertheless, at the end of the decade there remained a number of important differences between white and non-white labor-force characteristics.

Table 13 shows labor-force participation rates, by sex and color, for the two census years. In both 1940 and 1950 a somewhat higher

Table 13.—Observed and Age-standardized Percentage of the Population Fourteen Years Old and Over in the Labor Force, by Color and Sex, for the City of Chicago, 1950 and 1940

Sex and Color	Observed		Standardized for Age*	
	1950†	1940	1950†	1940
Male:				
White	82.4	82.4	82.4	84.1
Non-white . . .	79.1	78.1	76.9	75.3
Female:				
White	37.2	33.3	37.2	31.1
Non-white . . .	40.6	35.7	37.9	32.8

*Using the age distribution of the white population in 1950 as the standard.

†Statistics based on 20 per cent sample.

proportion of white males than of non-white males fourteen years old and over were in the labor force. The difference was in the opposite direction among females, where the non-white exceeded the white rate of labor-force participation in both years.

These comparisons for all persons fourteen years old and over disregard the patterns of differences by age. Among males the white was higher than the non-white labor-force participation rate at all ages in both 1940 and 1950 (see Appendix Table A-6). However, white-non-white differences among females were not in the same direction at all ages. The non-white rate was the higher only at ages twenty-five to sixty-four in 1940 and twenty-five to fifty-four in 1950. At the ages where the female rate of labor-force participation is highest—eighteen to twenty-four—the rate for white females was much higher than for non-white females. Evidently, it is easier for white females to enter the labor force at an early age (in part because they marry and begin childbearing later, on the average), but non-white females tend to remain in the labor force longer.

Because labor-force participation rates vary so greatly by age, in any over-all comparison for persons aged fourteen and over it is desirable to take account of differences in age distribution. Thus Table 13 shows labor-force participation rates standardized for age. The age standardization increases the difference between whites and non-whites for males in both years but decreases the differences for females. However, the direction of the differences remains the same as in the unstandardized comparisons. Even more important, the age standardization reveals a convergence of the white and non-white labor-force participation rates between 1940 and 1950. The differences between the white and non-white rates were smaller for both sexes in 1950 than in 1940.

Non-white members of the labor force had much higher rates of unemployment than did white members in both 1940 and 1950 (see Table 14). The relative disadvantage of non-whites was somewhat more pronounced among females than among males. This may simply reflect a greater tendency of white females to withdraw from the labor force when they are unsuccessful in finding work.

It is difficult to say whether the non-white position improved or deteriorated over the decade relative to the white. The unemployment rate for both groups was only about one-third as great in 1950 as in 1940. But this means that the rate observed for non-whites in 1950, a year of relative prosperity, was about as high as the rate for whites

Table 14.—Per Cent of the Labor Force Unemployed, by Color and Sex, for the City of Chicago, 1950 and 1940

Sex and Color	1950*	1940†
Male:		
White	4.1	14.4
Non-white . . .	11.3	35.2
Female:		
White	3.3	11.1
Non-white . . .	12.6	35.0

*Statistics based on 20 per cent sample.

†Persons on public emergency work are
classified as unemployed, as well as those
seeking work.

in 1940, when the economy was only beginning to emerge from the depression. It is possible that the comparatively high rate for non-whites
in 1950 reflects some degree of "normal" instability in employment
on the part of migrants still in the process of working out a job adjustment.

A considerable part of the higher rate of unemployment among
non-whites is due to the fact that they are concentrated in occupations
with a comparatively high incidence of unemployment. Some convergence of white and non-white employment rates, therefore, is to be
expected as non-whites improve their occupational status. Incidentally,
the over-all white-non-white differences in unemployment cannot be
explained by age differences, since non-whites had substantially higher
unemployment rates at all ages (Appendix Table A-6).

Table 15 shows the distributions of white and non-white employed
persons by class of worker. The decline in the proportions of unpaid
family workers and self-employed workers, for both whites and non-
whites, no doubt reflects the improvement of employment opportunities between 1940 and 1950. Especially noteworthy is the decrease in
the percentage of non-white self-employed females from 9.5 in 1940
to 2.8 in 1950. This is related to the sharp decrease, noted below, in

Table 15.—Percentage Distribution of Employed Persons by Class of Worker, by Color and Sex, for the City of Chicago, 1950 and 1940

Sex and Class of Worker	1950		1940	
	White*	Non-white†	White	Non-white
Male:				
Total employed............	100.0	100.0	100.0	100.0
Private wage and salary workers	81.5	85.6	81.7	83.7
Government workers........	7.7	10.1	5.8	8.4
Self-employed workers	10.7	4.2	12.2	7.7
Unpaid family workers.......	0.1	0.1	0.3	0.2
Female:				
Total employed............	100.0	100.0	100.0	100.0
Private wage and salary workers	88.3	88.6	86.9	85.6
Government workers........	7.0	8.4	6.0	4.2
Self-employed workers	4.0	2.8	5.2	9.5
Unpaid family workers.......	0.7	0.2	1.9	0.7

*Includes non-whites residing in census tracts with fewer than 250 non-white inhabitants.

†Excludes non-whites residing in census tracts with fewer than 250 non-white inhabitants.

the proportions of non-white females working in the personal services. The proportion of government workers increased from 1940 to 1950 for both whites and non-whites. In 1950 the proportion of government workers was substantially higher for non-whites than for whites of both sexes, but the difference was in the opposite direction for females in 1940. As a result of all these changes, the distribution of non-white males by class of worker was more dissimilar to that of white males in 1950 than in 1940, whereas the white-non-white dissimilarity for females was considerably reduced over the decade.

Tables 16 and 17 show the industry distributions of the white and non-white employed labor force in 1940 and 1950. It is apparent, first of all, that there were substantial shifts in industrial composition over the decade, particularly for non-whites. The extent of these shifts can be illustrated as follows: If the employed labor force had consisted of the same persons in 1950 as in 1940, at least 34.8 per cent of the non-white females would have had to change their industry classification to produce the change in industry distribution which occurred over

Table 16.—Percentage Distribution of Employed Males by Major Industry Group, by Color, for the City of Chicago, 1950 and 1940

Major Industry Group	1950		1940	
	White*	Non-whitet	White	Non-white
Total employed males	100.0	100.0	100.0	100.0
Agriculture, forestry, fisheries, and mining...............	0.2	0.2	0.2	0.1
Construction................	6.0	4.4	5.5	3.7
Manufacturing..............	38.6	38.3	37.5	24.7
Transportation.............	10.1	12.0	9.5	13.8
Communications and other public utilities.................	2.6	1.0	2.5	0.7
Wholesale trade.............	5.3	3.3	4.7	2.5
Retail trade................	15.2	13.0	17.5	18.9
Finance, insurance, and real estate	4.4	2.3	5.2	4.1
Business and repair services....	3.2	3.6	2.9	4.9
Personal services	3.1	8.0	4.0	13.8
Entertainment and recreation services	1.1	1.3	1.1	2.3
Professional and related services	4.8	3.6	4.5	3.3
Public administration..........	4.4	7.2	4.1	6.5
Industry not reported	1.0	1.8	0.8	0.7
Manufacturing detail:				
Furniture, and lumber and wood products	1.6	1.6	2.0	1.2
Metal industries	8.1	12.0	8.2	7.3
Machinery, except electrical	5.8	2.6	4.6	1.0
Electrical machinery, equipment, and supplies..............	4.3	1.4	2.7	0.2
Transportation equipment	1.7	1.7	1.5	0.5
Food and kindred products......	4.6	10.4	5.4	8.8
Apparel and other fabricated textile products	1.0	0.7	1.3	0.6
Printing, publishing, and allied industries.................	4.2	1.6	4.2	1.1
Chemicals and allied products ...	1.4	1.4	1.3	0.9
All other manufacturing industries (including not specified)	5.9	4.9	6.3	3.1

*Includes non-whites residing in census tracts with under 250 non-white population.

tExcludes non-whites residing in census tracts with under 250 non-white population.

Table 17.—Percentage Distribution of Employed Females by Major Industry Group, by Color, for the City of Chicago, 1950 and 1940

Major Industry Group	1950		1940	
	White*	Non-white†	White	Non-white
Total employed females	100.0	100.0	100.0	100.0
Agriculture, forestry, fisheries, and mining...............	0.1	0.1	0.1	0.0
Construction	0.6	0.2	0.4	0.1
Manufacturing	33.3	30.0	29.4	9.3
Transportation	2.6	1.6	1.8	0.9
Communications and other public utilities.................	3.9	0.6	3.6	0.1
Wholesale trade.............	3.7	1.8	3.0	0.3
Retail trade................	21.5	13.3	23.0	9.7
Finance, insurance, and real estate	7.3	1.7	6.1	2.7
Business and repair services....	2.3	0.6	1.5	0.3
Personal services	6.5	34.0	13.9	67.2
Entertainment and recreation services	0.8	0.7	0.9	1.3
Professional and related services.	13.0	9.2	12.8	5.7
Public administration	2.9	4.6	1.9	1.7
Industry not reported	1.5	1.6	1.6	0.7
Manufacturing detail:				
Furniture, and lumber and wood products	0.7	0.9	0.8	0.6
Metal industries	3.4	2.5	2.5	0.7
Machinery, except electrical	2.4	0.7	1.3	0.0
Electrical machinery, equipment, and supplies..............	7.0	2.2	3.2	0.0
Transportation equipment	0.7	0.4	0.5	0.0
Food and kindred products......	4.3	7.1	5.1	1.6
Apparel and other fabricated textile products	3.4	6.6	5.1	3.7
Printing, publishing, and allied industries	3.4	1.9	3.1	0.2
Chemicals and allied products ...	1.3	0.7	1.2	0.2
All other manufacturing industries (including not specified)	6.7	7.0	6.6	2.3

*Includes non-whites residing in census tracts with under 250 non-white population.

†Excludes non-whites residing in census tracts with under 250 non-white population.

the decade. The indexes of net redistribution between 1940 and 1950, calculated on this basis, are as follows:

	Male	Female
White	6.0	11.7
Non-white	17.6	34.8

Actually, of course, the amount of shifting between industries was much greater than is implied by these net figures, and there was movement into and out of the employed labor force, particularly that engendered by non-white migration. The figures serve, however, to demonstrate that major changes in the industrial attachments of Chicago's non-white labor force took place over the decade.

The most striking single change was the marked decrease in the proportion of non-white females employed in personal services. In 1940 this industry claimed two-thirds (67.2 per cent) of the non-white females, but the proportion was only one-third (34.0 per cent) in 1950.

Another significant change was the gain in the proportion of non-whites employed in manufacturing industries. In 1940, non-white females were greatly underrepresented in manufacturing, and the proportion of non-white males in manufacturing was only two-thirds as high as that of white males. But by 1950, with an increase in the proportion in manufacturing for whites and non-whites of both sexes, the proportion in manufacturing was only slightly lower for non-white than for white females, and the white and non-white proportions were nearly the same for males.

In terms of the major subdivisions of manufacturing, in 1940 the proportion of non-whites was less than the proportion of whites in all categories except for food manufacturing among males. By 1950, non-white males were equally or disproportionately represented relative to white males, in food, chemicals, transportation equipment, furniture and wood products, and metal manufacturing; and non-white females had achieved proportional representation, or more, in food, furniture, apparel, and the residual category of "all other" manufacturing industries.

There were few shifts in the pattern of over- and underrepresentation of non-whites in non-manufacturing industries. In 1940 there was a higher proportion of non-white males than of white males in transportation, communication, and other public utilities, retail trade, business and repair services, personal services, entertainment and recreation services, and public administration. The list of industries with non-white males disproportionately represented remained the same in 1950, except for the loss of retail trade. Non-white females were substantially overrepresented in personal services in both 1940 and 1950; in entertainment and recreation in 1940 only; and in public administration in 1950 only.

The net effect of all the changes between 1940 and 1950 was to make the non-white much more like the white industry distribution. In 1940, 21.1 per cent of the non-white males would have had to change to a different industry to make their industry distribution the same as that of white males; the figure was only half as large, 11.0 per cent, in 1950. For females the corresponding figures were 53.7 per cent in 1940 and only 29.3 per cent in 1950. In part, this rapid movement toward similar industry distributions of whites and non-whites can be attributed to the improvement of economic conditions between 1940 and 1950 and the abnormal demand for labor during World War II. However, it seems likely that a substantial part of the difference in industry distributions has been more or less permanently eliminated; and still further reductions of the difference would not be surprising, though the rate of change of the 1940-50 decade could hardly be repeated.

The changes in occupational composition accompanying the industrial shifts are revealed in Table 18. In quick summary, one could say that non-whites "moved up a rung on the occupational ladder" between 1940 and 1950. At the beginning of the decade non-whites were overrepresented in the three occupation groups—service workers, laborers, and private household workers—generally conceded to be lowest in socioeconomic status. By 1950 they were employed in dis-

Table 18. — Percentage Distribution of Employed Persons by Major Occupation Group, by Color and Sex, for the City of Chicago, 1950 and 1940

Sex and Major Occupation Group	1950		1940	
	White*	Non-white†	White	Non-white
Male:				
Total employed	100.0	100.0	100.0	100.0
Professional, technical, and kindred workers	9.2	2.8	7.0	3.4
Managers, officials, and proprietors (including farm)	11.9	2.9	10.7	3.1
Sales workers	7.9	2.3	9.3	3.4
Clerical and kindred workers	11.3	8.6	13.0	6.7
Craftsmen, foremen, and kindred workers	22.7	11.0	20.3	8.9
Operatives and kindred workers	22.1	28.1	22.2	20.0
Service workers, except private household	7.8	21.0	8.8	33.2
Laborers (including farm)	6.2	21.0	8.1	19.4
Private household workers	0.1	0.5	0.1	1.5
Occupation not reported	0.8	1.8	0.5	0.4
Female:				
Total employed	100.0	100.0	100.0	100.0
Professional, technical, and kindred workers	10.3	4.9	10.2	4.6
Managers, officials, and proprietors (including farm)	4.2	1.6	3.5	1.7
Sales workers	7.6	2.6	8.2	2.7
Clerical and kindred workers	41.3	11.6	35.3	4.5
Craftsmen, foremen, and kindred workers	2.3	1.9	1.5	0.5
Operatives and kindred workers	21.4	36.9	21.7	20.4
Service workers, except private household	9.0	19.6	11.6	25.7
Laborers (including farm)	0.7	3.8	1.3	1.7
Private household workers	2.1	15.5	6.1	37.7
Occupation not reported	1.1	1.6	0.6	0.5

*Includes non-whites residing in census tracts with fewer than 250 non-white inhabitants.

†Excludes non-whites residing in census tracts with fewer than 250 non-white inhabitants.

proportionate numbers in one additional occupation, operatives and kindred workers. However, they continued to have smaller proportions than did whites employed in the white-collar occupations and as craftsmen, foremen, and kindred workers. The substantial increase in the proportion of non-white operatives is, of course, related to the rise in the proportion in manufacturing, since manufacturing employs a large share of all persons in the occupations classified in this group.

The net shifts in occupational classification over the decade were greater for non-whites than for whites, and greater for females than for males, as shown by the following indexes of net redistribution between 1940 and 1950:

	Male	Female
White.	6.1	8.1
Non-white	15.1	28.5

The rank order of these index values is the same as that observed for the index of net redistribution with respect to industry classification.

As a result of the occupational changes of the decade, the non-white was more like the white occupation distribution in 1950 than in 1940. In 1940, 37.1 per cent of the non-white males would have had to move to a different major occupation group to make their occupational distribution identical with that of white males; by 1950, this figure was reduced to 35.4 per cent. Similarly, there was a reduction in the index of dissimilarity between the white and the non-white occupation distributions for females, from 46.1 per cent in 1940 to 43.1 per cent in 1950.

It should be noted that the dissimilarity between the white and non-white occupation distributions cannot be explained, to any great extent, by their industry attachments. If white and non-white males had the same occupation distribution within each major industry group (i.e., that of all employed males in the Chicago Standard Metropolitan Area in 1950), their over-all occupation distributions would be very similar; in fact, it would be necessary to shift only 5.1 per cent of the non-whites to a different major occupation group to make the two distributions identical. Thus the amount of dissimilarity between the two occupation distributions attributable to differences in industrial affiliation in 1950 was only one-seventh as large as the total index of dissimilarity, 35.4 per cent, as noted previously. A similar computation for females shows that industry differences between whites and non-whites would have produced an index of dissimilarity between the two occupation distributions of only 18.6 per cent, as compared to the total index of 43.1 per cent.

Income

It is not possible to study income changes over the 1940-50 decade, since the income figures for 1940 and 1950 are not comparable. Table 19 shows summary figures, by color, for 1950. But, inasmuch

Table 19.—Median Income in 1949, by Color, for Various Reporting Units, for the City of Chicago, 1950

Unit Reporting Income	White	Non-white
Families*.	$4,189†	$2,526†
Unrelated individuals*.	1,819†	1,412†
Families and unrelated individuals*	3,614†	2,150†
Persons with income§	2,666	1,924
Male§	3,292	2,370
Female§	1,764	1,294

*Based on 20 per cent sample.

†Includes non-whites living in census tracts with fewer than 250 non-white residents.

‡Excludes non-whites living in census tracts with fewer than 250 non-white residents.

§Based on 3 1/3 per cent sample.

as non-whites improved their occupational status, relative to whites, during the 1940-50 decade, it seems probable that the income difference was smaller, on a relative basis, in 1950 than in 1940. The median family income (i.e., income of all members of the family treated as a single amount) for non-whites was only three-fifths as large as the median family income for whites. There was a difference of about the same order for all consumer units, families and unrelated individuals. Using income figures compiled on the basis of persons' own incomes, non-white persons with income had a median income about 72 per cent as large as white persons. Table 20 shows the percentage distribution of families and of persons with income by 1949 in-

Table 20.—Percentage Distribution of Families by 1949 Family Income, by Color, and Percentage Distribution of Persons Fourteen Years Old and Over with Income by 1949 Personal Income, by Color and Sex, for the City of Chicago, 1950

1949 Income (Dollars)	Families*		Persons with Income†			
	White	Non-white	Male		Female	
			White	Non-white	White	Non-white
Total	100.0	100.0	100.0	100.0	100.0	100.0
Less than 500 . . .	4.3	10.4	5.1	6.0	17.9	17.1
500-999	2.0	6.2	5.3	8.7	13.9	22.2
1,000-1,999	5.4	17.2	10.4	20.5	23.8	36.4
2,000-2,999	12.8	29.3	21.0	40.0	30.9	19.9
3,000-3,999	21.8	19.4	28.2	19.4	9.1	3.5
4,000-4,999	17.0	8.6	14.2	3.6	2.3	0.6
5,000-5,999	13.4	4.5	7.4	1.0	1.0	0.1
6,000 or more . . .	23.3	4.4	8.4	0.8	1.1	0.2

*Based on 20 per cent sample; "white" includes non-white families living in census tracts with fewer than 250 non-white residents in 1950; "non-white" includes only those non-white families living in census tracts with 250 or more non-white residents in 1950.

†Based on 3 1/3 per cent sample.

come. Whereas 63 per cent of the non-white families had incomes of less than $3,000, only one-fourth of the white families had incomes below $3,000. Three-fourths of the non-white males with income, but

only two-fifths of the white males with income, received less than
$3,000; 76 per cent of the non-white females, but only 56 per cent of
the white females with income, received less than $2,000.

Housing Characteristics

During the 1940-50 decade, although the total population of Chicago increased by only 6.6 per cent, the number of occupied dwelling
units increased by 14.5 per cent. There was an increase of 9.4 per
cent in the number of dwelling units occupied by whites, despite the
fact that the white population decreased by 0.1 per cent over the decade. However, the number of dwelling units occupied by non-whites
increased less rapidly than did the non-white population, the rates of
increase being 72.3 per cent for non-white-occupied dwelling units
and 80.5 per cent for non-white population.

In the light of these differential changes, one would expect differentials as well in the change in average size of household. However,
the ratio of persons in households to number of households (equivalent to occupied dwelling units) decreased for both whites and non-
whites, as may be seen in the following figures:

	1950	1940
Total.	3.18	3.47
White	3.14	3.45
Non-white	3.47	3.69

The failure of the non-white average household size to show an increase is apparently explained by a change in census definitions. In
the 1940 Census, lodging houses with as many as 10 lodgers were included in the count of dwelling units (or households); whereas in the
1950 Census, lodging houses with 5 or more lodgers were regarded
as quasi-households and therefore excluded from the count of dwelling units. It seems likely that lodging houses with 5 to 10 lodgers
are more prevalent in non-white than in white residential areas. In
1940, 7 per cent of white families, but 31 per cent of non-white
families, had one or more lodgers in their households. Moreover,

the number of lodgers per family with lodgers was 1.7 for whites but 2.5 for non-whites. There seems to be little reason to doubt that the shift in classification of lodging houses with 5 to 10 lodgers involved more than enough persons to account for the apparent decrease in average household size for non-whites, which was, in any case, not so great as the parallel decrease for whites.

Table 21 shows the distribution of dwelling units occupied by

Table 21.—Percentage Distribution of Occupied Dwelling Units by Number of Persons in Unit, by Color of Occupant, for the City of Chicago, 1950 and 1940

Number of Persons in Dwelling Unit	1950*			1940		
	Total	White	Non-white	Total	White	Non-white
All units	100.0	100.0	100.0	100.0	100.0	100.0
1 person	11.5	11.0	15.6	8.2	7.6	14.0
2 persons	29.6	29.8	27.3	26.0	26.1	25.5
3 persons	23.2	23.9	17.6	23.4	23.9	17.5
4 persons	18.3	18.9	14.2	19.3	19.8	13.7
5 and 6 persons . .	13.8	13.5	16.3	17.2	17.2	17.2
7 persons or more	3.6	2.9	9.0	5.9	5.4	12.1
Median number of persons. . .	2.9	2.9	2.9	3.2	3.2	3.1

*Figures for whites include dwelling units occupied by non-whites living in census tracts with fewer than 250 non-white residents; figures for non-whites based on non-whites living in census tracts with 250 or more non-white residents.

whites and non-whites by number of persons per unit in 1950 and 1940. Given these distributions, one can see that the similarity of the white and non-white median household size in each year was produced by counteracting tendencies. Non-whites had the larger proportions both of 1-person households and of households comprising 7 persons or more; consequently, the clustering of household sizes around the average or median was less for non-whites than for whites. The changes in the distributions are, of course, affected by the reclassification of lodging houses with 5 to 10 lodgers; but it is not possible to determine

how much of the decline in the proportion of large households, observed for both whites and non-whites, is due to this factor.

In sum, the supply of housing available to non-whites did not ex-
pand so rapidly as did the non-white population over the 1940-50 decade. The consequence was that non-whites remained in an unfavorable
position, as compared with whites, with respect to the doubling-up of
families and the incorporation of non-family members into the household. One would expect the proportion of crowded dwelling units to
increase under these conditions, and the data given subsequently con-
firm this inference.

Table 22 shows the distribution of dwelling units occupied by

Table 22.—Percentage Distribution of Occupied Dwelling Units by
Number of Persons per Room, by Color of Occupant, for the City
of Chicago, 1950 and 1940

Persons per Room	1950*			1940		
	Total	White	Non-white	Total	White	Non-white
All dwelling units reporting . . .	100.0	100.0	100.0	100.0	100.0	100.0
1.00 or less	84.8	87.8	61.5	83.1	84.7	64.7
1.01 to 1.50	8.8	8.0	14.8	11.0	10.6	16.1
1.51 or more	6.4	4.2	23.7	5.9	4.7	19.2

*Figures for whites include dwelling units occupied by non-whites
living in census tracts with fewer than 250 non-white residents; figures
for non-whites based on non-whites living in census tracts with 250 or
more non-white residents.

white and non-white households by number of persons per room. In
both 1940 and 1950, non-whites had the higher proportions of crowded
units, regardless of whether the term "crowded" refers to units with
more than 1 person per room or to units with more than 1.5 persons
per room. Over the 1940-50 decade the proportion of crowded units
decreased slightly for whites but increased somewhat for non-whites.
The contrast is especially marked in terms of the proportion of units
with 1.51 or more persons per room; the ratio of the non-white to the
white proportion was about 4 to 1 in 1940 but nearly 6 to 1 in 1950.

These figures take on greater significance when it is recalled that non-whites have a larger proportion of one-person households, because these households, by definition, cannot have a person-room ratio in excess of unity. Thus the difference in crowding by color would be even greater if calculated for multiperson households. Another indication of crowding or doubling up is given by the fact that, in 1950, 22 per cent of non-white married couples did not have their own households, as compared with only 8 per cent of white married couples.

Homeownership increased for both white and non-white households between 1940 and 1950, as is shown in Table 23. No doubt this general increase is explained by the improvement in economic con-

Table 23.—Per Cent of Occupied Dwelling Units Owner-occupied, by Color of Occupant, for the City of Chicago, 1950 and 1940

Color	1950		1940 (Observed Per Cent)
	Observed Per Cent	Per Cent Standardized for Type of Structure*	
Total. . .	30.4	30.4	24.3
White. . . .	32.9	31.0	25.8
Non-white.	12.1	21.8	7.5

*Standardized by the indirect method on the basis of percentages of owner occupancy by type of structure for all occupied dwelling units in the city.

ditions over the decade, since homeownership is positively related to income. However, the considerable difference in favor of whites was maintained; in fact, in terms of absolute percentage points, the difference increased somewhat. It is of interest to note that a considerable part of the color difference in homeownership is related to the difference in pattern of occupancy by type of structure. (For example, in 1950, 18.7 per cent of white-occupied dwelling units, but only 4.7 per cent of non-white-occupied units, were in one-unit detached structures.) Since a larger proportion of white than of non-

white households live in one- and two-unit structures, one would expect their percentage of homeownership to be higher. In fact, when
homeownership percentages are standardized for type of structure
(Table 23), the percentage-point difference between whites and non-
whites is less than half as large as on the basis of observed percentages of homeownership. This calculation, of course, does not provide
an unambiguous causal inference. It may be that the disproportionate
tendency of non-white households to live in multiunit structures
merely reflects their inability to purchase single-family homes. But,
whether by choice or by necessity, non-whites reside in residential
areas where relatively few units appropriate for owner occupancy
are available. When this factor of limited availability is taken into
account, the discrepancy between white and non-white homeownership
does not appear so great as it does on first inspection.

The great majority of both white and non-white households in
Chicago live in rented dwelling units. Hence a good indication of the
financial aspects of housing is given by an examination of data on
rentals paid; these are shown in Table 24. During the 1940-50 decade
rents increased for both whites and non-whites, along with the general rise in the level of consumer prices. However, in both absolute
and relative terms the increase was greater for non-whites than for
whites. Whereas, in 1940, the white median contract monthly rent of
$33 exceeded the non-white median by $9, the 1950 white median of
$45 was only $4 greater than the non-white median (see Table 24). In
1940 there was a concentration of non-white rentals in the range of
$10-$29, and in 1950 in the $20-$49 range, while in both years there
were disproportionate numbers of whites paying rents lower and
higher than the cited intervals. The data suggest, though they do not
conclusively demonstrate, that the demand for non-white housing occasioned by the rapid influx of population during the decade placed
non-white households in a less favorable market position, vis-à-vis
whites, in 1950 than in 1940.

One thing seems quite clear: non-whites get less desirable
housing for a given rent than do whites. Table 25 shows that a much
larger proportion of non-whites than of whites occupy dwelling units
that either lack a private bath, are in a dilapidated structure, or fail

Table 24.—Percentage Distribution of Renter-occupied Dwelling Units by Contract Monthly Rent, by Color of Occupant, for the City of Chicago, 1950 and 1940

Contract Monthly Rent	1950*			1940		
	Total	White	Non-white	Total	White	Non-white
All units reporting . . .	100.0	100.0	100.0	100.0	100.0	100.0
Less than $10 .	0.4	0.4	0.2	2.6	2.6	2.1
$10-$19	8.6	8.9	6.7	22.0	20.8	33.0
$20-$29	16.1	15.8	17.7	21.4	20.5	30.6
$30-$39	15.4	14.3	21.3	19.6	20.3	13.8
$40-$49	20.8	20.9	21.4	19.1	19.8	12.2
$50-$59	16.4	16.5	15.5	7.9	8.1	5.8
$60-$74	12.0	12.0	11.9	4.2	4.4	2.0
$75-$99	6.3	6.7	3.9	1.8	2.0	0.4
$100 or more. .	4.0	4.5	1.4	1.4	1.5	0.1
Median contract rent .	$44	$45	$41	$32	$33	$24

*Figures for total and white-occupied units include vacant non-seasonal not dilapidated units for rent; figures for white-occupied units include units occupied by non-whites living in census tracts with fewer than 250 non-white residents; figures for non-white-occupied units based on non-whites living in census tracts with 250 or more non-white residents.

to meet acknowledged housing standards in both these respects. In 1950, over half, or 53 per cent, of non-white households, as against 15 per cent of white households, lived in units with no private bath or which were dilapidated. This difference prevailed despite the fact that non-white median rental was only slightly below white median rental, and non-white households were proportionately less frequent in the lowest rent intervals, $10-$19 and less than $10. If the percentage of units with no private bath or dilapidated is standardized for homeownership and amount of rent paid, as in Table 25, the difference in white and non-white proportions remains as high as 29 percentage points, as compared with 38 percentage points on the basis of observed proportions. Clearly, white-non-white differences in proportions of homeownership and level of rent explain only a minor

Table 25.—Observed Percentage of Dwelling
Units with No Private Bath or Dilapidated,
and Percentage Standardized for Owner Occupancy and Rent, by Color of Occupant, for
the City of Chicago, 1950

Color*	Per Cent with No Private Bath or Dilapidated	
	Observed	Standardized†
Total.	19.2	19.2
White.	14.8	15.3
Non-white.	52.6	44.1

*Figures for total and white-occupied units
include vacant non-seasonal not dilapidated units
for rent; figures for white-occupied units include
units occupied by non-whites living in census
tracts with fewer than 250 non-white residents;
figures for non-whites based on units occupied by
non-whites living in census tracts with 250 or
more non-white residents.

†Standardized by the indirect method on the
basis of percentages with no private bath or
dilapidated by tenure and rent for all occupied
dwelling units in the city.

part of the difference in prevalence of substandard housing.

In summary, non-white housing conditions are less satisfactory
than white; the difference appears to have increased, if anything,
over the 1940-50 decade (though relevant data are scanty); and the
difference is by no means accounted for solely by the relative economic advantage of the white population. Going somewhat beyond
a strict interpretation of the data, one infers that non-white housing
conditions reflect both the economic disadvantage of the Negro and
the non-economic restrictions on his access to the housing market.
Partly in order to pool incomes and partly because of the limited
housing supply, Negroes resort to doubling-up of families and incorporation of non-family members into their households. By ex-
pending a larger proportion of its aggregate income for rent, the
average Negro household can pay a rent nearly equal to that of the

average white household. But the quality of housing received for this
expenditure is inferior, and the Negro household must more often en-
dure a crowding of the dwelling unit to a degree that is generally
recognized as undesirable. It does not seem farfetched, therefore,
to attribute some of the irregularity in Negro family life and the so-
cial-personal disorganization related thereto to the predicament of
the Negro engaged in the search for adequate living quarters. No
doubt the causal relationships in this situation are complex, but it
can hardly be doubted that the housing problem is integrally related
to other problems of Negroes in the metropolis.

Mortality and Fertility

The vital processes, as well as spatial movement and social
mobility, are involved in the redistribution of population and changes
in its composition. However, it has already been shown (chap. iii)
that migration has been a more important factor than natural increase in the growth of the Negro population in Chicago. The importance of residential mobility in bringing about a redistribution of the
Negro population within the city is demonstrated in a later chapter.
Moreover, although the Negro and white populations of the city have
very different levels of mortality and fertility, it seems evident that
these differentials and changes thereof played only a subordinate
role in bringing about the shifts in the relative social status of the
two groups over the 1940-50 decade. It seems unnecessary, therefore, to develop an extensive analysis of racial differentials in fertility and mortality for the purposes of this monograph, particularly
in view of the fact that extensive studies of the subject are available
elsewhere and are continuing.[2]

---

2.   Philip M. Hauser and his associates have in progress longitudinal studies of differential fertility and mortality according to
race, nativity, and socioeconomic status in the city of Chicago. Two
reports on the study have been published to date: Albert J. Mayer
and Philip M. Hauser, "Class Differentials in Expectation of Life at
Birth," Revue de l'Institut International de Statistique, Vol. XVIII,
Nos. 3/4 (1950); Evelyn M. Kitagawa, "Differential Fertility in Chicago, 1920-40," American Journal of Sociology, LVIII (March, 1953),
481-92. See also the following unpublished doctoral dissertations at

Some summary measures of differentials in vital rates are reviewed here. In so far as mortality and fertility levels are related to social and economic characteristics of the population, the mortality and fertility levels for the white and Negro populations might be expected to converge as white-Negro differentials with respect to social and economic characteristics decrease.

The 1950 life-expectancy at birth for non-whites in Chicago was only slightly higher than the 1930 life-expectancy at birth for whites

Table 26.—Expectation of Life at Birth (in Years), by Color and Sex, for Chicago, 1930-50

Year	White Population		Non-white Population	
	Male	Female	Male	Female
1950*....	64.7	70.8	58.2	63.5
1940†....	62.6	67.2	51.0	56.3
1930†....	57.8	61.7	42.5	46.7

*Computed from unpublished tabulations of the Illinois Department of Public Health, Bureau of Statistics.

†From Albert J. Mayer and Philip M. Hauser, "Class Differentials in Expectation of Life at Birth," Revue de l'Institut International de Statistique, Vol. XVIII, Nos. 3/4 (1950).

in Chicago. But, as Table 26 shows, increases in non-white life-expectancy over the period 1930-50 were substantially greater than those in white life-expectancy. Consequently, the white-non-white difference in expectation of life at birth dropped from fifteen to seven years in the twenty-year period.

However, there is no evidence of convergence in the total fertility rates for the non-white and the white populations. The total fertility rate for non-whites as a percentage of the rate for whites was

the University of Chicago: Philip M. Hauser, "Differential Fertility, Mortality, and Net Reproduction in Chicago, 1930" (1938); Albert J. Mayer, "Differentials in Length of Life, City of Chicago, 1880 to 1940" (1950); Evelyn M. Kitagawa, "Differential Fertility in Chicago, 1920-40" (1951).

80 in 1920, 102 in 1930, 128 in 1940, and 133 in 1950. As Table 27 shows, total fertility rates for both non-whites and whites increased during the decade 1940-50, but the increase was greater, in both absolute and relative terms, for the non-white population.

Table 27.—Total Fertility Rates, by Color, for Chicago, 1920-50

Year	Births per 100 Women*	
	White	Non-white
1950†......	248	329
1940‡......	155	198
1930‡......	180	184
1920‡......	235	188

*Standardized for age, with a rectangular age distribution as the standard population.

†Computed from data in Table 21, Vol. II, Vital Statistics of the United States, 1950 (Washington: Government Printing Office, 1953).

‡From Evelyn M. Kitagawa, "Differential Fertility in Chicago, 1920-40," American Journal of Sociology, LVIII (March, 1953), 481-92.

Chapter V

Expansion of the Negro Community, 1920-50

The rapid growth of Chicago's Negro population was described in earlier chapters. Between 1920 and 1950 the number of Negro residents increased from 109,000 to 492,000; as a proportion of total population, Negroes increased from 4 per cent in 1920 to 14 per cent in 1950. Migration has played a relatively more important role in Negro population growth in Chicago than has natural increase; over four-fifths of the growth during the decades 1920-30 and 1930-40 and over seven-tenths of the population increase between 1940 and 1950 resulted from the excess of in-migrants over out-migrants.

This chapter concerns the spatial counterpart of the population increase. The rapidly growing Negro population of the city had to be housed. The question can be posed—in which areas of the city did the Negroes secure dwellings?

It might be found that Negroes secured for their occupancy the same proportion of dwellings in each area of the city. In this case their residences would be widely dispersed, and the distributions of Negro and non-Negro residences by area would correspond. On the other hand, it might be found that Negroes secured all dwellings in some areas of the city but no dwellings in the remainder of the city. Under these circumstances the residences of Negroes would be highly concentrated within the city and would be highly segregated with respect to the residences of non-Negroes. Innumerable distributional patterns, ranging between the extremes of a dispersed even distribution and a concentrated complete segregation, might be postulated.

The spatial distribution of Negro population in Chicago is examined at four points in time: 1920, 1930, 1940, and 1950. Theoretically, the distributional patterns observed at the four points could differ

markedly from one another. In fact, the high rates of residential mobility among Negroes suggest that this might be the case. Large numbers of in-migrants were entering the city and securing housing for
the first time; and among non-whites who were residing in Cook
County, of which Chicago comprises the bulk, in both 1949 and 1950,
at least 16 per cent were living in a different dwelling in 1950 than
in 1949.

The expansion of the Negro community which has accompanied
the growth of Negro population in Chicago is described in the sections which follow.

Background

During the last half of the nineteenth century, Chicago's Negro
population increased from 300 to 30,000; but Negroes as a proportion
of the city's population increased only from 1.1 to 1.8 per cent during
the fifty-year period. Between 1900 and 1910 the Negro population increased by 14,000; yet, at the latter date, Negroes comprised only
2.0 per cent of Chicago's total population.

One-fifth of the Negroes residing in Chicago in 1910 had been
born in Illinois; not over one-third had been born in the Deep South
states of North and South Carolina, Georgia, Alabama, Mississippi,
Arkansas, and Louisiana. One-half of the Negro males were engaged
in domestic and personal service occupations—7 per cent as janitors
and sextons, 8 per cent as servants, 9 per cent as waiters, and 20
per cent as porters; one-sixth were engaged as laborers; and 4 per
cent were in professional occupations. Of the children seven to thirteen years of age, 92 per cent were enrolled in school; only 5 per
cent of the population twenty-five years of age and over were illiterate.[1]

In 1910, Negroes resided in sixty of the sixty-three subareas

---

1. From published materials of the Thirteenth Census of the
United States and the Bureau of the Census report, Negro Population
of the United States, 1790-1915 (Washington: Government Printing
Office, 1918).

into which the city had been divided.[2] In fifteen contiguous communities Negroes comprised more than 1 per cent of the resident population—Near North Side, Near West Side, Loop, Near South Side, Armour Square, Douglas, Oakland, Fuller Park, Grand Boulevard, Kenwood, Washington Park, Hyde Park, Woodlawn, West Englewood, and Englewood. (The location of these communities can be ascertained from Fig. 23.)

The core of the 1910 Negro residential area stretched south from Twelfth to Fifty-fifth streets, extending a few blocks either side of State Street. Yet probably not more than a dozen blocks in the core could have been considered areas of exclusive Negro residence.[3] In the South Side area, running eastward from the core to Lake Michigan, were the residences of roughly three-fourths of the city's 1910 Negro population; but only one of ten residents in this South Side area was Negro.

In the Near West Side community north of Madison Street and stretching from Halsted Street to Western Avenue was a settlement of some 3,000 Negroes. In the Englewood area, centered between Halsted Street and Ashland Avenue, Fifty-ninth and Sixty-seventh streets, was a settlement of Negroes numbering about 2,000. The 1910 Negro

---

2. Unpublished tabulations of population by race for sixty-three subareas of the city of Chicago as delimited in 1910, on file at Chicago Community Inventory, University of Chicago.

3. Maps indicating the density and distribution of the 1910 Negro population are reproduced in Chicago Commission on Race Relations, The Negro in Chicago (Chicago: University of Chicago Press, 1922). Data on population by race for selected areas of the city in 1910 and 1920 are given in the text (pp. 107 ff.). However, the area bounded by Twelfth and Fifty-fifth streets, Wentworth, and Indiana is listed with a 1910 total population of 311,049 and a 1920 population of 376,171; the 1910 population for a much more extensive South Side area, reconstructed from community data, was only 331,032; and the 1920 population of the delimited area, as reconstructed with census-tract data, was but 103,923. In so far as the published figures for total population clearly refer to an area other than that stated, the data on population by race for selected areas have not been relied on in this analysis. However, it has been assumed that the maps prepared from special tabulations for enumeration districts are reliable.

population of the Near North Side was approximately 1,000. And
some 800 Negroes resided in the Loop. These areas were by no
means exclusively Negro, however; in the subareas of highest Negro
concentration, Negroes apparently made up no more than six of every
ten residents. The community of Morgan Park, then outside the
limits of the city of Chicago, had 126 Negro residents; its total population was slightly over 5,000.

There were, then, Negroes residing in most areas of the city;
but the distribution of Negro residents by area differed substantially
from that of non-Negro residents. If the 1910 Negro population had
been distributed by area in exactly the same way as the non-Negro
population, Negroes would have constituted 2 per cent of the population in each area. But in Douglas 30 per cent of the 1910 population
were Negro (16,997 Negroes in a population of 57,392); in the Near
South Side community 16 per cent of the 1910 population were Negro
(3,864 Negroes in a population of 23,864). Negroes constituted between 5 and 10 per cent of the population in the Loop, in Armour
Square, Grand Boulevard, and Washington Park; and they constituted
between 2 and 5 per cent of the population in Fuller Park, Oakland,
Kenwood, West Englewood, and Hyde Park. In each of the other fifty-
two communities, less than 2 per cent of the population were composed of Negroes.

Between 1910 and 1920 the Negro population of Chicago increased
by about 65,000—from 44,000 in 1910 to 109,000 in 1920. And as a
proportion of Chicago's population, Negroes increased from 2 to 4
per cent during the decade. The northward migration of Negroes during World War I accounted for this marked population increase and
resulted in changes in the composition of Chicago's Negro population.

The proportion of Negro residents born in the Deep South increased.[4] By 1920, only 15 per cent of the Negro residents had been
born in Illinois; perhaps two-fifths had been born in the Deep South.
By 1930, after another decade of heavy in-migration, 18 per cent of

---

4.   Published data of the Fourteenth Census of the United States
and from the Bureau of the Census report, Negroes in the United
States, 1920-1932 (Washington: Government Printing Office, 1935).

Chicago's Negro residents had been born in Illinois, whereas one-half had been born in the Deep South states.

Relatively more Negro males found employment in non-service industries. Whereas 51 per cent of the Negro males were engaged in domestic or personal service occupations in 1910, only 28 per cent were in such occupations in 1920. On the other hand, the proportion of Negro males engaged as laborers increased from 16 to 39 per cent during the decade; and the proportion engaged as semiskilled operatives in manufacturing rose from 1 to 6 per cent between 1910 and 1920.

But no improvement in the school enrolment or the illiteracy of Chicago's Negro population occurred during the decade 1910-20. In both years, 92 per cent of the children seven to thirteen years of age were enrolled in school. The percentage illiterate within age groups was as high in 1920 as in 1910 among Chicago's Negroes:[5]

Age (Years)	1920	1910
10-14........	0.2	0.2
15-24........	1.1	0.9
25-34........	1.7	1.3
35-44........	3.2	3.0
45-54........	7.6	8.5
55-64........	16.8	19.8
65 and over...	36.2	34.3

Comparisons of age cohorts—e.g., persons thirty-five to forty-four years old in 1910 with persons forty-five to fifty-four years old in 1920—make it clear that the incoming Negro population was less well educated than the 1910 Chicago Negro population.

Between 1910 and 1920 the Negro population in Chicago grew rapidly in both absolute and relative terms; the major source of growth was in-migration; the proportion of Negroes born in the Deep

5.   Data from Negro Population in the United States, 1790-1915, Table 30, "Illiteracy," and Fourteenth Census of the United States, Vol. II, Table 18, "Illiteracy."

South increased, whereas the proportion born in northern or border states decreased; non-service occupations became an important source of Negro employment; the educational status of the Negro population did not improve because of the inferior educational training of the incoming population.

Negro Residential Distribution

The 1910 pattern of Negro residential distribution has been sketched briefly. The major concentration of Negro residence stretched due south from the city's center for a distance of some 7 miles, extending eastward to Lake Michigan. In the Near North and Near West Side communities and in the far south communities of Englewood and Morgan Park there were spatially distinct and sizable Negro settlements. The pattern of Negro residence changed but slightly during the next decade; Lilydale in the Roseland community, a settlement of Negro homeowners in a hitherto undeveloped area of the city, came into existence between 1910 and 1920.

Hence the area of Negro residence expanded very little despite the influx of Negro population to Chicago. Rather, a consolidation of existing areas of Negro residence took place, i.e., the incoming Negro population was absorbed into areas in which a nucleus of Negroes already resided. This succession from white to Negro occupancy is illustrated for subareas of the Washington Park community in Table 28. In 1910 the areas ranged from 1 to 47 per cent with respect to proportion Negro; ten years later they ranged from 7 to 77 per cent. Yet Negroes as a proportion of the city's total population increased only from 2 to 4 per cent during the decade. It then follows that these areas, in which a core settlement of Negroes already existed, received a disproportionate share of the city's increase in Negro population.

Beginning with 1920, the spatial distribution of Negro residences can be examined in some detail. A series of four maps shows the distribution of Negro population with respect to the distribution of non-Negro population in Chicago by 935 census tracts for 1920, 1930, 1940, and 1950. A description of the estimates involved in distributing the 1920 data by census tracts is given in Appendix D.

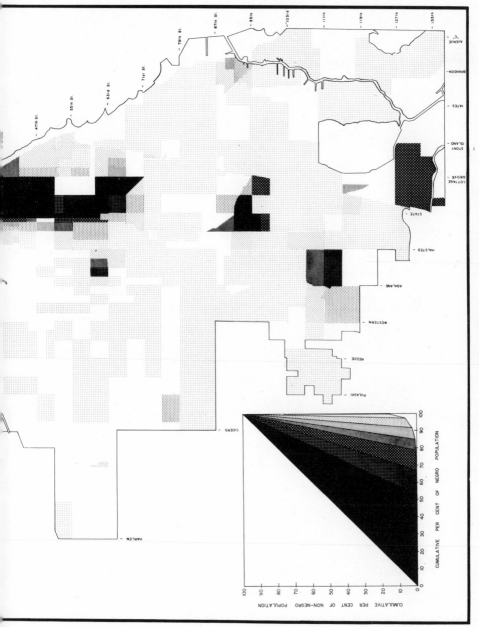

Fig. 8.—Negro Population, Chicago, 1950

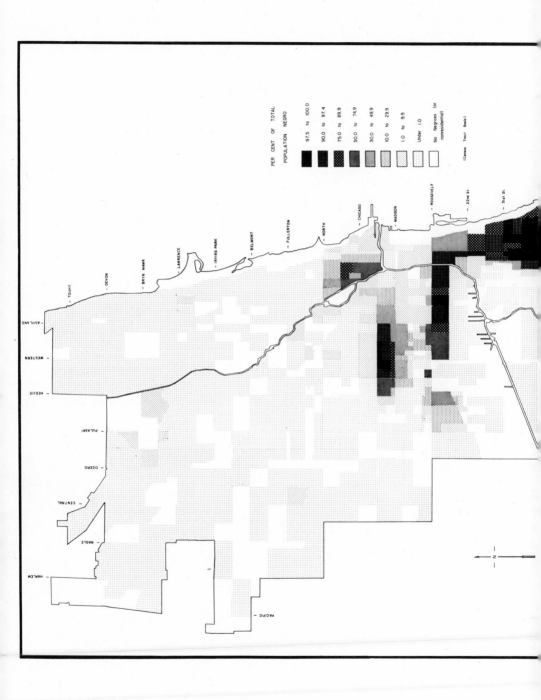

PER CENT OF TOTAL
POPULATION NEGRO

97.5 to 100.0

90.0 to 97.4

75.0 to 89.9

50.0 to 74.9

30.0 to 49.9

10.0 to 29.9

1.0 to 9.9

Under 1.0

No Negroes (or
nonresidential)

(Census Tract Basis)

Table 28.—Population by Race for Census Tracts in the Washington
Park Community and Vicinity, 1910 and 1920

1950 Census-Tract Number	1910 Population			1920 Population			Per Cent Negro	
	Total	White	Negro	Total	White	Negro	1910	1920
570, 600	3,928	2,068	1,860	3,410	778	2,632	47.4	77.2
601, 602	8,327	8,223	104	11,041	9,902	1,139	1.2	10.3
878, 606 (part)	3,825	3,707	118	3,711	1,989	1,722	3.1	46.4
603, 604	7,522	7,374	148	12,695	11,847	848	2.0	6.7
878, 606 (part)	2,059	2,037	22	1,933	1,683	250	1.1	12.9
605, 607	5,078	5,010	68	8,569	7,893	676	1.3	7.9
Combined tracts. .	30,759	28,439	2,320	41,359	34,092	7,267	7.5	17.6

Source: 1910 data from unpublished census tabulations on file at
Chicago Community Inventory, University of Chicago; 1920 data from
Ernest W. Burgess and Charles Newcomb (eds.), Census Data of the
City of Chicago, 1920 (Chicago: University of Chicago Press, 1931).

In constructing the maps, census tracts were classified into nine
intervals in terms of their proportions Negro; these intervals are
constant from map to map, ranging from census tracts in which no
Negroes reside to census tracts in which 97.5 per cent or more of the
residents are Negro. The curves, inset on the maps, show the cumu-
lative percentage distributions of Negro and non-Negro population
with respect to these constant intervals.

Figure 5 shows the spatial distribution of Negroes with respect
to non-Negro population in Chicago in 1920. There were no census
tracts in which Negroes amounted to more than 97.5 per cent of the
population at this date; nor were there any tracts in which Negroes
constituted between 90.0 and 97.4 per cent of the population. Consequently, no tracts are shaded in the patterns corresponding with
these intervals. But there were 24 census tracts in which Negroes
constituted between 75.0 and 89.9 per cent of the residents in 1920;
these tracts are shaded in the pattern corresponding with this interval. At the other extreme, there were no Negro residents in the 408
unshaded census tracts.

The distribution of Negro and non-Negro population with respect to these intervals is shown by the inset curve. The first segment of the curve, identified in the pattern corresponding with the interval 75.0-89.9 per cent, indicates the proportion of the city's Negro and non-Negro population residing in census tracts in which the proportion Negro falls between 75.0 and 89.9 per cent. In 1920, 44.8 per cent of the city's Negro population and 0.4 per cent of the city's non-Negro population resided in the 24 tracts with the specified proportion Negro. The second segment of the curve, identified in the pattern corresponding with the interval 50.0-74.9 per cent, indicates the proportion of the city's Negro and non-Negro population residing in census tracts in which between 50.0 and 74.9 per cent of the residents are Negro. In 1920, 15.4 per cent (60.2 minus 44.8 per cent) of the city's Negro population and 0.5 per cent (0.9 minus 0.4 per cent) of the city's non-Negro population resided in the 13 census tracts with Negro proportions ranging from 50.0 to 74.9 per cent. Or 60.2 per cent of the city's Negro population and 0.9 per cent of the city's non-Negro population resided in census tracts in which at least half the residents were Negro.

The extent to which the curve bows away from the diagonal indicates the degree to which Negroes are residentially concentrated with respect to non-Negroes and can be interpreted as an indicator of the degree of segregation.[6] If the Negro population were residentially distributed over the 935 census tracts of the city in precisely the same way as the non-Negro population, the curve would coincide with the diagonal; if all Negroes resided in exclusively Negro tracts and all non-Negroes resided in exclusively non-Negro tracts, the curve would coincide with the $\underline{X}$-axis (the horizontal base line) throughout.

The maps and curves in Figures 6, 7, and 8 show the residential distribution of Negro with respect to non-Negro population in 1930, 1940, and 1950, respectively. In general, the areas of Negro residential

---

6. See David A. Wallace, "Residential Concentration of Negroes in Chicago" (unpublished Ph.D. dissertation, Harvard University, 1953); and Otis Dudley Duncan and Beverly Duncan, "A Methodological Analysis of Segregation Indexes," American Sociological Review, XX (April, 1955), 210-17.

concentration are the same over the thirty-year period 1920-50. For example, 65 per cent of the census tracts in which Negroes amounted to 10 per cent or more of the 1950 population were tracts in which Negroes comprised 1 per cent or more of the 1920 population. In 1950, Negroes numbered 492,265 and constituted 13.6 per cent of the city's population; in 1920 they numbered 109,458 and constituted 4.1 per cent of the city's population.

The general outlines of the Negro residential area had been established by 1920. In so far as expansion of the Negro residential area has occurred, it has been in terms of adding areas contiguous to existing areas of Negro concentration. Most of the apparent exceptions reflect the locational pattern of publicly financed housing developments.

Curves for all four census years bow far from the diagonal, indicating a substantial concentration of Negro residences with respect to non-Negro residences. In fact, on the basis of any indexes proposed to measure the degree of residential segregation of Negro population, Chicago ranks high, if not the highest, among United States cities.[7]

Further, there is a suggestion that residential segregation of Negroes in Chicago has increased through time, particularly between 1920 and 1930.[8] Distributions of Negro and non-Negro population with respect to the intervals used for mapping are shown in Table 29; from these data the inset curves were constructed. In 1920 there were no Negroes residing in almost exclusively Negro tracts (tracts in which Negroes comprise 97.5 per cent or more of the residents); but the proportions of the city's Negro population residing in almost exclusively Negro tracts were 19.0 per cent in 1930, 49.7 per cent in 1940,

---

7.   Wendell Bell and Ernest M. Willis, tabular materials for "The Segregation of Negroes in American Cities: A Comparative Analysis," paper read at 1955 meetings of the American Sociological Society; Otis Dudley Duncan and Beverly Davis, Contributions to the Theory of Segregation Indexes ("Urban Analysis Series," No. 14 [Chicago: Chicago Community Inventory, University of Chicago, 1953]).

8.   For detailed analysis see Wallace, op. cit.

Table 29.—Percentage Distribution of Negro and Non-Negro Population, by Negro Proportion in the Census Tract of Residence, for Chicago, 1920, 1930, 1940, and 1950

Per Cent Negro	1920		1930		1940		1950	
	Negro	Non-Negro	Negro	Non-Negro	Negro	Non-Negro	Negro	Non-Negro
97.5-100.0..	0.0	0.0	19.0	0.0	49.7	0.0	52.9	0.1
90.0-97.4 ..	0.0	0.0	44.6	0.3	25.8	0.2	14.0	0.1
75.0-89.9 ..	44.8	0.4	15.8	0.2	11.3	0.2	11.7	0.3
50.0-74.9 ..	15.4	0.5	10.2	0.4	3.3	0.1	6.2	0.6
30.0-49.9 ..	18.4	1.2	2.5	0.3	3.2	0.5	7.0	1.6
10.0-29.9 ..	10.1	1.8	3.8	1.4	3.4	1.3	5.4	4.0
1.0-9.9....	8.3	10.9	2.8	7.3	2.2	6.5	2.2	9.2
Less than 1.0	3.0	64.7	1.3	51.9	1.1	54.6	0.6	66.7
No Negroes.	0.0	20.5	0.0	38.2	0.0	36.6	0.0	17.4
City of Chicago	100.0	100.0	100.0	100.0	100.0	100.0	100.0	100.0

and 52.9 per cent in 1950. On the other hand, the proportions of the non-Negro population residing in almost exclusively non-Negro tracts (tracts in which Negroes comprise less than 1 per cent of the residents) were 85.2 per cent in 1920, 90.1 per cent in 1930, 91.2 per cent in 1940, and 84.1 per cent in 1950.

Between 1920 and 1930 the proportion of Chicago's Negro population residing in almost exclusively Negro residential areas increased; and the proportion of non-Negroes residing in almost exclusively non-Negro residential areas increased. This increased segregation of the Negro population apparently did not result, in the main, from a contraction or shrinkage of the area in which Negroes resided. It is true that in some census tracts, particularly in the New City and the Hyde Park-Kenwood areas, the number of Negroes decreased; and the number of census tracts with no Negro residents increased from 408 in 1920 to 437 in 1930. But apparently the increased segregation of the Negro population resulted primarily from a disproportionate growth of Negro population in areas with substantial 1920 Negro populations and a disproportionate growth of non-Negro population in areas with no Negro residents in 1920.

For example, the city's Negro population increased by 125,000 during the decade 1920-30; in 65 census tracts in which Negroes made up 10 per cent or more of the 1920 population, the Negro population increased by 76,000. The city's non-Negro population increased by 550,000 during the decade, but the non-Negro population in the 65 tracts decreased by 78,000. In 1920, 532,000 non-Negroes resided in tracts with no Negro residents; ten years later, 1,198,000 non-Negroes resided in tracts with no Negro residents.

Change in the residential segregation of Negro with respect to non-Negro population was slight during the decade 1930-40. Nine-tenths of the city's Negro population and less than 1 per cent of the city's non-Negro population resided in tracts in which more than half the residents were Negro at both census periods, and nine-tenths of the city's non-Negro population resided in tracts with no Negro residents. It is probably relevant that the city's Negro population increased by only 44,000 during the ten-year period, as compared with 125,000 during the preceding decade, and the city's non-Negro population decreased slightly between 1930 and 1940.

Change in the residential segregation of Negro population between 1940 and 1950 is difficult to evaluate. The proportion of the city's Negro population residing in areas of almost exclusively Negro residence increased, whereas the proportion of the city's non-Negro population residing in areas of almost exclusively non-Negro residence decreased. There were, then, relatively fewer Negroes and relatively more non-Negroes residing in "mixed" tracts (tracts in which Negroes comprise between 1.0 and 97.4 per cent of the residents) in 1950 than in 1940.

The number of "mixed" tracts increased substantially between 1940 and 1950—from 135 in the former to 204 in the latter year. But this, in itself, does not constitute evidence that stable "mixed" tracts were emerging.

The city's Negro population increased by 215,000 between 1940 and 1950—from 277,731 in 1940 to 492,265 in 1950. The 1940 areas of Negro residence were congested, and the entire increase in Negro population could not be absorbed by these areas. As an indication,

the 1940 gross population density ranged from 46,000 persons per
square mile in areas of almost exclusively Negro residence to 15,000
persons per square mile in areas of almost exclusively non-Negro
residence. Yet the data summarized below (for non-white and white,
rather than Negro and non-Negro, populations) show that the bulk of
the Negro population increase was absorbed by already congested
areas in which Negroes comprised at least 1 per cent of the 1940
population.

Per Cent Non-white, 1940	Change in Population, 1940-50	
	Non-white	White
97.5 or more.......	22,493	- 204
90.0-97.4	22,491	- 333
75.0-89.9	21,217	- 4,074
30.0-74.9	22,776	-11,307
10.0-29.9	29,212	-15,550
1.0-9.9...........	50,987	-17,427
1.0 or less	58,017	45,856
City of Chicago....	227,193	- 3,039

Further, the data just given indicate that the white population decreased within each group of tracts in which non-whites composed 1
per cent or more of the 1940 population and that a gain in non-white
population, exceeding in magnitude the loss of whites, occurred within each group of tracts. Further, the net increase in total population
was greatest in those groups of tracts in which the 1940 proportion
non-white was highest; as a result, the largest absolute increase in
gross population density during the decade occurred in the areas of
highest initial density.

This suggests that the "mixed" areas observed in 1950 are transitory, i.e., that non-Negroes will continue to leave the areas and
Negroes will continue to enter the areas and that, with time, the
"mixed" areas will become almost exclusively Negro residential
areas. A highly segregated population, expanding under pressure of

sheer numbers, can appear "less segregated" during the expansion phase without any permanent change in residential patterns. Whether the 1950 "mixed" areas will stabilize or whether the succession from non-Negro to Negro occupancy will continue is unknown.

Patterns of Succession

Infrequently has the succession from non-Negro to Negro occupancy in Chicago been arrested, interrupted, or reversed, once it was under way. However, the rate at which succession takes place has varied widely among areas. The graphs in Figure 9 indicate that this is the case.

In the upper-left graph, census tracts in which between 10 and 70 per cent of the 1920 residents were Negro are plotted with respect to per cent Negro in 1920 and per cent Negro in 1930. If the Negro proportion decreased between 1920 and 1930, the point representing the census tract falls below the broken-line diagonal. If the Negro proportion increased between 1920 and 1930, the point falls above the broken-line diagonal. Three tracts fall below the diagonal; no tracts fall on the diagonal; 38 tracts fall above the diagonal. Hence succession from non-Negro to Negro occupancy continued between 1920 and 1930 in 38 of the 41 tracts in which Negroes constituted between 10 and 70 per cent of the 1920 population.

The graph in the upper-right corner shows that succession continued between 1930 and 1940 in 36 of the 41 tracts with 1930 proportions Negro of 10-70 per cent. Succession from non-Negro to Negro occupancy continued during the decade 1940-50 in 35 of the 39 tracts in which between 10 and 70 per cent of the 1940 residents were Negro, as indicated by the lower-left graph.

But it is evident that the rate of succession differs markedly among tracts. For example, among tracts with 1940 proportions Negro of 10-20 per cent, the 1950 proportions Negro ranged from 1 to 99 per cent. On the average, the rate of succession was more rapid during the decades 1920-30 and 1940-50, decades during which the city's Negro population grew rapidly, than during the decade 1930-40, a decade of comparatively slow growth of Negro population.

The lower-right graph indicates changes in proportion Negro be-

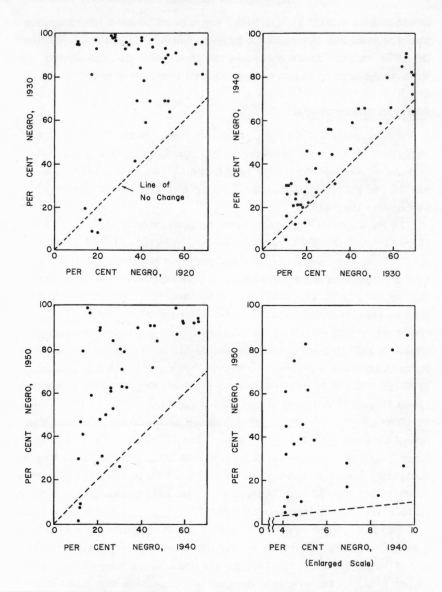

Fig. 9.—Decade Changes in Proportion of Negroes in the Population, for Groups of Selected Census Tracts in Chicago, 1920-50. (See text for definition of groups.)

tween 1940 and 1950 for the group of tracts with 1940 Negro proportions of 4-10 per cent, i.e., tracts which in 1940 were at an early
stage in the succession from non-Negro to Negro occupancy. An increase in the proportion Negro occurred during the decade in 20 of
the 21 tracts; and in 1950 these 20 tracts ranged from 5 to 87 per
cent with respect to proportion Negro.

Patterns of change in the Negro proportion through time are
examined for four groups of tracts: (1) the 153 census tracts in
which Negroes made up 1 per cent or more of the 1920 population;
(2) the 38 tracts with 1920 Negro proportions under 1 per cent and
1930 Negro proportions of 1 per cent or more; (3) the 13 tracts with
1920 and 1930 Negro proportions under 1 per cent and 1940 Negro
proportions of 1 per cent or more; and (4) the 74 tracts in which Negroes first constituted 1 per cent or more of the population in 1950.

1. As Table 30 shows, in over four-fifths of the tracts in which
Negroes made up 1 per cent or more of the 1920 population, the pro-

Table 30.—Census Tracts of the City of Chicago in Which Negroes
Comprised 1 Per Cent or More of the 1920 Population, Classified
by Direction of Change in Percentage Negro, 1920-30, 1930-40,
and 1940-50

Number of Tracts			Direction of Change				Per Cent of Tracts		
All Tracts*	Compa-rable†	Esti-mated‡	1920-50	1920-30	1930-40	1940-50	All Tracts*	Compa-rable†	Esti-mated†
153 .	33	120	...	...	...	...	100.0	100.0	100.0
74 .	13	61	+	+	+	+	48.3	39.3	50.9
14 .	2	12	+	-	+	+	9.2	6.1	10.0
13 .	6	7	+	+	-	+	8.5	18.2	5.8
12 .	2	10	+	+	+	-	7.8	6.1	8.3
13 .	4	9	+	-	-	+	8.5	12.1	7.5
1 .	0	1	+	-	+	-	0.7	0.0	0.8
4 .	0	4	+	+	-	-	2.6	0.0	3.3
22 .	6	16	-	...	...	...	14.4	18.2	13.4

*Excludes one tract in which no resident population was enumer-
ated in 1940 or 1950.

†No changes in census-tract boundaries 1920-30.

‡Change in census-tract boundaries 1920-30 (see Appendix D).

portion Negro was higher in 1950 than in 1920. In nearly half the
tracts in which at least 1 per cent of the 1920 population was Negro,
the proportion Negro increased during each decade of the thirty-
year period, i.e., there was no interruption in the succession process..

The most frequent pattern is, then, for the succession from
non-Negro to Negro occupancy to continue without interruption.
Further, succession is most likely to be arrested, interrupted, or
reversed during its initial stages. There were 131 tracts with 1920
proportions Negro of 1 per cent or more in which the proportion Negro increased between 1920 and 1950, and 22 tracts in which the proportion Negro decreased during the period. They are shown below,
classified by their 1920 proportion Negro:

Per Cent Negro, 1920	Change in Proportion Negro, 1920-50	
	Increase	Decrease
10 or more	66	0
1-10	65	22
All tracts.	131	22

In each of the 66 tracts in which the 1920 proportion Negro was 10
per cent or more, Negroes increased as a percentage of the total
population between 1920 and 1950; in 65 of the 87 tracts with 1920
proportions Negro of 1-10 per cent, or in only three-fourths of these
tracts, did the proportion Negro increase between 1920 and 1950.

Similarly, among tracts with long-run increases in the proportion Negro, the succession process was more frequently interrupted
or temporarily arrested during the initial stages. Of the 131 tracts
in which the proportion Negro increased between 1920 and 1950, 110
experienced an increase in proportion Negro between 1920 and 1930.
The 131 tracts are shown below, classified by their 1920 proportion
Negro:

Per Cent Negro, 1920	Change in Proportion Negro, 1920-30	
	Increase	Decrease
10 or more	61	5
1-10	49	16
All tracts	110	21

Succession was interrupted in 25 per cent of the tracts with 1920 proportions Negro between 1 and 10 per cent, as compared with only 7 per cent of the tracts with 1920 proportions Negro of 10 per cent or more.

2. There were 38 tracts in which Negroes made up 1 per cent or more of the population for the first time in 1930. Two-thirds, or 25, of these 38 tracts experienced an increase in proportion Negro between 1930 and 1940 and again between 1940 and 1950; one-fourth, or 9, of the 38 tracts experienced an increase in proportion Negro between 1930 and 1950, although the succession process was interrupted during the decade 1930-40. In only 4 tracts was the proportion of Negroes lower in 1950 than in 1930. Of the 10 tracts with 1930 Negro proportions of 10 per cent or more, each experienced an increase in proportion Negro from 1930 to 1940 and from 1940 to 1950. Of the 28 tracts with 1930 Negro proportions of 1-10 per cent, 15 evidenced an increase in proportion Negro during both decades, 9 showed an increase in proportion Negro between 1930 and 1950 but a decrease between 1930 and 1940, and 4 showed a decrease in the proportion Negro between 1930 and 1950.

3. In 13 census tracts, the 1940 proportion Negro was 1 per cent or more, whereas the 1920 and 1930 proportions Negro had been less than 1 per cent. Negroes constituted a larger proportion of the population in 1950 than in 1940 in 8 of these tracts and a smaller proportion in 5; the 1940 proportion Negro was low in all 13 tracts.

4. In 74 tracts, Negroes made up more than 1 per cent of the 1950 population but less than 1 per cent of the population in the pre-

ceding census years. Succession from non-Negro to Negro residence
had proceeded rapidly during the decade 1940-50 in the 74 tracts,
which are classified below in terms of their 1950 Negro proportions.

Per Cent Negro, 1950	Number of Tracts
50 or more	8
30 to 50	6
10 to 30	19
1 to 10	41
All tracts.	74

As has been indicated, the succession from non-Negro to Negro
occupancy during the thirty-year period was seldom arrested, once
it was under way. Of the 126 census tracts with Negro proportions
of 1 per cent or more in each census year from 1920 to 1950, only
20 experienced a change of less than 10 percentage points in the proportion of the population who were Negroes over the thirty-year period.
Four of these tracts which evidenced some stability in proportion Negro had 1920 proportions Negro of over 80 per cent; although the percentage-point increase had been less than 10 points, the succession
from mixed to exclusive Negro occupancy had been nearly completed
by 1950.

In the remaining 16 tracts, the 1920 Negro proportions were low,
none exceeding 8 per cent. In at least 5 of these tracts the Negro population consisted primarily of domestic service workers apparently
living in or near their workplaces. The proportion of Negroes never
exceeded 4 per cent in these tracts; and in 3 tracts the 1950 Negro
proportion was lower than that in 1920. Excluding these 5 tracts, 10
tracts in proximity to areas of Negro concentration and 1 tract spatially isolated from the major Negro residential areas evidenced
moderate stability between 1920 and 1950 with respect to the proportion of population consisting of Negroes.

In the 10 tracts located near Negro residential concentrations,

succession from non-Negro to Negro occupancy appears to have occurred slowly on a block-by-block basis. Some indicators that suggest this are (1) in each tract the 1950 Negro proportion was greater
than that of 1940, 1930, or 1920; (2) in each tract the number of Negro
residents increased between 1940 and 1950, whereas the number of
non-Negro residents decreased during the decade; (3) the residences
of Negroes were segregated within tracts and concentrated in blocks
adjacent to larger areas of Negro residential concentration; and (4)
the number of blocks within each tract in which 10 per cent or more
of the dwellings were occupied by Negroes increased between 1940
and 1950 for each of the 10 tracts.

The stability of a single isolated census tract, No. 23, is indicated by the data summarized here:

Year	Population		Per Cent Negro
	Total	Negro	
1920.	5,082	124	2.4
1930.	4,521	233	5.2
1940.	5,775	268	4.6
1950.	6,184	244	3.9

In 1950, 85 per cent of the tract's Negro population resided within
two blocks; however, Negroes made up less than one-third of the
population residing in the two-block area. It appears that in this one
case the succession from non-Negro to Negro occupancy was arrested at an early stage, and the pattern of mixed occupancy stabi-
lized. It may be noted that this tract, which had a small number of
non-whites other than Negroes in 1920, 1930, and 1940, was invaded
by Japanese between 1940 and 1950. Negroes were, consequently,
outnumbered by other non-whites in the latter year (see Appendix
F).

In summary, the data of this chapter show that the spatial outline of the Negro community in Chicago had been established by 1920,
if not by 1910. Further expansion of the Negro community has occurred within this framework, i.e., the additional Negro residents

have, in the main, secured housing in areas which already had a nucleus of Negro residents in 1920. Apparently, this pattern of expansion
has resulted in an increase of residential segregation for Negroes
in Chicago and a consolidation of the Negro community.

The succession of areas from non-Negro to Negro occupancy
has infrequently been arrested, interrupted, or reversed, once under
way, although areas have differed widely in the rate at which this
succession has taken place. The invasion phase virtually always has
been followed by consolidation. Cursory examination suggests that
the patterns of succession occurred on a block basis in a similar
manner to that observed on a tract basis, i.e., with invasion followed
by consolidation and, ultimately, by a complete turnover of population from white to Negro occupancy.[9]

Other aspects of the spatial pattern of the Negro community in
Chicago can be noted. The residences of Negroes tend to be concentrated toward the center of the city, whereas those of non-Negroes
tend to be concentrated away from the city's center. The percentage

---

9. It is entirely possible that patterns of expansion of Negro
residential areas in the future will differ from those of the past, in
view of changes in the legal status of agreements to restrict the access of Negroes to housing. Such a possibility is recognized, though
regarded as improbable in the immediate future, in the following
remark: "On May 3, 1948, in two decisions, Shelley v. Kraemer,
arising in Missouri, and Hurd v. Hodge, arising in the District of
Columbia, the U.S. Supreme Court held that neither state nor federal
courts can enforce race restrictive covenants. The rulings, of course,
will neither end residential segregation nor readily open up existing
housing supplies to additional Negro residence, except where appreciable additions to the over-all supply take place. Even the latter re-
mote possibility is subject to the realities of various other devices
designed to prevent Negro entry" (quoted from George B. Nesbitt,
"Relocating Negroes from Urban Slum Clearance Sites," Land Economics, XXV [August, 1949], 275-88, n. 1). Whether or not one
agrees with Nesbitt's estimate of the effect of the Supreme Court decisions, it is evident that measurement of that effect with presently
available census data presents a difficult, if not insuperable, task.
Coming within two years of the 1950 Census, the court action left
little time for its effects, if any, to be registered in movements observed over the decade 1940-50. It may be that a comparison of the
decade 1950-60 with the decade 1940-50 will permit some rough inference as to the effect of the legal change; but the situation will, of
course, be complicated by other concurrent changes in the housing
supply, Negro purchasing power, and numerous other factors.

distribution of non-white and white population by distance zone from
the center of the city is shown below.[10]

Distance from City's Center (Mi.)	1950		1940	
	Non-white	White	Non-white	White
Less than 2......	8.3	5.7	5.0	5.9
2-4	32.0	16.4	28.1	17.8
4-6	34.1	26.0	42.0	27.3
6-8	19.2	24.7	21.3	25.5
8 or more.......	6.4	27.2	3.6	23.5

These figures do not show so clearly as do the maps in this chapter
the fact that the expansion of the Negro community has been predominantly along radial lines from the center of the city. The major axis
of growth has been southward along State Street, the secondary one
being westward along Lake and Twelfth streets. Since the West Side
growth has lagged somewhat behind the South Side growth and since
the West Side area of Negro concentration lies somewhat nearer to
the Loop than the South Side area, an over-all zonal distribution somewhat obscures the fact that radial growth occurred within both these
areas. Even so, however, the figures indicate that over half the Negro population lives within 5 miles of the city center, as compared
with only about one-third of the white population.

---

10. Beverly Duncan, Growth and Redistribution of the Resident
Population in the Chicago Standard Metropolitan Area (Chicago:
Chicago Plan Commission, 1954), Appendix C.

Chapter VI

Stages of Succession

Concept of Succession

An area undergoes "succession" when one type of land use replaces another. The term "residential succession" means, more specifically, the replacement of one population group in an area by another. The initial population and its successor may differ with respect to economic function, social status, ethnic or national background, race, or other socially significant characteristics or a combination of characteristics.[1] In this study, of course, attention is focused on racial succession, and the question is raised of whether racial succession is associated with changes in other aspects of population composition. Accompanying residential succession may be changes in the density of population, the composition of households, the way in which residential structures are used, the character of local institutions, and the like. Such changes, however, are not assumed to be invariable concomitants of succession; their occurrence and intensity must be established by research.

Succession is a normal aspect of city growth.[2] Growth requires areal expansion, hence a shift of some areas from non-residential to residential use. Growth of commercial and industrial functions leads

---

1. For a discussion of the concept of succession see Harold A. Gibbard, "The Status Factor in Residential Successions," American Journal of Sociology, XLVI (May, 1941), 835-42.

2. See E. W. Burgess, "The Growth of the City," in R. E. Park et al., The City (Chicago: University of Chicago Press, 1925); E. W. Burgess, "Residential Segregation in American Cities," Annals of the American Academy of Political and Social Science, CXL (November, 1928), 105-15.

them, in turn, to encroach upon previously residential areas, particularly in the belt surrounding the center of the city, which is referred to as the "zone in transition," but in other parts of the city as well. A population group with high socioeconomic status often vacates a residential area, as the area ages and its housing becomes less desirable, in favor of newer residential developments; the area may then be taken over by a group of somewhat lower status. Cressey has shown that each of the major groups of immigrants to Chicago originally took up residence near the city's center and then moved toward the periphery over a period of years. Many areas near the center have therefore undergone residential succession, in terms of ethnic characteristics, several times.[3]

To make the notion of residential succession quite explicit, consider the following simplified situation: During year t_0 a given area is exclusively inhabited by members of population group A. In year t_1, some members of group B move into the area, and, by the end of year t_n all the residents of the area are members of group B. We would then say that over an n-year period the area underwent a succession from an area of A residents to an area of B residents. In practice, the initial and terminal dates of a succession cycle can seldom be dated precisely, both for lack of data and because the displacement of group A by group B may never be 100 per cent complete. Other complications may arise, too. The area under study may, throughout its history, be inhabited by several groups. Yet a unidirectional change in the relative importance of these groups may signify that succession is occurring, even though an entire, simple cycle of succession may never be completed. For example, group C may begin to take over the area from group B before the latter has completely superseded group A. There is also the theoretical possibility that population turnover may cease at some point short of complete replacement of one group by another. The area may then have a mixed population in relatively stable proportions for a period of years. Little is known about the conditions necessary to produce a stable mixed

3. Paul F. Cressey, "Population Succession in Chicago, 1898-1930," American Journal of Sociology, XLIV (July, 1938), 59-69; Richard G. Ford, "Population Succession in Chicago," American Journal of Sociology, LVI (September, 1950), 156-60.

area, and one must be careful not to assume that a given area is, in fact, one of this type, without making certain that the mixture is homogeneous, i.e., that there are no subdivisions of the area in which practically complete succession has occurred.

The concept of succession, as defined here, does not intrinsically involve considerations of conflict between the initial population and its successor or of resistance by the former. In some instances succession does indeed involve overt conflict and organized resistance, but these phenomena may be so unimportant as to go unnoticed in other cases. Rather than beg the question by definition, it seems best to regard succession as involving population turnover, pure and simple, and to leave it an open question for research to determine whether and under what conditions succession is accompanied by intergroup friction.[4]

It should be clear that the rate of succession may be quite variable, i.e., the complete cycle may take only a short while or may occur over a long period of years. Moreover, the population turnover may be rapid at first and then slow down, or vice versa. Hence the time relationships involved in succession become a subject for study. Another possibility is that at any period group B may move into an area more rapidly than group A moves out, and the gross population density may consequently increase. Unless there is simultaneously a succession from non-residential to residential uses of land, net density must likewise increase. In fact, in some types of succession it may well be that an increase in residential density is a necessary concomitant, if it is true that only by using the land more intensively can the incoming group afford to occupy the area.

------

4. Both Burgess, "Residential Segregation in American Cities," and Gibbard, "The Status Factor in Residential Successions," describe stages of succession that involve resistance of the old residents of the area to the influx of new residents. In this study it has seemed preferable to delineate stages solely on the basis of the extent of population turnover (see subsequent parts of this chapter). For a methodological study of racial tension in relation to succession see Shirley A. Star, "Interracial Tension in Two Areas of Chicago: An Exploratory Approach to the Measurement of Interracial Tension" (unpublished Ph.D. dissertation, University of Chicago, 1950).

Ideally, to study residential succession in an area, one would like to have a large number of observations on the characteristics of the area in the form of a time series covering the period during which succession occurs. In practice, data are likely to be available only for a few, widely separated points in time. When succession occurs rapidly, this may mean that an entire cycle takes place within a period between two observations, and one has, so to speak, only "before and after snapshots" of the situation rather than the ideal "moving picture" of the succession process.

Specifically, with the decennial census data used in this study, one can identify areas which turned over from virtually complete white occupancy in 1940 to virtually complete non-white occupancy in 1950. In other areas succession may have been well advanced by 1940 and completed by 1950; or the turnover of population may not have begun by 1940 but be well on its way by 1950; and so on.

Examples of Succession

Some of the many possible variations in the time pattern of succession are illustrated in Figure 10, which shows the proportion of the population who were Negroes for selected census tracts at ten-year intervals, 1920-50. (For a map showing location of these tracts, see Fig. 23, chap. viii.) Census tract 587 already had a substantial proportion—one-fifth—of Negroes in 1920. During the 1920-30 decade, population turnover was rapid, so that by 1930 its population was 92.6 per cent Negro and, by 1940, 97.7 per cent. During the 1940-50 decade the tract's Negro proportion increased only slightly, from 97.7 to 98.8 per cent. Nevertheless, in absolute terms there was a considerable increase in Negro residents, from 6,203 in 1940 to 6,733 in 1950, or a rate of increase of 8.5 per cent for the decade. One might, therefore, conclude—somewhat arbitrarily, to be sure—that in this tract the succession from white to Negro residence was virtually completed by 1940, with the subsequent increase in Negro population representing a "piling up" of Negroes in the area. This "piling up" is all the more significant because there was no new housing constructed in the tract between 1940 and 1950.

A second example of an area in which virtually complete succes-

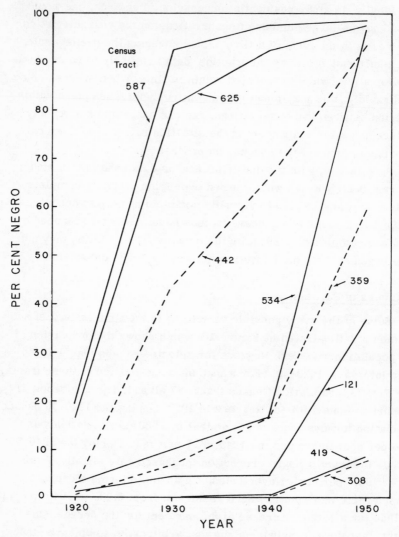

Fig. 10.—Change in Proportion of Negroes in the Total Population, for Selected Census Tracts in Chicago, 1920-50.

sion occurred is tract 625. The increase in the Negro proportion in this tract roughly paralleled that in tract 587, but the turnover of population was not quite completed by 1940, when 92.3 per cent of the residents were Negroes. Between 1940 and 1950 the Negro proportion continued to increase, reaching 97.6 per cent in 1950. In absolute terms, the increase of 1,570 in the Negro population more than compensated for the decline of 657 in the number of white inhabitants, and, as in tract 587, there was scarcely any new residential construction during the decade. This example, then, might be characterized as one of a late phase of consolidating the succession from white to Negro occupancy, coupled with a piling up of Negro population.

Census tracts 359, 442, and 534 provide instances of areas in which succession was barely under way in 1920 and continued over the thirty-year period, but at varying rates. Consolidation of Negro occupancy in tract 442 was more rapid in the first two decades than in the other two tracts, but the latter areas experienced the more rapid turnover of population from 1940 to 1950. In tract 534 the Negro proportion increased from 16.5 per cent in 1940 to 96.9 per cent in 1950, while in tract 359 the increase was from 16.5 to only 59.1 per cent. If attention is focused on the last decade, all three of these tracts may be characterized as being in the midst of a process of consolidating the succession from white to Negro occupancy.

Tract 121, likewise, exemplifies the consolidation of Negro occupancy but is at an earlier stage of succession, with a Negro proportion of only 4.5 per cent in 1940 and 36.7 per cent in 1950. In view of the variability in time patterns of succession, one would hesitate to forecast the rate of succession in this tract beyond 1950 on the basis of previous changes alone. It is, of course, logically possible for the succession process to come to a halt at an early stage, with a stabilization of the proportion of Negroes in the tract. However, there is nothing in the history of Negro succession in Chicago to indicate that this is a likely outcome.

An example of an area which underwent "invasion" by Negroes between 1940 and 1950 is afforded by tract 419. There were only three Negroes reporting residence in this tract in 1920 and two in 1930. There was a penetration of Negroes into the tract between 1930 and 1940, with 0.6 per cent of the population Negro in the latter year, but only between 1940 and 1950 was there any substantial invasion. At the end of the decade 8.4 per cent of the inhabitants were Negroes.

Finally, tract 308 illustrates the case of penetration by Negroes only during the final decade of the series 1940-50. The Censuses of 1920 and 1940 reported no Negroes in the tract, and there was only one in 1930. By 1950, however, 7.7 per cent of the tract's residents were Negroes.

The actual variety of succession patterns is, of course, much greater than is represented by these eight examples. The examples were chosen, in fact, to illustrate fairly clearly the contrasts between areas undergoing succession at different times and at different rates. It is evident that any classification of tracts according to stage or rate of succession must be to some degree arbitrary, but even a crude classification should serve to disclose whether there are significant differences between areas in different stages of succession.

Selection of Census Tracts for Analysis

The study of succession in this monograph is confined to the 1940-50 decade, because the changes occurring during this ten-year period can be documented much more fully by census data than those of any previous decade. A second restriction on the scope of the study arises from its interest in population characteristics of areas undergoing racial succession. Census-tract data showing separately the demographic, economic, and housing characteristics of whites and non-whites are available only for tracts with 250 or more non-white residents. There were 102 such tracts in Chicago in 1940, and 175 in 1950. A third restriction was to confine the study to instances in which there was a population turnover involving succession of whites by Negroes rather than, for example, succession involving non-whites other than Negroes or succession from non-residential to residential land use. Situations like these were noted in several tracts, and these, together with certain miscellaneous circumstances impairing comparability, required the elimination of 21 tracts from the analysis. A list of these tracts, with a discussion of reasons for their exclusion, appears in Appendix F.

The universe of the succession study, then, comprises 154 census tracts that, in 1950, had 250 or more non-white residents and in which the non-whites were preponderantly Negroes rather than members of other races.

Classification of tracts.—As already shown, census tracts exhibit a wide variety of succession patterns from the standpoint of rate and timing of succession. This means that any classification of areas according to stages of succession must be along more or less arbitrary lines. The classification problem here is somewhat simplified by considering only the changes in racial composition between 1940 and 1950. Moreover, certain categories in the classification scheme are virtually dictated by the limitations of the available data; comparable data must be at hand for all tracts grouped in any given category.

Succession is considered to have four main stages: penetration, invasion, consolidation, and piling up—recognizing, of course, that succession logically need not continue through all stages and may be interrupted at any point and that there is no sharp dividing line between any two consecutive stages.

"Penetration" is the stage of initial entry of Negroes into an area occupied by whites. "Invasion" occurs when penetration is followed by the movement into the area of substantial numbers of Negroes; in this study no tract is considered "invaded" until it has at least 250 non-white residents. "Consolidation" refers to the continued increase in number and proportion of Negroes in an area, after invasion has been accomplished. Consolidation may proceed to virtually complete occupancy of the area by Negroes, after which, if Negroes continue to increase in numbers, the stage of "piling up" is reached.

The first stage—penetration—is disregarded in the analysis. Data on non-white population characteristics are not available for a tract until it has sufficient numbers of non-whites to place it beyond the penetration stage.

Tracts classified as having undergone invasion between 1940 and 1950 are those with fewer than 250 non-white residents in 1940 and having a non-white proportion of less than 2 per cent in 1940 and with 250 or more non-white residents in 1950. The non-white proportions in these tracts ranged from 4.5 to 98.4 per cent in 1950.

Primarily for methodological reasons, three subcategories of the consolidation stage are recognized. With but one exception, however, all tracts in the three groups had the common characteristic of increasing in proportion of non-whites between 1940 and 1950; in the exceptional case the tract had an increase in absolute number of non-whites, along with a disproportionate increase in white population. The tracts classified as "early consolidation" are those having 250 or more non-white residents in 1950 and fewer than 250 in 1940, but with a non-white proportion of 2 per cent or more in 1940. As shown in Figure 11, the bulk of the early-consolidation tracts—20 of

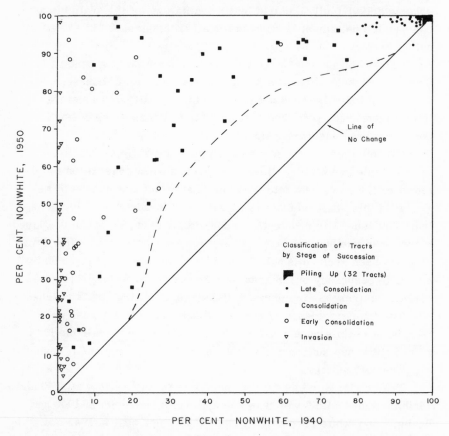

Fig. 11.—Per Cent of Population Non-white, 1940 and 1950, for 154 Census Tracts in Chicago Having 250 or More Non-white Inhabitants in 1950, by Stage of Succession.

the 26 tracts in this category—had between 2 and 10 per cent non-whites in 1940. It will be noted that the only difference between the definitions of invasion and early-consolidation tracts is in respect to the non-white proportion in 1940. Actually, the early-consolidation tracts were not completely invaded—in terms of attaining a non-white population of 250—until some time after 1940. The main reason for separating them from the invasion tracts is that their non-white pro-portions were too high to allow one to interpret data on the total popu-lation in 1940 as essentially white population, while separate data on non-white population characteristics are not available for 1940.

The second group of tracts undergoing consolidation will be re-ferred to simply as "consolidation tracts." These tracts had 250 or more non-whites in both 1940 and 1950, but a non-white proportion under 80 per cent at the beginning of the decade. Only 5 of the 35 tracts in this group had non-white proportions under 10 per cent in 1940. By 1950 the non-white proportions in these tracts ranged from 12.0 to 99.4 per cent.

The third group of tracts undergoing consolidation are called "late-consolidation tracts." These differ from the "consolidation" tracts only in that the 1940 non-white proportion was 80 per cent or more. By the end of the decade all these tracts had non-white pro-portions exceeding 92 per cent, and in all but 3 of the 28 tracts non-whites constituted over 95 per cent of the population. One tract, No. 935, was kept in this group even though its non-white proportion de-clined from 94.7 to 92.2 per cent over the decade. This is a tract of larger than average area size in which there was some new housing construction for white occupancy during the decade, increasing the white population from 153 in 1940 to 348 in 1950. Meanwhile non-whites increased in number from 2,709 to 4,133.

The final category, the piling-up tracts, includes 32 tracts with 97.5 per cent or more non-whites in both 1940 and 1950. Two tracts included in this group had small decreases in absolute numbers but not in proportion of non-whites over the decade. All the others con-form with the notion of "piling up," i.e., further increase in numbers of non-whites after virtual completion of succession. There were, however, 7 tracts in this group in which the non-white proportion de-

Table 31. —Criteria for Classifying Census Tracts According to Stage of Succession: 175 Census Tracts with 250 or More Non-white Inhabitants in 1950

Stage	Definition	Interpretation	Methodological Characteristics
Piling up (32 tracts)	97.5 per cent or more of population non-white in both 1940 and 1950 250 or more non-white residents in both years	Succession cycle already virtually completed in 1940, but Negro population may continue to increase, resulting in higher population density	Data for total population of tract essentially represents non-white population in both years
Late consolidation (28 tracts)	80.0-97.4 per cent of population non-white in 1940 90.0 per cent or more of population non-white in 1950 250 or more non-white residents in both years	Succession cycle is virtually completed between 1940 and 1950, for tracts where succession was already very advanced by 1940	Data are available for white and non-white population separately in both 1940 and 1950
Consolidation (35 tracts)	Less than 80.0 per cent of population non-white in 1940 250 or more non-white residents in both 1940 and 1950	Invasion occurred before 1940; further increase in per cent of population non-white between 1940 and 1950	Data are available for white and non-white population separately in both 1940 and 1950
Early consolidation (26 tracts)	2 per cent or more of population non-white in 1940 250 or more non-white residents in 1950 but less than 250 in 1940	Invasion occurred before 1940, but succession had not advanced very far by then; further increase in per cent of population non-white between 1940 and 1950	Data are available for white and non-white population separately only in 1950; these are generally census tracts with smaller populations than the average tract

Table 31 (continued)

Stage	Definition	Interpretation	Methodological Characteristics
Invasion (33 tracts)	Less than 2 per cent of population non-white in 1940 and less than 250 non-white residents in 1940 250 or more non-white residents in 1950	Tract may have been penetrated by non-whites before 1940, but significant degree of invasion occurred only after 1940	Data are available for white and non-white population separately only in 1950; data for total population of tract in 1940 essentially represents white population in that year
Excluded from analysis (21 tracts) a (11 tracts)	a - Tracts in which other races outnumbered Negroes in 1950 (see Appendix F)	a - Negroes and other non-whites probably have different succession patterns	a - Tract data on population characteristics not available separately for Negroes and other non-whites
b (1 tract)	b - Total population less than 100 in 1940	b - Pattern of change not interpretable	b - Insufficient numbers for analysis
c (2 tracts)	c - Non-whites are nearly all residents of institutions	c - Institutional population's residence determined by location of institutions	c - Data for institutional and non-institutional population not comparable in many respects
d (7 tracts)	d - Unusual changes, 1940-50 (see Appendix F)	d - Indicates presence of factors that may disturb typical pattern of succession	d - Data do not fall into patterns followed by majority of tracts

creased slightly, despite the increase in number of non-whites. It is doubtful that such decreases are significant. One must remember that even a small increase in absolute numbers of whites in these tracts may suffice to diminish the percentage of non-whites. For example, in tract 592 the non-white proportion decreased from 99.6 to 98.4 per cent as a consequence of an increase from 20 to 96 whites and from 5,277 to 6,092 non-whites.

Table 31 summarizes the criteria used to classify tracts by stage of succession. The tracts falling in each group are shown on a map, Figure 12, and are listed numerically in Appendix Table E-1. These materials are largely self-explanatory, but a few additional remarks may clarify the way in which they are interpreted in this study.

In Figure 11 the diagonal line is drawn to separate tracts increasing from those decreasing in percentage non-white over the 1940-50 decade. All tracts above the line showed an increase, and the figure demonstrates graphically the point already made, i.e., that a decrease in proportion non-white is exceptional among tracts having attained a substantial number or proportion of non-whites. The dotted line on the chart is designed to emphasize another fact: census tracts with non-white proportions between 25 and 75 per cent in 1940 uniformly experienced a large increase in their non-white proportions between 1940 and 1950. In all cases but one, this increase amounted to 20 percentage points or more. This observation bears on the question of whether tracts having "mixed" populations —i.e., substantial proportions of both whites and Negroes—may, under certain circumstances, retain their "mixed" character for a period of years. If the 1940-50 experience were a reliable indication, one could certainly say that such a development is unlikely. In other words, the data for this decade reveal no instance of a tract with "mixed population" (25-75 per cent non-white) in which succession from white to Negro occupancy was arrested, though, to be sure, the succession was more rapid in some tracts than in others. No doubt the 1940-50 experience is, at most, typical of periods of large increases in the Negro population of the whole city, and instances of relatively stable mixed neighborhoods might appear during a period of less rapid growth of Negro population.

The spatial arrangement of the tracts in the five categories (Fig. 12) is about what one would expect from a knowledge of the pattern of expansion of Negro settlement in Chicago (chap. v). The piling-up tracts, with the exception of one in the northwest corner of the Near West Side community, are located in the center of the South Side "Black Belt." Most of the late-consolidation tracts are adjacent or near to the piling-up tracts in the "Black Belt" and on the Near West Side; the remainder are found in the southern part of the Near West Side, in the "Lilydale" Negro community, and in the Negro settlement in Morgan Park. The consolidation tracts are more widely scattered, appearing not only on the periphery of the piling-up and consolidation tracts in the "Black Belt" and in the Near West Side community, but also in the Near North Side, Englewood, West Englewood, South Chicago, and Morgan Park communities and adjacent to the older portion of the Lilydale settlement. The early-consolidation and invasion tracts are also somewhat scattered, although the bulk of them appear to be extensions of the "Black Belt" and Near West Side areas of Negro settlement.

In interpreting the results of the succession study, several things need to be kept in mind. First, the concept of stages of succession is an abstract and somewhat idealized scheme which, at best, can describe the actual process only approximately. Second, census tracts are arbitrary units, not at all homogeneous in size of area or population. Their classification according to stage of succession is to a considerable extent a matter of judgment, tempered by the necessity of working within the limits of the available data. Above all, the fact that the time period covered is fixed at ten years means that some tracts may proceed through a whole cycle of succession or several stages thereof, while others go through but a single stage. For example, tract 624 changed from 0.2 to 98.4 per cent non-white between 1940 and 1950, while tract 450 changed from 0.3 to 12.4 per cent non-white over the decade: Yet both are classified as "invasion" tracts because both were invaded only after 1940. To some extent, the study design overcomes the limitations of the data, for both cross-sectional comparisons among the several categories of tracts and measures of change over a ten-year period are possible. Even this combination, however, affords only an approximation to the theoretically preferable plan of following each tract through an entire succession cycle.

A further limitation on the study is occasioned by the lack of certain data. The tabulation below summarizes the situation in this regard for the five classes of tracts.

	1940	1950
Piling up.	a,b	a,b
Late consolidation	a	a
Consolidation.	a	a
Early consolidation.	x	a
Invasion	b	a

The symbol "a" means that census data on population and housing characteristics are available separately for whites and non-whites. The symbol "b" means that data on characteristics of the total population essentially represent non-whites only (piling-up tracts) or whites only (invasion tracts, 1940). The symbol "x" refers to the absence of data adequate to describe either the white or the non-white population separately (except for one or two characteristics). The most complete data are those for the total tract population in 1950, the second most complete those for total population in 1940. The data available by color are materially less detailed, especially those for 1940. This means that the best information (in terms of coverage of the data) is available for the piling-up tracts, and the poorest information for the early-consolidation tracts, with the other three groups falling in an intermediate position.

Population growth by stage of succession.—The distribution of total and Negro population over the categories of tracts used in the succession study is shown in Table 32. The 154 tracts analyzed contained over 95 per cent of the city's Negro population in 1940 and about 93 per cent in 1950. The small minority of Negroes remaining are those residing in tracts with special characteristics precluding their analysis according to the scheme of succession stages and those living in tracts with fewer than 250 non-white residents. The

Table 32.—Population by Race, for Census Tracts Classified by Stage of Succession, Chicago, 1940 and 1950

Group of Census Tracts	Number of Tracts	Population (Thousands)						Per Cent Negro	
		1940			1950			1940	1950
		Total	Negro	Other	Total	Negro	Other		
All tracts	935	3,397	278	3,119	3,621	492	3,129	8.2	13.6
With 250 or more non-whites, 1950	175	651	273	378	796	482	314	41.9	60.6
Piling up	32	139	138	1	161	160	1	99.0	99.3
Late consolidation	28	102	93	9	136	134	3	91.5	97.8
Consolidation	35	113	30	83	138	86	52	26.2	62.1
Early consolidation	26	58	3	55	74	29	44	4.9	39.5
Invasion	33	154	1	153	173	50	124	0.5	28.6
Other*	21	84	8	76	113	24	89	10.0	21.1
With less than 250 non-whites, 1950	760	2,746	5	2,741	2,825	10	2,815	0.2	0.4

*Excluded from analysis (see Appendix F).

latter tracts include those logically classifiable as in the stage of penetration. At this time, of course, it is impossible to know whether succession will continue in these tracts, and little can be learned from census data about the characteristics of Negroes living in them. There is some indirect evidence, summarized in Appendix C, that Negroes living in tracts with fewer than 250 non-white residents do not differ greatly from Negroes in the remainder of the city with respect to educational attainment. Presumably, the same conclusion would hold regarding social characteristics highly correlated with education.

Role of Residential Mobility in Succession

In each of the five categories of tracts in the succession analysis there was a substantial increase in Negro population, the increase being greatest in relative terms, of course, in the invasion and early-consolidation tracts, which contained few Negroes in 1940. In each group there was a decrease in non-Negro population, but in no case was this decrease as large as the Negro increase. In this sense, one might say that "piling up" is a concomitant of succession at all stages rather than a distinct stage of succession.

It is evident that the bulk of the increase in Negro population in the invasion, early-consolidation, and consolidation tracts must have resulted from the movement of Negroes into these areas between 1940 and 1950 rather than from the natural increase (excess of births over deaths) of Negroes already residing there in 1940. In the late-consolidation and piling-up tracts, however, the Negro population of 1940 was large enough to produce a considerable natural increase. Consequently, it is desirable to estimate the respective contributions of residential movement and natural increase to the growth of the Negro population in these areas. The preparation of such an estimate also affords an occasion for supplementing the analysis of migration for the city as a whole (in chap. iii) with analyses for selected subareas of the city.

Components of population growth.—The Negro population of the city of Chicago increased by 77 per cent during the decade 1940-50. The analysis of the components of this increase (chap. iii) indicates

that 72 per cent of the total increase was accounted for by net in-
migration—the excess of in-migrants over out-migrants—and only
28 per cent was accounted for by natural increase—the excess of
births over deaths.

Components of the growth of the Negro population in groups of
census tracts of the city can be ascertained in the same way. The
growth of the Negro population between 1940 and 1950 in any group
of census tracts can be broken into growth due to natural increase
and growth due to net in-movement (the difference between the number of persons moving into the tracts and the number of persons
moving from the tracts during the decade).

Three cautions in the interpretation of the results should be indicated. First, estimates of net residential movement are not estimates of population turnover. If the number of persons moving into
the tracts equals the number of persons leaving the tracts, net movement, the difference, is zero; however, gross movement or population turnover, the sum, is not necessarily zero. Second, it cannot be
ascertained whether the origin of persons moving into the tracts
was in other tracts inside the city or whether their origin was outside the city; similarly, it cannot be ascertained whether the destination of persons moving out of the tracts was to other tracts inside
the city or whether their destination was outside the city. Finally,
the results of the analysis are subject to substantial error, somewhat more so than the migration estimates for the city as a whole.
However, it is unlikely that the error is so great as to vitiate the
conclusions drawn.

The sources of growth of the Negro population in the piling-up
tracts, the late-consolidation tracts, and the remainder of the city
are compared in Table 33. Both the percentage increase in Negro
population and the proportion of the increase in Negro population
accounted for by net in-movement[5] during the decade 1940-50 were
smaller in the areas that were almost exclusively Negro in 1940

---

5. The term "in-movement" is meant to include both migration into an area originating outside Chicago and change of residence
from one area to another within the city.

Table 33.—Estimated Components of Negro Population Growth, for
Selected Groups of Census Tracts of the City of Chicago, 1940-50

Group of Census Tracts and Distance from Loop	Per Cent Increase in Population	Per Cent Increase Due to		Increase Due to Net In-movement as Per Cent of Total Increase
		Natural Increase	Net In-movement	
Piling up.	16	6	10	60
Within 5 miles .	53	17	36	67
5 miles or more	7	4	3	46
Late consolidation	43	15	28	65
Within 5 miles .	52	21	31	60
5 miles or more	34	9	25	72
Remainder of city.	326	81	245	75
Entire city	77	22	55	72

than in the remainder of the city. But in each group of tracts net in-
movement was quantitatively a more important source of growth than
natural increase.

In both the piling-up and the late-consolidation tracts, the percentage increase in Negro population was greater in the tracts located within 5 miles of the Loop than in the tracts located 5 miles
or more from the Loop. In the piling-up tracts, net migration was a
more important source of growth in the centralized than in the de-
centralized tracts, whereas in the late-consolidation tracts the reverse was true.

Figure 13 shows rates of net in-movement, i.e., estimated net
in-movement per 100 survivors of the population residing in the
tracts in 1940, by age, for the Negro population in each group of
census tracts. At each age the net rate of in-movement for both the
piling-up and the late-consolidation tracts was below the rate for
the city as a whole, whereas the rate for the remainder of the city
was substantially higher than that for the city as a whole.

The peak rate of net in-movement for each group of tracts,
as for the city as a whole, occurred for persons fifteen to nineteen
years of age in 1940 or twenty-five to twenty-nine years of age in
1950. But, as Figure 13 shows, there were differences among the
groups of tracts in the pattern of rates by age. In the piling-up tracts

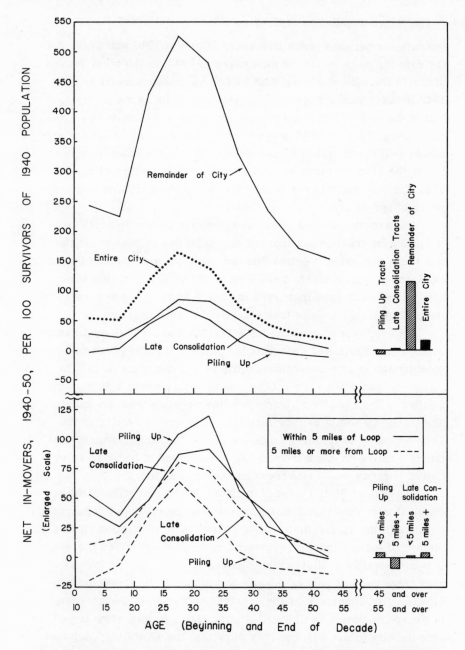

Fig. 13.—Estimated Rate of Net In-movement, 1940-50, per 100 Survivors of the 1940 Population, by Age, for the Negro Population in Census Tracts Grouped by Stage of Succession.

the rate for persons under five years of age in 1940 was lower than
the rate for persons five to nine years in 1940; in the other groups
of tracts the rate was somewhat higher for persons under five in
1940 than for persons five to nine years in 1940. In the piling-up
tracts the rate of net in-movement for persons twenty to twenty-
four years of age in 1940 was markedly lower than that for persons
fifteen to nineteen years of age in 1940. But in the other groups of
tracts the rate for persons twenty to twenty-four years of age in
1940 was only slightly lower than that for persons fifteen to nineteen
years of age in 1940.

The pattern of rates of net in-movement by age indicates that
the piling-up tracts were more highly selective of persons in the
late teens and early twenties than were the other areas. On the other
hand, the piling-up tracts were less selective of children and persons in the adult ages than were the other areas. This suggests that
the piling-up tracts were less selective of family groups.

However, the lower panel of Figure 13 and the data summarized
in Appendix Table A-7 show that the pattern of rates of net in-movement by age in late-consolidation tracts was the same as that in
piling-up tracts when the comparison is restricted to tracts within
5 miles of the Loop or to tracts 5 miles or more from the Loop.
The piling-up and late-consolidation tracts within 5 miles of the
Loop appeared to be more selective of family groups, whereas the
tracts 5 miles or more from the Loop appeared to be more selective of persons in the late teens and early twenties.

Residential distribution of migrants.—The foregoing material
demonstrates the importance of residential mobility in producing
changes in the spatial distribution of the Negro population. With the
method of estimating net residential movement described therein,
it is not possible to distinguish between persons coming into an
area from another part of the city and migrants coming from outside the city. Inasmuch as the greater proportion of the increase
in Negro population in Chicago is attributable to migration from outside the city (chap. iii), one may infer that the spatial expansion of
the area of Negro settlement in the city is caused, directly or indirectly, by the influx of Negro migrants. It would be of considerable

interest, from the standpoint of the succession process, if one could determine, in addition, whether the movement of Negroes into areas hitherto inhabited by whites involves primarily the older residents of the city or a disproportionate number of recent migrants to the city.

Data on the intra-city distribution of 1935-40 migrants to Chicago are available for a set of 24 large "migration areas," selected ones of which are shown in Figure 14. The census-tract data on distribution of 1949-50 migrants to Chicago can be consolidated into comparable area groupings. Unfortunately, the "migration areas" are so large that they may obscure some important differences. Table 34 shows that in both 1940 and 1950 migration area 14 contained a larger

Table 34.—Distribution of Non-white Migrants to Chicago, 1935-40 and 1949-50, by Selected Areas

Migration Area	1935-40		1949-50	
	Per Cent of Total Migrants	Migrants as Per Cent of 1940 Non-white Population	Per Cent of Total Migrants	Migrants as Per Cent of 1950 Non-white Population
City, total . . .	100.0	5.3	100.0	1.8
4	2.6	7.6	3.9	2.1
10	2.3	5.0	7.6	2.2
11	8.4	5.2	14.4	2.1
13	2.2	5.2	4.4	2.0
14	57.1	5.2	38.0	1.5
15	1.2	15.8	4.2	4.7
16	16.7	4.9	13.9	1.9
23	1.9	3.9	5.5	2.3
Remainder of city	7.6	7.8	8.1	1.4

proportion of recent non-white migrants than any other area. This area takes in a large section of the South Side "Black Belt." It is significant that the proportion of the city's total migrants living in this area dropped from 57 per cent in 1940 to 38 per cent in 1950. The second largest concentration of recent non-white migrants in 1940

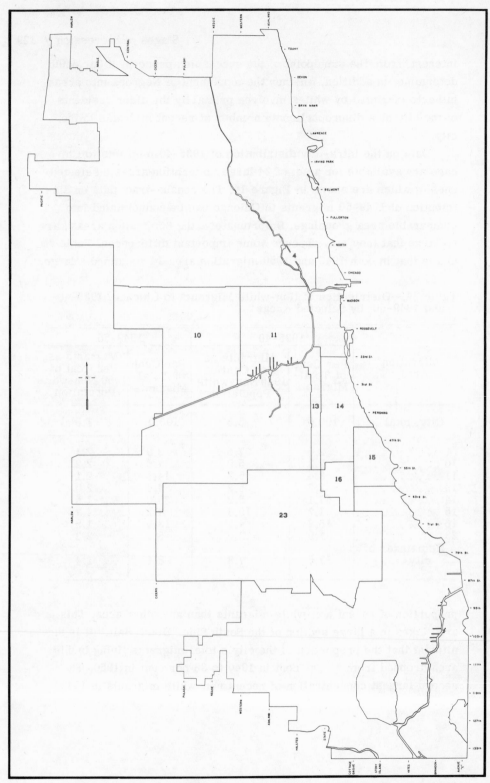

Fig. 14.—Selected Areas Used in Migration Analysis, Chicago

was in migration area 16—the southern extremity of the "Black Belt"
—which contained one-sixth of the recent migrants. But by 1950 this
area had dropped to third rank, being displaced by area 11, which
includes most of the area of Negro settlement on the West Side. These
three areas (14, 16, and 11) together contained 82 per cent of the recent migrants in 1940, but only 66 per cent in 1950. It is clear, therefore, that the major areas of concentrated Negro settlement receive
the bulk of the migrants. But by 1950, with the considerable expansion
of Negro settlement in areas peripheral to these, their importance
as a "port of entry" had diminished somewhat.

If one relates the number of migrants in each area to its non-
white population at the end of the decade, to form a crude rate, the
results (Table 34) reveal that migration areas 14, 16, and 11 did not
receive disproportionate numbers of migrants. Their 1940 in-migration rates were, in fact, slightly below that of the entire city, and
their 1950 rates were not greatly different from the city rate. On the
other hand, relatively high migration rates were observed in 1940
for areas 4 (on the Near North Side) and 15 (Kenwood-Hyde Park
communities, to the east of the "Black Belt") and in the residual
part of the city obtained by subtracting out the eight main areas of
non-white in-migration. In 1950 the only conspicuously high in-migration rate was in area 15 (Kenwood-Hyde Park). This high rate, however, may have been due to in-migration of other races rather than
Negroes.

These data, though crude, indicate that while the bulk of Negro
migrants enter areas of established Negro settlement, recent migrants are just as important an element in areas of recent or less
concentrated Negro settlement as in areas in which Negroes constitute a very large proportion of the population.

There is, however, another way to interpret the residential distribution of migrants, which places a somewhat different light on
the matter. A given area within the city may increase its population
through natural increase (births minus deaths), net in-movement
from other parts of the city, or net in-migration from outside the
city. The statistics are not detailed enough to permit this kind of
breakdown, but the following calculations yield some indirect evidence.

Between 1940 and 1950 the non-white population of the city increased by about 227,000. In 1950 about 9,000 non-whites in the city reported their 1949 residence as being outside the city. There were, therefore, 4.0 in-migrants during 1949-50 per 100 of the 1940-50 population increase. If one makes a similar computation for each census tract with 250 or more non-white inhabitants in 1950 and groups the tracts by stage of succession, he finds that three-fourths of the piling-up tracts had ratios in excess of 4.0, as compared with only one-fifth of the early-consolidation and invasion tracts. By stage of succession, these are the percentages of tracts with ratios above 4.0:

Piling up.	75
Late consolidation	64
Consolidation	37
Early consolidation.	23
Invasion	21

Despite the fact that the migration data pertain to but one year of the decade over which non-white population increase is measured, these results indicate that in the early stages of succession the movement of Negroes into formerly white areas is led by those who have lived in the city for some time rather than by recent migrants. This is not in contradiction to the observation that tracts in the later stages of succession have a higher proportion of migrants in their total population than those in the early stages. The proportion of migrants in the former group is low because their Negro population is large to begin with and they may be unable to absorb as many migrants relative to their initial population as can areas where Negroes are displacing whites.

In summary, the fragmentary data on migration that are available permit the following inferences: The bulk of the Negro migrants to Chicago enter areas of established Negro settlement—by and large, tracts in the late stages of succession. The migrants contribute disproportionately to the Negro population growth of these areas, as contrasted to areas of invasion and early consolidation. Conversely, older residents, rather than recently arrived migrants, constitute a disproportionate number of the Negroes moving into areas of former white occupancy.

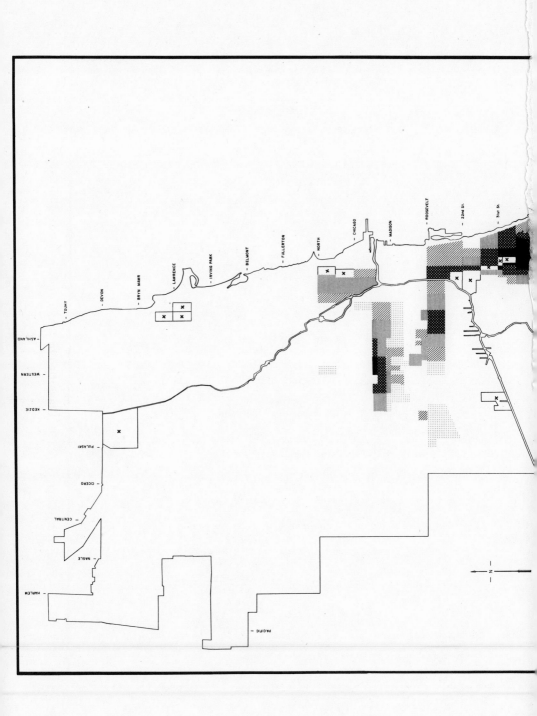

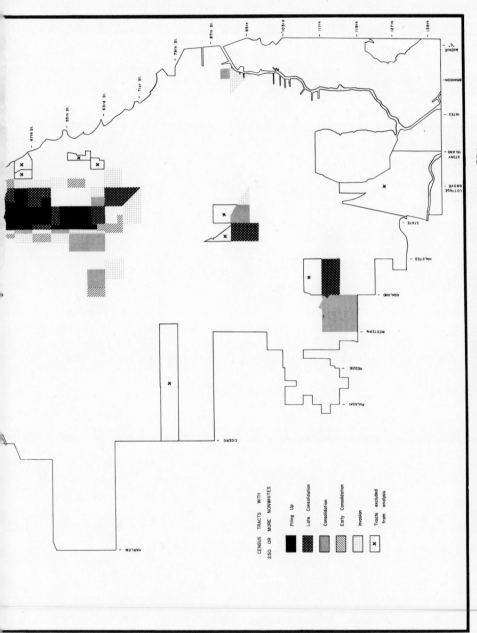

Fig. 12.—Census Tracts Classified by Stage of Succession, Chicago, 1950.

Chapter VII

Concomitants of Succession

Introduction

This chapter deals with changes in population and housing characteristics in areas undergoing succession from white to Negro residence
during the 1940-50 decade. Not all these changes, of course, can be
regarded as "effects" of succession. In fact, several of them are quite
evidently due to forces that have little or nothing to do with changes
in residential patterns within the city—e.g., the decline in the rate of
unemployment or the rise in level of educational attainment over the
interval of ten years. Nevertheless, one may hypothesize that the rate
of change in the characteristics of an area's population is affected
by residential succession, even if the source of change must be sought
in general social trends or economic fluctuations.

One primary focus of interest in the succeeding analysis is the
measurement of the degree of "stability" of area characteristics. In
all areas undergoing succession there is, by definition, a turnover
of population. Yet it is conceivable that the population moving into an
area may resemble the population moving out in its social and economic characteristics. The area, then, may be regarded as "stable"
with respect to these characteristics, even though its racial composition changes. There are two major reasons for expecting to find
some degree of stability despite the turnover of population. The first
may be termed the "situational" factor. Each local area of the city
has a functional position in the organization of the city as a whole. If,
for example, a neighborhood is served by rapid-transit facilities, it
is suitable as a residence for persons whose occupations require
long or frequent movements about the city. If it is located near large

manufacturing establishments, then its residences are likely to be in demand by the workers in those establishments. The second factor making for stability may be called the "site" factor. Once an area has been built up, there is a considerable inertia in its pattern of land use, because most structures have a useful life of a human generation or more. Thus a neighborhood in which most residences are in apartment houses is likely to remain an apartment-house neighborhood for many years. A census tract with a mixed pattern of commercial, industrial, and residential uses is likely to have such a mixture of uses for some time. This is not to deny the obvious fact of changes in general land-use patterns but rather to assert that the time scale of changes in these patterns is long compared with that of the changes in ethnic composition of residents.

If, then, the situational relationships and site characteristics of an area remain somewhat the same over a period of time, new residents entering the area can be expected to make a type of residential adjustment which is similar to that of the older residents. Moreover, areas differing with respect to site and situational factors are likely to differ in regard to the characteristics of persons who move into them. In this sense areas may be said to be "selective" of their residents, the degree of selectivity being indicated by the extent of the differences in the social and economic characteristics of persons moving into them.

The term "stability" may be construed in at least two senses. In the first, it has reference to the absolute level of a given measured characteristic. In this sense, if the prevalence of a given attribute in an area changes in proportional frequency from 10 to 30 per cent over a ten-year period, one would perhaps consider the area unstable with respect to this characteristic. But under the second sense of the term "stability," which essentially involves a comparative point of view, the mere fact of change in level is not incompatible with stability. If one is comparing, say, fifteen neighborhoods that have a clear rank order with respect to a given characteristic and if, in all the neighborhoods, there is a uniform change over a specified period, then the rank order would be unchanged, i.e., there would be a pronounced "stability" of the pattern of interarea variation. In the discussions to follow, attention is given both to changes in absolute level and to changes in relative position within sets of census tracts being compared. The concept of "stability," however, is used only in the second sense of maintenance of relative position in a comparison. The two points of view correspond, respectively, to the analysis of changes in average values and to the analysis of regression relationships or correlation.

Plan of analysis.—In chapter vi all the census tracts with 250 or more non-white residents in 1950 were classified into five stages of succession and a sixth category of tracts excluded from the analysis for various reasons. In this chapter each of the five sets of tracts is considered as a unit for expository purposes. This amounts to the presentation of five separate studies of the succession process; in chapter viii the findings of these five analyses are compared, and differences among the five sets of tracts are examined.

The treatment of the five stages of succession is not entirely uniform. In the first place, as already noted, the available data do not have the same coverage and detail for all five sets of tracts. Second, certain comparisons that are appropriate for one stage of succession are inappropriate for another. For example, for the consolidation tracts, which had a substantial proportion of non-whites in 1940 as well as in 1950, one may examine changes in the characteristics of non-whites over the decade; but such an analysis does not make sense for the invasion tracts, which had virtually no non-whites in 1940. In any case, the latter comparison could not be made for lack of data. In particular, then, the breakdown of the data by color varies from one stage of succession to another.

The map showing location of tracts in each of the five stages of succession (Fig. 12) reveals that in each case the tracts are distributed over several zones and often in two or three sectors. Previous research has shown that the Negro population of Chicago is differentiated by zones,[1] and the same may well be true of sectors. In working with the succession stages, therefore, one wants to be as-

---

1. E. Franklin Frazier, The Negro Family in Chicago (Chicago: University of Chicago Press, 1932), chaps. vi and vii.

sured that the apparent concomitants of succession, as revealed by the analysis, do not obtain only for the particular zone or sector in which the tracts at that stage are most heavily represented. In each analysis there is an area breakdown, but the area classification is not the same for all five sets of tracts. This variation in the classification is necessary to permit each areal subgroup of tracts to be represented in sufficient numbers for analytical purposes—a requirement, it must be admitted, that is only marginally fulfilled, at best, in certain cases. An outline of the area classification follows.

Piling up:

> Zone 3-4, 11 census tracts located between 2 and 4 miles from the center of the city (State and Madison streets), one of them being on the Near West Side and the remainder on the South Side
> Zone 5, 11 tracts between 4 and 5 miles from the center, all on the South Side
> Zone 6-7, 10 tracts between 5 and 7 miles from the center, all on the South Side

Late consolidation:

> Zone 2-3, 8 tracts located between 1 and 3 miles from the center, 4 of them on the Near West Side and 4 on the South Side
> Zone 4-5, 10 tracts located between 3 and 5 miles from the center, 2 on the West Side and 8 on the South Side
> Zone 6-14, 10 tracts located between 5 and 14 miles from the center, all on the South Side

Consolidation:

> North Side, 6 tracts, all in community area 8, Near North Side, and within 2 miles of the city center
> West Side, 14 tracts, 12 in community area 28, Near West Side, 2 in community area 27, East Garfield Park, and all between 1 and 4 miles from the city center
> South Side, 15 tracts, 6 of them located 2-4 miles from the city center and 9 of them 4-14 miles from the center

Early consolidation:

> North and West Side, 14 tracts, 3 in the Near North Side community area, 10 in the Near West Side community area, and 1 in community area 29, North Lawndale, and all of them located within 5 miles of the city center
> South Side, 12 tracts, 8 of them located between 1 and 6 miles of the center and 4 between 6 and 8 miles

Invasion:

West Side, 17 tracts located in four Near West Side and West Side

community areas, but all between 1 and 5 miles of the city center
South Side, 16 tracts, 7 between 4 and 6 miles of the center and 9
between 6 and 12 miles of the center

Evidently, the areal distribution of these census tracts is such
that a uniform zone-sector classification would have small or zero
frequencies in some categories for each of the five stages of succession. Although some of the classifications are based on zonal location
and others on sector location, it may be noted that a rough zonal ordering is implicit in the latter, inasmuch as the North Side and West Side
tracts are comparatively close to the center of the city, whereas the
South Side tracts extend to relatively great distances from the center.

Nine variables or characteristics of census tracts were subjected
to a systematic scrutiny of changes and stability over the 1940-50
decade. These include population density, room crowding of dwelling
units, educational attainment, unemployment, white-collar employment, homeownership, rent, and housing equipment—central heating
and mechanical refrigeration. More explicit designations of these
variables appear in the text and tables of this chapter, and their
complete technical definitions are given in Appendix G, along with
some notes on the way they were handled in the study, including computational procedures and techniques of "standardization." Two factors governed the choice of these variables: foremost, the availability and comparability of the requisite data and, second, the assumption that they reflect significant physical and social aspects of the
residential adjustment of populations. Although one can think of other
characteristics worth examination in the context of succession, it is
likely that many of them would be correlated in some degree with
those studied here.

The analysis relies on the elementary techniques of descriptive
statistics—comparison of averages and calculation of regression
equations. The description of results is made as non-technical as
possible, but, in formulating interpretations, several technical problems were kept in mind. Some of these are described in succeeding
paragraphs and in Appendixes G and H.

Figure 15 will serve as a general illustration of the approach
and mode of interpreting results. It involves data on the piling-up

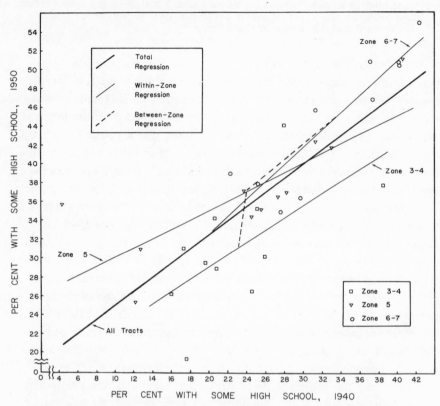

Fig. 15.—Scattergram and Regression Lines Showing Relationship of 1950 to 1940 Percentages of the Population Having Completed One Year or More of High School, for 32 Piling-Up Tracts, by Zone. (Persons twenty-five years old and over; percentages standardized for age.)

tracts and, for that reason, does not cover all the kinds of comparisons made in later sections of the chapter. These, however, are explained as they appear. The figure is a scattergram showing the relationship of the 1950 to the 1940 percentage of adults with at least some high-school education (standardized for age) in the 32 piling-up tracts. For example, the point in the upper right-hand corner of the diagram represents census tract 605, in which 42.4 per cent (standardized) of the population twenty-five years old and over reported having completed one year or more of high school in 1940 and 55.0 per cent (standardized) in 1950. Three symbols are used in plotting the points for the tracts, to distinguish them according to zonal location.

The heavy straight line is the line of regression of the 1950 on the 1940 percentages for all 32 tracts. Its equation is $\underline{Y}=17.4 + 0.75\underline{X}$, where $\underline{Y}$ is the 1950 percentage with one year or more of high school and $\underline{X}$ is the 1940 percentage. It is evident from the graph that this linear equation adequately describes the average relationship of the 1950 to the 1940 percentages, although some points deviate from the line to a considerable degree. The correlation coefficient provides a measure of the adequacy of the regression line as a basis for infer- ring the 1950 percentage if the 1940 percentage is given. For the en- tire group of 32 tracts the correlation is .80, and one may state, consequently, that 64 per cent (the square of .80) of the variance in the 1950 percentages is accounted for by the 1940 percentages. Or, to express the relationship another way, the correlation indicates that there is a moderately strong tendency for census tracts to main- tain their relative positions according to educational status over the decade.

The interpretation of the regression line is facilitated by examin- ing the mean values for the two census years. The (unweighted) mean percentage with one year or more of high school was 26.6 in 1940 $(\underline{M_X})$ and 37.4 in 1950 $(\underline{M_Y})$, i.e., there was an average increase of 10.8 percentage points. However, the slope of the regression line (0.75, in the equation in the preceding paragraph) indicates that the amount of the increase varied systematically according to the level of educational attainment in 1940. Tracts with low percentages in 1940, on the average, made larger gains over the decade than did those with relatively high percentages at the beginning of the decade.[2]

---

2. A slope of unity (1.0) would mean that, on the average, the change over the decade was the same, irrespective of a tract's po- sition at the beginning of the decade. If, for example, each tract in- creased by 10 points, the regression equation would be $\underline{Y}=10 + (1.0)\underline{X}$. In the special case where there were no changes at all over the decade, the equation would be, of course, $\underline{Y}=(1.0)\underline{X}$. When the calcu- lation of the regression constants shows the slope to be unity, or

The three lighter straight lines are the regressions for the three sets of tracts by zone, the equations for which are shown subsequently, in Table 36. These within-zone regressions and the correlations corresponding thereto are interpreted in the same way as the regression for the total group of 32 tracts.

The dashed line in Figure 15 connects the means for the three zonal sets of tracts and is referred to as the "between-zone" regression. This regression is not required to be linear. The 1940 (unweighted) means are 23.1 for Zone 3-4, 24.0 for Zone 5, and 33.3 for Zone 6-7; the corresponding 1950 (unweighted) means are 31.1, 37.0, and 44.7. Thus in both 1940 and 1950 average educational attainment was higher, the greater the zonal distance from the city center. Moreover, there was an increase in average level of schooling in each of the three sets of tracts between 1940 and 1950, the greatest increase being for the tracts in Zone 5.

The substantive interpretation of the data shown in Figure 15 appears in a later section of this chapter. Here attention is called to several technical aspects of the analysis that affect the interpretation. First, none of the computations involves weights for tract size, despite the fact that there is considerable variation in both size of area and number of residents among the census tracts. In some cases it

---

negligibly different from unity, it can generally be assumed that all tracts tended to change by about the same amount (whether an increase or a decrease) on the average. However, since the regression slope is an average, the same caution must be exercised as in interpreting any average, i.e., to accept it as a representative figure only if the value is not distorted by a few deviant cases. Thus, in the text, all interpretations of regression slopes depend not only on the calculated value of the slope but also on a careful inspection of scattergrams to rule out the possibility that peculiar changes in one or two tracts unduly affected the relationship observed over all tracts.

The interpretation of a slope appreciably below unity is that tracts initially low tended to increase more (or decrease less) than tracts with initially high values of the given characteristic. Similarly, a slope appreciably above unity signifies that, on the average, increases were greater (or decreases smaller) for tracts with initially high values than for tracts with initially low values. Again, in drawing a conclusion from the finding that the slope departs substantially from unity, one must be sure that the average relationship which the slope represents is not unduly affected by a few tracts with extremely atypical changes.

was possible to supplement the regression analysis by computing
weighted means (actually, computing means from the aggregated
tract distributions, which amounts to the same thing). But this could
not be done for all the variables considered, nor was it feasible to
calculate regressions and correlations on a weighted basis. To avoid
misleading conclusions from the unweighted summary statistics, the
original data have been examined for their consistency with the conclusion in each case. Second, the fact that adjacent tracts or tracts
located near one another are not statistically independent means
that conventional tests of significance for means, regression coefficients, and correlations are not applicable. This circumstance also
precludes the use of analysis of covariance, which otherwise would
be the appropriate technique for comparing the total regressions
with the within-zone regressions and for testing the significance of
differences among zone means. In lieu of formal tests of significance,
reliance has been placed on inspection of the summary statistics for
pattern and consistency of results. These two problems—size of unit
and lack of independence—are discussed more fully in Appendix H.

Third, all regressions, except the between-zone regressions,
are taken to be linear in form. It is clear that the linear equations,
if extrapolated beyond the range of the data from which they were
computed, often give impossible or unreasonable results. However,
for purely descriptive purposes this circumstance is not especially
undesirable. Moreover, inspection of scattergrams revealed no instances of clearly curvilinear relationships over the range of the observations; these would be difficult to identify, in any case, with the
relatively small samples of tracts analyzed here. A fourth problem,
more important than the preceding one, is that many of the distributions of tracts according to their population characteristics are not
normal. In some cases it can be seen from the scattergram that two
or three tracts with relatively extreme values unduly influence the
slope of the regression or size of the correlation. In such cases the
interpretation of the regression analysis is appropriately qualified.
Still, one must exercise considerable caution in comparing regression and correlation coefficients for different sets of tracts. A related problem is that the sets of tracts grouped by stage of succession

differ somewhat in degree of internal variability. For example, most
of the piling-up tracts are clustered together in an area of less than
3 square miles, extending from 3 to 7 miles from the center of the
city; by contrast, the late-consolidation tracts are more widely scattered and appear at zonal distances of 1-13 miles from the city center. Since the characteristics of the resident population are known to
exhibit considerable zonal differentiation, one might expect greater
variability among the late-consolidation tracts than among the piling-
up tracts. As is well known, extending the range of variability tends
to increase the correlation; for this reason appropriate precautions
must be taken not to misinterpret differences in correlations between
different sets of tracts.

Piling Up

The piling-up process.—The concept of "piling up" rests on the
observation that an area may continue to experience an influx of Negro population after succession from white to Negro population is
virtually completed. Whether or not piling up should be considered
the final stage of succession or a phenomenon that follows succession
need not be argued, since this is a matter of definition. But it can be
demonstrated rather quickly that piling up is a typical concomitant
of the completion of the succession cycle, as well as, in some measure, of the earlier stages of succession.

It has already been noted that in all but 2 of the 32 census tracts
classified in the piling-up category there were increases in the absolute numbers of non-whites between 1940 and 1950. The total population of this group of tracts increased from 139,000 to 161,000, or an
increase of 15.6 per cent, over the decade. Three-fifths of the increase is attributable to net in-movement of population rather than
to an excess of births over deaths. Hence there was a considerable
influx of population to these tracts from outside the city or from
other areas within the city. The growth in population entailed an increase in the already high gross residential density, from 46,700 persons per square mile in 1940 to 54,000 persons per square mile in
1950. Net residential density would have been considerably higher in
both years, since the gross land area includes Washington Park, as

well as numerous smaller parcels of non-residential land.

There was no corresponding increase in the supply of housing to accommodate the expanding population. The only tract with any substantial amount of new construction during the decade was 557, which includes part of the Chicago Housing Authority's Ida B. Wells homes, first occupied in 1941. The only other tract where the number of dwelling units constructed in 1940 or later, as reported in the 1950 Census, amounted to as much as 4 per cent of the number of dwelling units existing in 1940 was tract 547, which reported 60 new units, or 4.2 per cent of the number existing in 1940. No new dwelling units were reported for 18 of the 32 piling-up tracts. By contrast, the population increased by more than 4 per cent in all but 5 of the tracts in the piling-up category. There was actually a decrease in the total number of dwelling units reported in 7 tracts, in all but 1 of which, nevertheless, there was an increase in population.

Despite the lack of new housing construction and the decrease in the total number of dwelling units in certain tracts, the total number of dwelling units in the piling-up tracts increased from 39,967 in 1940 to 45,888 in 1950, or an increase of 14.8 per cent, a slightly lower rate of increase than that of the population (15.6 per cent). But this apparent increase in number of dwelling units actually added very little, in net terms, to the available living space. A total of 1,155 of the dwelling units enumerated in 1950 were reported to have been constructed in the preceding ten-year period. But, at the same time, there were net decreases in the number of dwelling units in several tracts, attributable to demolition, conversion to non-residential use, and the like. The total of these net losses amounted to 587 units, more than half as many as those added by new construction. On balance, therefore, the entire set of tracts had an increase of 5,921 dwelling units over the decade, of which new construction contributed only 568 units in net terms. The remainder of the increase in dwelling units, 5,353, must have resulted from one or another kind of conversion. There are several ways of increasing the number of dwelling units other than by construction of new units. A dwelling unit may be partitioned into two or more smaller units. Non-residential structures may be converted to residential use. The rooms in a transient hotel or lodging house may be furnished with minimal cooking equipment, leading to their classification as "dwelling units." No doubt a good deal of the latter type of conversion occurred. In 20 census tracts there was a net increase in number of dwelling units between 1940 and 1950, exclusive of new construction, amounting to 4 per cent or more of the number of dwelling units reported in 1940.

It should be understood that the net increase in number of dwelling units, exclusive of those produced by new construction, indicates only the minimum amount of conversion which actually occurred. In many cases addition of units by conversion was partially compensated for by demolition of structures, conversion to non-residential use, and the like. A careful comparison of 1940 and 1950 block statistics reveals that in many blocks there were decreases in the number of dwelling units, from whatever cause, compensated for by increases in other blocks in the same tract.

One way in which the number of dwelling units is apparently diminished is through a change in census definitions. In the 1940 Census, lodging houses with more than 10 lodgers were classified as quasi-households and were therefore excluded from the count of dwelling units. In the 1950 Census, lodging houses with 5 or more lodgers were classified as quasi-households. Consequently, lodging houses with 5-10 lodgers were counted as dwelling units in 1940 but not in 1950. It seems probable that there was a considerable number of such lodging houses in the piling-up area in both years. In 1940 the ratio of the (estimated) non-institutional population living in quasi-households to the (estimated) total population living in households was 1.4 per 100; in 1950 the corresponding ratio (based on enumerated, not estimated, population) was 10.1 per 100. No doubt there was an actual increase in the ratio of quasi-household to household residents in the area, but it is probable that the apparent increase reflects in large part the afore-mentioned change in definition. Whatever the quantitative importance of the reclassification of lodging houses, its only possible effect on the count of dwelling units would be to decrease it.

Because the population in the 32 piling-up tracts increased at a slightly faster rate than the number of dwelling units, one would expect to find an increase in the average number of persons per household. However, this did not occur, primarily because there was an increase in the number of persons residing in quasi-households, other than institutions, from 1,861 (estimated) in 1940 to 14,769. As already indicated, part of this change resulted from reclassification of small lodging houses. Thus the decrease in mean population per household from 3.6 to 3.2 persons cannot be interpreted literally. It is significant that, despite the decrease in average size of household, the room crowding of dwelling units increased. Considering only households in which 2 or more persons resided (because 1-person households, by definition, cannot have more than 1 person per room), the proportion with 1.51 or more persons per room increased from an estimated 29.3 per cent in 1940 to 31.9 per cent in 1950 in the piling-up tracts. At the same time, there was an increase in the proportion of residents of households living in 1-person households, from 4.5 per cent (estimated) in 1940 to 6.0 per cent in 1950. (This change, too, reflected in part the reclassification of small lodging houses, by decreasing the denominator of the proportions, i.e., the population living in households.)

In summary, piling up represents an increase of Negro population without a corresponding increase in living space. It is reflected in the heightening of gross and net residential density, the creation of additional dwelling units by one or another kind of conversion, and an increase in room crowding in dwelling units. The latter effect would doubtless appear even more striking if measured in terms of unit floor space rather than on a per room basis. The piling-up tracts have an appreciably larger ratio of population living in quasi-households, except institutions, to population in households than do other areas of non-white residence: 10.1 as compared to 8.7 per 100. This at least suggests that the pressure generated by piling up forces some people into living arrangements other than those of a normal household.

Density and crowding.—In the piling-up tracts as a whole, population density and room crowding of dwelling units increased between 1940 and 1950. In discussing the regression analysis, summarized in Table 35, some attention will be given to the consistency of these changes on a tract-by-tract basis.

Table 35.—Summary of Regression Analysis for Density and Crowding: Piling-Up Tracts, by Zone

Characteristic and Zone	Mean 1950 $\underline{My}$	Regression Constants*			Correlation $\underline{r}$
		Mean 1940 $\underline{Mx}$	Inter-cept $\underline{a}$	Slope $\underline{b}$	
Density (population in hundreds per square mile of gross land area):					
All tracts (32)	615	523	111.9	0.96	.92
Zone 3-4 (11 tracts)	597	418	32.7	1.35	.93
Zone 5 (11 tracts)	642	581	40.8	1.04	.99
Zone 6-7 (10 tracts)	606	575	46.7	0.97	.98
Crowding (per cent of dwelling units with 1.51 or more persons per room):†					
All tracts	31.1	25.3	17.0	0.56	.64
Zone 3-4	35.4	23.2	21.0	0.62	.55
Zone 5	30.5	25.7	15.3	0.59	.91
Zone 6-7	27.1	27.1	8.9	0.67	.93

*For regression equation, $\underline{Y} = \underline{a} + \underline{b}\underline{X}$; all data are for combined white and non-white population in each tract; tracts not weighted by size.

†Based on dwelling units occupied by two or more persons.

In 29 of the 32 piling-up tracts, gross density increased between 1940 and 1950; all three exceptions were in Zone 6-7. In general, there was little change in the relative positions of the tracts with respect to density, as indicated by the high correlation, .92, between the 1940 and the 1950 densities. The correlations within each zone were even higher. Over the entire group of tracts the average tendency was for density to increase by a constant amount, irrespective of the density at the beginning of the decade. This also held for Zones 5 and 6-7 taken individually, as is indicated by the regression slopes near unity in value. However, within Zone 3-4 the slope of 1.35 means that there was a tendency for increases in density to be somewhat greater in the tracts which already had the highest densities in 1940.

One must be cautious in interpreting the mean densities shown in Table 35. Density is a ratio of population to area, and the census tracts vary enormously in gross land area, with a tendency for the highest gross densities to be found in the smallest tracts. For example, the largest tract in the group contains nearly a half square mile of non-residential land (Washington Park). The density figures, by zone, obtained by dividing the aggregate population of each zone by its aggregate land area, are as follows:

	1950	1940
All zones	540	467
Zone 3-4.	650	398
Zone 5	636	584
Zone 6-7.	447	427

From these figures it is evident that the greatest increases in density occurred for the areas nearest the center of the city. In fact, the innermost zone had the lowest gross density in 1940 but the highest in 1950. This shift in the relative densities of the zones appears to contradict the earlier statement that the relative ranking of the individual tracts did not change greatly. The explanation is that virtually all the tracts with increases greater than the average for the 32 tracts were in Zone 3-4. The average change was from 52,350 to 61,500 persons per square mile, or a change of 9,200. This change was exceeded by 12 of the 32 piling-up tracts—9 of the 11 tracts in Zone 3-4, 2 of the 11 tracts in Zone 5, and 1 of the 10 tracts in Zone 6-7.

Room crowding—here defined as the proportion of households consisting of 2 or more persons living in dwelling units with 1.51 or more persons per room—increased in 21 of the 32 piling-up tracts. Of the tracts failing to increase in room crowding, 1 was in Zone 3-4, 4 were in Zone 5, and 6 in Zone 6-7. The sole tract in Zone 3-4 which decreased in room crowding was 557, a portion of which is in the Wells public housing project, where occupancy standards prevent room crowding. It is significant, however, that crowding increased in the portion of the tract not included in the housing project.

In Zone 3-4 changes in crowding over the decade were somewhat erratic, resulting in several large shifts in rank among the component tracts. Hence the correlation between the 1950 and 1940 percentages of crowded units was only .55. Even when computed with tract 557 omitted, the correlation was no higher than .66. In Zones 5 and 6-7, on the contrary, there was considerable stability in the relative positions of the tracts, with the correlations between 1950 and 1940 crowding percentages exceeding .90.

In each of the three zones, as well as in the piling-up tracts as a group, the regression slope was well below unity. Thus, on the average, the largest increases in crowding took place in the tracts with initially low crowding. Actually, all the tracts in which decreases in crowding occurred had 20 per cent or more crowded units in 1940, whereas 9 of the tracts with increasing crowding began the decade with a percentage under 20. These differential changes resulted, of course, in a reduction of the heterogeneity of the 32 tracts with respect to crowding. Thus the standard deviation of the tract percentages dropped from 10.9 in 1940 to 9.5 in 1950. At the same time, the average percentage of crowding increased the most in the zone where it was initially lowest, so that, at the end of the decade, Zone 3-4 had the highest percentage of crowding.

The variables considered in this section—population density and room crowding—reflect the piling-up process in sheerly physical terms. It is significant, therefore, that they agree in pointing to the innermost zone as the locus of the most severe piling up. Perhaps equally significant is the fact that this zone manifests the least stability over the decade in terms of the ranking of the component tracts in the two census years, as is indicated by the comparatively low correlations for this zone in Table 35. Another way of stating this finding is that the changes in Zone 3-4 on a tract-by-tract basis were more erratic than those in the other two zones. As between the two variables under discussion, the greater relative stability was manifested by gross density, despite the large average increase in density in absolute terms. This comparison holds within zones, as well as for the entire set of piling-up tracts.

Socioeconomic characteristics.—The marked improvement between 1940 and 1950 in the level of educational attainment of Negroes in the city as a whole was noted in chapter iv. This change likewise characterized the piling-up tracts, among which 31 showed a gain in the proportion with at least some high-school education, and only 1 (in Zone 3-4) a loss. The regression analysis in Table 36 includes both the observed percentages with some high school and the percentages standardized for age. The major effect of the standardization is to reduce somewhat the figures for tracts in Zone 6-7, where the age distribution was favorable for high levels of educational attainment. On the whole, however, the results for the observed and the standardized percentages are quite similar. A graphic presentation of the regression analysis of the standardized percentages was shown earlier (Fig. 15).

In general, and especially in the two inner zones, there was a tendency for the largest increases in the percentage with some high school to occur in tracts with the lowest initial levels of educational attainment, as is indicated by the regression slopes of less than unity. However, the tracts tended to maintain their relative positions over the decade, especially those in Zone 6-7, where the correlation between 1950 and 1940 percentages with some high school was .90. Although the average gains in level of educational attainment varied among the three zonal groups of tracts, there was, at the end of the decade, as at the beginning, an upward zonal gradient, with the highest percentages with some high school occurring in Zone 6-7.

Table 36.—Summary of Regression Analysis for Socioeconomic Characteristics: Piling-Up Tracts, by Zone

Characteristic and Zone	Mean 1950 M_Y	Mean 1940 M_X	Regression Constants*		Correlation r
			Intercept a	Slope b	
Education:					
Per cent completed 1 year of high school or more†					
All tracts (32)	38.8	28.1	18.9	0.71	.83
Zone 3-4 (11 tracts)	32.6	23.3	15.8	0.72	.66
Zone 5 (11 tracts)	37.8	25.5	26.4	0.45	.81
Zone 6-7 (10 tracts)	46.6	36.2	17.6	0.80	.90
Per cent completed 1 year of high school or more, standardized for age†					
All tracts	37.4	26.6	17.4	0.75	.80
Zone 3-4	31.1	23.1	16.2	0.64	.63
Zone 5	37.0	24.0	25.1	0.50	.79
Zone 6-7	44.7	33.3	13.9	0.93	.90
Unemployment (per cent of male labor force unemployed):‡					
All tracts	12.5	40.0	6.5	0.15	.48
Zone 3-4	14.8	50.0	19.5	-0.09	-.23
Zone 5	11.9	38.9	4.4	0.19	.57
Zone 6-7	10.5	30.0	2.4	0.27	.80
White-collar employment (**per** cent of male employed labor force in white-collar occupations):					
All tracts	15.5	15.5	3.2	0.79	.73
Zone 3-4	14.4	15.5	2.4	0.77	.70
Zone 5	14.7	15.1	2.7	0.79	.88
Zone 6-7	17.8	15.9	6.4	0.71	.64

*For regression equation, $Y = a + bX$; all data are for combined white and non-white population in each tract; tracts not weighted by size.

†For persons twenty-five years old and over.

‡Unemployed includes persons on public emergency work in 1940.

The improvement in business conditions between 1940 and 1950 brought about a marked reduction in the unemployment rate in each of the piling-up tracts, as well as among Negroes in the entire city. In absolute terms the reduction in the unemployment rate was greatest in those zones and individual tracts having the highest rates at the beginning of the decade. In Zone 6-7 and to a very moderate extent in Zone 5, the individual tracts tended to have much the same rank with respect to unemployment in 1950 and 1940, despite the marked drop in the over-all level of the unemployment rate. However, in Zone 3-4 there was practically no relationship on a tract-by-tract basis between the 1950 and the 1940 unemployment rates. The pattern of zonal averages was the same in both years, with comparatively high rates of unemployment toward the center of the city and low rates in the outer zone. This pattern was maintained despite the fact that the lowest zonal average for 1940 was twice as great as the highest one for 1950.

The data in chapter iv show that there was no change between 1940 and 1950 in the proportion of non-white employed males in white-collar occupations in the city as a whole; it was 16.6 per cent in 1950 as in 1940, although there were changes in occupational distribution within the white-collar category. In the piling-up tracts as a group there was likewise no change in the average proportion of white-collar workers; and exactly half the tracts had an increase in proportion of white-collar workers and half of them a decrease. However, the average for Zone 3-4 declined slightly, while that for Zone 6-7 increased; 8 of the 11 tracts in Zone 3-4 showed a decreasing proportion of white-collar workers, compared with 6 of the 11 tracts in Zone 5 and 2 of the 10 tracts in Zone 6-7. These changes were sufficient to establish an upward zonal gradient in proportion of white-collar workers at the end of the decade, though there was none at the beginning.

The correlations between 1940 and 1950 percentages of white-collar workers indicate only a moderate tendency for tracts to maintain their relative positions. Moreover, inspection of the scattergrams suggests that the correlations would be considerably lower but for the influence of a few tracts with extremely high or low values. Because all the regression slopes are below unity, one would infer a tendency for increases in the white-collar proportion to be larger (or decreases smaller) among tracts with initially low percentages. But this is true only on the average, and there are numerous exceptions.

Of the three socioeconomic characteristics, education appears to be the most stable and unemployment the least stable, in terms of the consistency with which tracts are ranked in the comparison between 1940 and 1950. One possible explanation is that the indicator of educational level used here—per cent having completed at least one year of high school—cuts the status distribution toward its middle, whereas unemployment (in 1950) and white-collar employment mark off the extremes. In general, a measure of central tendency is likely to be more stable than a measure of the frequency of a somewhat rare characteristic.

This qualification does not apply to the comparison among zones. For each of the three socioeconomic characteristics Zone 3-4 showed the least stability. For two of the characteristics Zone 6-7 showed the greatest stability.

Housing characteristics.—The piling-up tracts as a group have a low proportion of homeownership, in comparison with the non-whites of the entire city. In 1950, 12.1 per cent of the non-white-occupied dwelling units were owned by their occupants in the city as a whole; in the 32 piling-up tracts the (unweighted) mean of the tract proportions was 9.6 per cent. In working with a characteristic that appears so infrequently, a high degree of stability is not to be expected. The low correlations for Zones 3-4 and 5 in Table 37 show that there was, in fact, little consistency between the 1950 and 1940 rankings of tracts on homeownership in these zones..In Zone 6-7, however, the 1940 ranking was maintained in 1950, as indicated by the correlation of .95.

In all three zones (and in 29 of the 32 tracts) there was an increase in the proportion of homeownership over the decade, with the amount of increase varying inversely with zonal distance from the center of the city. These changes resulted in a gradient pattern for 1950 such that the highest average percentage of homeownership occurred in Zone 3-4 and the lowest in Zone 6-7. This gradient disappears, how-

Table 37.—Summary of Regression Analysis for Housing Characteristics: Piling-Up Tracts, by Zone

Characteristic and Zone	Mean 1950 M_Y	Mean 1940 M_X	Regression Constants* Intercept a	Slope b	Correlation r
Homeownership (per cent of occupied dwelling units owner-occupied):					
All tracts (32)	9.6	5.9	3.6	1.03	.73
Zone 3-4 (11 tracts)	10.3	5.9	7.7	0.44	.32
Zone 5 (11 tracts)	9.5	5.3	4.4	0.97	.44
Zone 6-7 (10 tracts)	9.0	6.5	1.0	1.23	.95
Rent (median contract monthly rent, tenant-occupied dwelling units, dollars):					
All tracts	37.23	24.79	14.14	0.93	.89
Zone 3-4	33.08	19.64	10.17	1.17	.72
Zone 5	36.40	24.39	5.88	1.25	.97
Zone 6-7	42.74	30.88	19.89	0.74	.86
Equipment:					
Per cent of dwelling units with central heating†					
All tracts	73.1	67.2	14.2	0.88	.98
Zone 3-4	60.6	53.2	7.3	1.00	.97
Zone 5	73.6	66.8	16.8	0.85	.99
Zone 6-7	86.2	82.9	23.1	0.76	.99
Per cent of dwelling units with mechanical refrigeration†					
All tracts	64.3	29.7	37.6	0.90	.75
Zone 3-4	47.7	14.3	19.9	1.95	.71
Zone 5	67.7	28.1	48.3	0.69	.84
Zone 6-7	78.8	48.4	62.8	0.33	.38

*For regression equation, $Y = a + bX$; all data are for combined white and non-white population in each tract; tracts not weighted by size.

†Percentages based on dwelling units reporting on this equipment item.

ever, if the homeownership percentages are standardized for type of structure. After standardization, the average percentage of home-ownership for 1950 in Zone 3-4 was 15.1, compared with 16.7 and 16.5 in Zones 5 and 6-7, respectively. Incidentally, the average standard-ized percentage for all 32 piling-up tracts in 1950 was 16.1, com-pared with 21.8 for all non-white-occupied units in the city. Hence standardization does not alter the finding that the piling-up tracts as a group are low in homeownership.

The vast majority of dwelling units in the piling-up tracts are occupied by tenants. There was a considerable increase in average rent paid for tenant-occupied units over the 1940-50 decade; aver-age rent increased in each of the 32 piling-up tracts. However, the pattern of intertract differences within the piling-up area was gener-ally maintained, as was the pattern of zonal variation. Over the en-tire 32 tracts, the correlation near .9 and the regression slope near unity indicate the general tendency for median contract monthly rent to increase by a constant amount, irrespective of the rent level in 1940. In Zones 3-4 and 5 the rent increases were somewhat greater, on the average, in tracts with comparatively high rents in 1940, but in Zone 6-7 the differential was in the opposite direction.

The pattern of an upward zonal gradient in rental values, evident in 1940, was maintained in 1950, with only a small decrease in the difference between the averages for Zones 3-4 and 6-7. Within zones, the rank pattern of individual tracts was quite stable in Zone 5, some-what less so in Zone 6-7, and still less in Zone 3-4. Even in the lat-ter zone, however, there was a moderately high correlation between 1950 and 1940 median rentals.

Of the two items of housing equipment considered, central heat-ing would be expected to have greater stability than mechanical re-frigeration, because the former is often installed at the time of the original construction and affects all units in a given structure, where-as the latter may not be installed until long after construction and need not depend on installation in other units of the same structure. Moreover, if conversion occurs in a structure with central heating, the additional dwelling units are likely to have central heating. This expectation is clearly verified by the correlations between the 1950 and 1940 percentages of dwelling units with these items of equipment, .98 for central heating and .75 for mechanical refrigeration over all 32 piling-up tracts.

The pattern of changes in the proportion of units with central heating reflects the variation in proportion of units with central heating at the beginning of the decade. In Zone 6-7, where there were only two tracts with under 90 per cent of the units having central heating in 1940, the major change was an increase in percentage of units with central heating in these two tracts. Similarly, in Zone 5 there were 5 tracts with percentages above 90 in 1940, and the increases in proportion with central heating naturally were more conspicuous in the remaining tracts. However, in Zone 3-4, only one tract was essentially "saturated" in 1940, and, on the average, there was an equal change in the percentage of units with central heating irrespective of the 1940 percentage; by coincidence, the regression slope of the 1950 on the 1940 percentages was exactly 1.0. In summary, in all zones there were considerable increases in the proportion of units with central heating, where there was room for such increases to occur. These changes reduced, but by no means eliminated, the differences among zones observed in 1940. In both 1940 and 1950 the proportion of units with central heating rose with increasing distance from the center of the city.

In 1940 none of the 32 piling-up tracts had as much as two-thirds of its dwelling units equipped with mechanical refrigeration. Between 1940 and 1950 there was a substantial increase in the average proportion with mechanical refrigeration and an increase in the proportion in all but one of the 32 piling-up tracts. The zonal gradient—a rise in the proportion with increasing distance from the city center —was maintained despite these changes. But the changes were somewhat erratic among the tracts within zones. In Zone 3-4 the regression slope of the 1950 on the 1940 percentage with mechanical refrigeration was extraordinarily high, 1.95. In this zone there were 3 tracts which deviated markedly from the pattern of the remaining 8. All 3 had low percentages in 1940, 1 decreased between 1940 and 1950, and the other 2 increased comparatively little. If these 3 tracts were excluded from the analysis, the regression slope would be near unity, since in all the other tracts there were substantial increases, of a fairly uniform amount, in the percentage with mechanical refrigeration. In Zone 5 there was fair consistency in the ranking of tracts as between the 1950 and 1940 percentages. But in Zone 6-7 the changes, though positive in all cases, resulted in a number of large shifts in rank and consequently in a low correlation between the 1950 and 1940 percentages with mechanical refrigeration.

The housing characteristics analyzed here present a mixed picture with respect to the pattern of changes accompanying the piling-up process. It is noteworthy that there were increases in homeownership and improvements in housing equipment in most of the 32 tracts, despite the increased pressure of population on living space. At the same time, in line with the general trend for the whole city, there was a substantial increase in average rentals paid.

It seems impossible to suggest a significant generalization about the pattern of homeownership, since this characteristic showed great stability in the outermost zone but not in the other two zones. Moreover, there was no consistent zonal gradient in the percentage of homeownership as there was for the other three housing characteristics. On the other hand, rent was a relatively stable characteristic in all zones, but not so stable as the proportion of units with central heating (construing the term "stability" to refer to the pattern of intertract variation rather than the average level over all tracts). The percentage of units with mechanical refrigeration exhibits a deviant pattern, in that this characteristic was least stable in Zone 6-7, whereas on all other characteristics examined for the piling-up tracts the least stability was found in Zone 3-4. Of the four housing characteristics, rent and percentage with central heating were clearly the more stable ones.

Late Consolidation

Changes in population and dwelling units.—In census tracts classified as in the late-consolidation stage of the succession process, over four-fifths of the residents were non-white in 1940; by 1950 the late-consolidation tracts were areas of almost exclusive non-white occupancy. At the beginning of the decade, 91.5 per cent

of the population residing in the late-consolidation group of tracts
was Negro; by the end of the decade, 97.8 per cent of the residents
were Negroes.

The white population residing in the late-consolidation group of
tracts decreased during the decade; however, the increase in non-
white population was substantially greater than the decrease in white
population, and, as a result, the total population residing in this
group of tracts increased by one-third between 1940 and 1950. The
net population increase of 34,613 resulted from a loss of 5,711 whites
and a gain of 40,324 non-whites. About 65 per cent of the absolute increase in non-white population can be attributed to the in-movement
of non-whites from other areas of the city or from areas outside the
city. The influx of non-whites far exceeded the out-movement of
white population in absolute terms.

Increasing population densities were coupled with the shift from
mixed to almost exclusive Negro occupancy in these tracts. Gross
residential density rose from 24,800 to 33,200 persons per square
mile during the ten-year period. Although these gross density figures are substantially lower than those of the tracts in the piling-up
stage, they are well above the gross densities observed in tracts
less advanced in the succession process or in tracts not undergoing
succession from white to Negro occupancy.

The number of households or occupied dwelling units in the late-
consolidation tracts increased slightly less rapidly than did population. During the decade, occupied dwelling units increased by 8,141,
or 30.9 per cent, as compared with a 34.0 per cent increase in resident population. Furthermore, less than one-fourth of the net increase
in occupied dwelling units can be accounted for by new residential
construction. Well over 6,000 units were added from sources other
than new construction; in so far as there were slightly fewer than
1,000 vacant units in the late-consolidation tracts in 1940, the bulk
of the increase in dwelling units between 1940 and 1950 must have
resulted from conversion of non-residential structures to residential
use, from the conversion of existing dwelling units to smaller units,
or from the conversion of rooms in hotels and lodging houses to dwelling units for households.

The number of households experiencing room crowding increased in both absolute and relative terms during the decade 1940-50. Whereas 17.2 per cent of the households were crowded in 1940, 24.7 per cent were crowded in 1950. Although the proportion of crowded households in the late-consolidation tracts was lower than that in the piling-up tracts in both 1940 and 1950, the percentage-point increase during the decade 1940-50 was greater in the late-consolidation tracts than in the piling-up tracts—6.6 and 2.6 points in the respective groups.

These general comments indicate that, at the late-consolidation stage of the succession process, there was not only a replacement of white by non-white residents but also a substantial increase in population congestion. A "piling up" of population accompanied the shift from mixed to exclusive Negro occupancy.

Density and crowding.—Increases in gross residential density accompanied the change from mixed to exclusive Negro occupancy in 27 of the 28 late-consolidation tracts. The single tract in which gross residential density decreased, census tract 541, is bounded by Thirty-second, State, Thirty-fifth, and Federal streets and is located in a South Side redevelopment area. Two of the five blocks in the tract which were devoted to residential use in 1940 had been completely cleared of residential structures by 1950; the number of dwelling units in the remaining three blocks dropped during the decade, which suggests that selective demolition was being carried on. It is unlikely that any decrease in net residential density occurred.

In the main, the relative positions of the tracts with respect to density changed little during the decade, as indicated by the high correlation, .92, between the 1940 and 1950 densities. Over the entire group of tracts the average tendency was for density to increase by a constant amount, irrespective of the density at the beginning of the decade. The regression analysis is summarized in Table 38. Among the 8 tracts in Zone 2-3, there was relatively little shift in the positions of tracts with respect to one another; but the absolute increases in density were somewhat greater in the tracts that had the highest densities at the beginning of the decade. Shifts in relative position with respect to density were somewhat greater among the 10 tracts in Zone 4-5, as indicated by the correlation of .84 between

Table 38.—Summary of Regression Analysis for Density and Crowding: Late-Consolidation Tracts, by Zone

Characteristic and Zone	Mean 1950 M_y	Mean 1940 M_x	Regression Constants*		
			Inter-cept a	Slope b	Corre-lation r
Density (population, in hundreds, per square mile of gross land area):					
All tracts (28)	374	287	88.8	0.99	.92
Zone 2-3 (8 tracts)	296	197	9.6	1.46	.92
Zone 4-5 (10 tracts)	437	344	105.4	0.96	.84
Zone 6-14 (10 tracts)	374	303	92.1	0.93	.99
Crowding (per cent of dwelling units with 1.51 or more persons per room):†					
All tracts	24.8	14.4	12.3	0.92	.58
Zone 2-3	34.0	13.2	19.5	1.10	.70
Zone 4-5	24.9	15.7	13.9	0.71	.61
Zone 6-14	17.4	14.2	3.2	1.00	.94

*For regression equation, $Y = a + bX$; all data are for combined white and non-white population in each tract; tracts not weighted by size.

†Based on dwelling units occupied by two or more persons.

the 1940 and 1950 densities; there was no consistent variation in the absolute increase in density over the ten-year period with the density at the beginning of the decade.

The tracts which deviated most from the regression line in Zone 4-5 were the one discussed above, in which gross density decreased during the decade, and census tract 559, roughly bounded by Thirty-fifth, Cottage Grove, Pershing, and Vincennes streets, which is the site of one part of the Chicago Housing Authority's Wells project. The land on which the project was constructed, making up roughly half the land area of the tract, had been cleared of its former slum residences before the 1940 Census enumeration; in 1950, over 500 dwellings were enumerated in this part of the tract. The gross density of the tract more than doubled during the decade, obviously as a result of the project. The special changes in these tracts probably account for the somewhat lower correlation between 1940 and 1950 density in Zone 4-5 than in the other two zones.

There was scarcely any change in the relative positions of the 10 tracts in Zone 6-14 with respect to density, as indicated by the high correlation, .99, between 1940 and 1950 density. The apparent slight tendency for tracts with the lowest initial density to experience a greater absolute increase in density between 1940 and 1950 is accounted for by a single tract, 685, in which large parcels of land were changed from non-residential to residential use through new construction between 1940 and 1950.

Problems of interpreting the unweighted mean densities were considered in the analysis of density in the piling-up tracts. The weighted mean densities, obtained by dividing the aggregate population of each group of tracts by the aggregate land area of the group, are summarized below (in hundreds of persons per square mile).

	1950	1940
All tracts	332	248
Zone 2-3.	275	186
Zone 4-5.	453	340
Zone 6-14.	308	240

When tracts are classified into three groups in terms of distance from the center of the city, the highest densities in both 1940 and 1950 and the greatest absolute increase in density over the ten-year period are observed in Zone 4-5. The least increase in gross density, in both absolute and relative terms, occurred in Zone 6-14; yet the bulk of the new residential construction took place in these tracts. If net residential density had been employed as the variable, the increase in density for Zone 6-14, as compared with the increase in Zones 2-3 and 4-5, would have been even less, because increments to the land in residential use occurred in the outer zone. In both 1940 and 1950 the lowest densities were observed in Zone 2-3; these low densities probably reflect the fact that the ratio of non-residential to residential land use is higher toward the center of the city.

Room crowding, i.e., the proportion of households comprising two members or more with 1.51 persons per room or more, increased in 26 of the 28 late-consolidation tracts. The 2 tracts in which crowding did not increase during the decade are in Zone 6-14; new residential construction occurred in both tracts between 1940 and 1950.

Over the entire late-consolidation group of tracts, considerable shifting in the relative positions of tracts with respect to room crowding occurred, as indicated by the correlation of only .58. The correlations between the 1950 and 1940 proportions of crowded units were slightly higher in Zones 2-3 and 4-5. In view of the fact that the correlations are not high and the scatter of points around the regression lines is somewhat irregular for both zones, it seems best to place no substantive interpretation on the departure of the regression slopes from unity.

In Zone 6-14 there was considerable stability in the relative positions of tracts with respect to room crowding, as indicated by the correlation of .94. The average tendency was for crowding to increase by a constant amount, irrespective of the level of crowding at the beginning of the decade, as indicated by the slope of 1.00; and, on the average, the increase in the proportion of crowded units was only 3 percentage points.

Examination of the unweighted means, shown in Table 38, indicates that the average increase in crowding over the ten-year period

varied from 20.8 percentage points in Zone 2-3 to 3.2 points in Zone
6-14. In 1940 the range of variation in crowding by zones was only
2.5 percentage points; in 1950 the level of crowding in Zone 2-3 was
9.1 points higher than in Zone 4-5 and 16.6 points higher than in
Zone 6-14.

The regression of the 1950 level on the 1940 level of crowding
was analyzed for non-white households separately. The results of
the analysis were virtually identical with those summarized for all
households. The correlation of 1950 on 1940 level of crowding for
non-white households was .61 over all 28 late-consolidation tracts,
as compared with a correlation of .58 for all households. Within
zones, the correlations for non-white households approximated those
for all households. However, no consistency in the relative positions
of tracts with respect to level of crowding was found among white
households, as indicated by a correlation coefficient of only .12
over all 28 late-consolidation tracts. The low correlation can be
anticipated because the numbers of white households in the late-
consolidation tracts in 1940, and especially in 1950, were very small.

The absolute level of crowding was substantially higher among
non-white households than among white households in both 1940 and
1950. In the former year the average level of crowding in the late-
consolidation tracts was 14.8 per cent for non-white households and
9.9 per cent for white households; in 1950 the average level of crowding was 25.0 per cent for non-white households and 18.8 per cent for
white households. The level of crowding increased during the decade
among both white and non-white households, but the absolute increase
was somewhat greater for non-white than for white households. These
comments apply within zones as well as for the late-consolidation
tracts as a whole.

Socioeconomic characteristics.—The educational level of the
population, as measured by the proportion of the population twenty-
five years of age or older having completed at least one year of high
school, increased in each of the 28 late-consolidation tracts during
the decade. The regression analysis in Table 39 includes both the observed percentages and the percentages standardized for age.

There was considerable stability in the relative positions of

Table 39.—Summary of Regression Analysis for Socioeconomic Characteristics: Late-Consolidation Tracts, by Zone

Characteristic and Zone	Mean 1950 M_Y	Mean 1940 M_X	Regression Constants*		Correlation r
			Intercept a	Slope b	
Education:					
Per cent completed 1 year of high school or more†					
All tracts (28)	38.9	26.9	11.3	1.03	.89
Zone 2-3 (8 tracts)	29.0	18.7	15.6	0.71	.61
Zone 4-5 (10 tracts)	34.4	22.4	7.4	1.20	.92
Zone 6-14 (10 tracts)	51.4	38.0	20.4	0.82	.76
Per cent completed 1 year of high school or more, standardized for age†					
All tracts	36.3	26.6	8.5	1.05	.92
Zone 2-3	25.9	18.6	15.6	0.56	.55
Zone 4-5	32.4	22.5	6.4	1.15	.91
Zone 6-14	48.7	37.2	15.3	0.90	.90
Unemployment (per cent of male labor force unemployed):‡					
All tracts	12.3	39.3	5.5	0.17	.60
Zone 2-3	15.2	46.0	6.4	0.19	.49
Zone 4-5	12.4	44.4	9.0	0.08	.22
Zone 6-14	9.8	28.8	5.9	0.14	.80
White-collar employment (per cent of male employed labor force in white-collar occupations):					
All tracts	15.6	17.8	6.2	0.53	.53
Zone 2-3	12.3	13.7	5.1	0.52	.48
Zone 4-5	12.4	18.2	15.7	-0.18	-.34
Zone 6-14	21.6	20.8	4.8	0.80	.92

*For regression equation, $Y = a + bX$; all data are for combined white and non-white population in each tract; tracts not weighted by size.

†For persons twenty-five years old and over.

‡Unemployed includes persons on public emergency work in 1940.

tracts with respect to the educational attainment of the resident population in 1940 and in 1950, as indicated by the correlations of .89 between the 1940 and 1950 percentages with some high-school education
and of .92 between the 1940 and 1950 percentages standardized for
age. The two most deviant tracts were subject to special changes
during the decade. Tract 434 in Zone 2-3 is the site of Chicago Housing Authority's Brooks project; a slum area was cleared and the
834-unit housing project erected between 1940 and 1950. The marked
increase in the educational level of the population in tract 434 does
not appear to be accounted for by changes in age composition. Tract
685, in Zone 6-14, had only 228 households in 1940; by 1950, as a result of substantial new construction during the decade, households
numbered 1,207. The marked increase in educational level of the
population appears to be accounted for, in part, by the more favorable age distribution of the 1950 population.

The correlation of the 1950 with the 1940 level of education was
somewhat lower in Zone 2-3, which includes tract 434—.61 on the
basis of observed percentages and .55 on the basis of percentages
standardized for age. Within Zone 4-5, tracts were quite stable in
their relative positions with respect to educational level, with correlations of .92 and .91 observed for the crude and standardized percentages, respectively. The moderate correlation of .76 between
1950 and 1940 crude percentages with some high-school education
for Zone 6-14 reflects primarily the deviancy of tract 685; however,
on the basis of the standardized percentages, there was considerable
stability in the relative positions of tracts, as indicated by the correlation of .90.

The average tendency for the 28 late-consolidation tracts was
for the absolute increase in educational attainment between 1940 and
1950 to be a constant, irrespective of level of educational attainment
in 1940. However, this over-all regression relationship averages out
inconsistent tendencies observed with a zonal breakdown. The within-
zone regression slopes depart from unity in both directions. The between-zone regression shows some tendency for the largest absolute
increase to occur in the outer zone, which had the highest level of
educational attainment initially.

In both 1940 and 1950 there was a sharp upward zonal gradient in educational attainment. For tracts in Zone 2-3, the average proportion with some high-school education was roughly 19 percentage points lower than that in Zone 6-14 in 1940 and about 22 points lower in 1950.

For the non-white population, the educational level increased in all late-consolidation tracts. But for the white population, educational level as measured by the crude percentage with some high school decreased in 6 of the 28 tracts, and as measured by the standardized percentage with some high school it decreased in 10 of the 28 tracts.

The regression of 1950 on 1940 educational level for the non-white population was virtually identical with that for total population, with correlations of .90 and .94 based on crude and standardized percentages, respectively. However, for the white population, the 1950 level of education was largely independent of the 1940 level—correlations of .12 and .26 for crude and standardized percentages, respectively.

The absolute increase in percentage with some high-school education was about the same for non-whites as for whites. In both years the educational attainment of the non-white population was lower than that of the white population. The average tract percentages with some high-school education were 25.9 for non-whites and 31.8 for whites in 1940 and 38.9 and 44.9 for the respective groups in 1950; the average tract percentages with some high-school education standardized for age were 25.3 for non-whites and 35.4 for whites in 1940 and 36.0 and 45.1 for the respective groups in 1950. In 1950 there is evidence of an upward zonal gradient in educational level for both non-white and white populations; however, in 1940, an upward zonal gradient is observed only for non-whites. In fact, a slight downward zonal gradient is apparent for the white population in 1940, and it would appear that in Zone 6-14 the educational attainment of the non-white population was somewhat greater than that of the white population in that year.

The unemployment rate for males dropped substantially between 1940 and 1950 in each of the late-consolidation tracts; in absolute terms the reduction in level of unemployment was greatest in those tracts having the highest unemployment rates at the beginning of the decade.

Over the 28 late-consolidation tracts, there was considerable shifting in the relative positions of tracts with respect to level of un-employment, as is shown by the correlation of .60 between 1950 and 1940 unemployment rates. Within Zones 2-3 and 4-5, there was little relationship on a tract-by-tract basis between the 1950 and 1940 un-employment rates; but within Zone 6-14, the ranking of tracts with respect to unemployment was fairly stable over the decade, as indicated by the correlation of .80 between 1950 and 1940 rates.

The average unemployment rate for late-consolidation tracts was 39.3 per cent in 1940; ten years later it was only 12.3 per cent. In both years there is evidence of a strong downward zonal gradient in level of unemployment. At the beginning of the decade 1940-50, 46.0 per cent of the males in Zone 2-3, but only 28.8 per cent of those in Zone 6-14, were unemployed; at the end of the decade, 15.2 per cent of the males in Zone 2-3, but only 9.8 per cent of those in Zone 6-14, were unemployed.

When the regression analysis of 1950 on 1940 unemployment rates is carried out for non-whites and whites separately, somewhat the same patterns emerge. The correlations between 1950 and 1940 rates are consistently higher for non-whites than for whites—correlations of .62 and .27, respectively, for the 28 late-consolidation tracts; .67 and .46 for Zone 2-3; .21 and .15 for Zone 4-5; and .79 and .39 for Zone 6-14. The within-zone correlations of 1950 on 1940 unemployment rates for Zones 2-3 and 6-14 are considerably higher for the non-white population than for total population as well. The absolute decrease in unemployment rates during the decade was greatest for tracts with a high level of unemployment at the beginning of the decade for both non-white and white populations.

Unemployment rates were consistently higher for the non-white population than for the white population. In 1940 an average of 40.8 per cent of the non-white males and 22.8 per cent of the white males were unemployed in late-consolidation tracts; by 1950 the average unemployment rate was only 12.5 for non-white males and 4.5 for white males. A strong downward zonal gradient in unemployment rates is observed for both non-white and white populations in 1940; in 1950 a downward zonal gradient is observed for the non-white population, but virtually no variation in unemployment level by zone is observed for the white population.

The proportion of employed males in white-collar occupations decreased between 1940 and 1950 in 17 of the 28 late-consolidation tracts; as a result, the average proportion in white-collar occupations dropped from 17.8 to 15.6 per cent during the decade.

Over the 28 late-consolidation tracts, tract-by-tract variation in the 1950 proportion in white-collar occupations was only slightly dependent on the 1940 occupation level. This was the case within Zones 2-3 and 4-5 as well. However, in Zone 6-14 considerable stability in the relative positions of tracts with respect to percentage of white-collar workers is evident, with a correlation of .92 observed. In this zone slight decreases in the white-collar proportions for two tracts with comparatively high proportions at the beginning of the decade combined with increases in tracts with initially low proportions to produce a regression slope somewhat below unity. In the two remaining zones the changes were too erratic to permit a summary statement.

Between 1940 and 1950 the percentage of white-collar workers dropped in 5 of the 8 tracts making up Zone 2-3; the average tract percentage of white-collar workers similarly dropped, from 13.7 in 1940 to 12.3 in 1950. In Zone 4-5, 9 of the 10 tracts decreased with respect to percentage of white-collar workers; the average tract percentage dropped markedly during the decade, from 18.2 to 12.4 per cent. Only 3 of the 10 tracts in Zone 6-14 decreased in occupational level during the ten-year period, and the net result was a slight increase in percentage of white-collar workers: 20.8 in 1940 as compared with 21.6 in 1950.

The percentage of white-collar workers in 1940 is not available for the non-white and white populations separately. In 1950 the percentage of white-collar workers was lower in the non-white than in the white population in virtually every late-consolidation tract, and the average percentage of white-collar workers for the 28 late-consolidation tracts was only 15.1 for non-whites as compared with 33.1 for whites.

Housing characteristics.—The percentage of owner-occupied
dwelling units increased in 22 of the 28 late-consolidation tracts during the decade 1940-50. The average proportion of homeowners increased from 13.8 per cent in 1940 to 14.0 in 1950.

A fair stability in the ranking of tracts with respect to level of
homeownership is evident for the late-consolidation tracts as a group
and within each zone as well (see Table 40). Correlation coefficients
of .86 are observed for the group as a whole and for Zones 2-3 and
4-5, and the correlation between 1950 and 1940 percentages of homeowners is .82 in Zone 6-14. In general, there was no consistent variation between absolute increase in homeownership during the decade
and level of ownership in 1940, although in Zone 4-5 there was some
tendency for the largest increases to occur in tracts with a high proportion of owners in 1940.

A rather steep upward zonal gradient in proportion of homeowners appeared in both 1940 and 1950; only one-twentieth of the dwellings in Zone 2-3 but over one-fifth of the dwellings in Zone 6-14
were owned by their occupants in both years. The average proportion
of owner-occupants in Zone 2-3 increased by less than one percentage point during the decade, the proportion in Zone 4-5 increased
by four points, and a decrease of four points is observed in the percentage of owner-occupants in Zone 6-14. The decrease in Zone
6-14 results from the marked drop in homeownership which occurred
in tracts 683 and 685; these were tracts in which a substantial volume of new construction took place during the decade, the bulk of
which appears to have been renter-occupied in 1950. However, the
absolute number of owner-occupied units in both tracts increased
between 1940 and 1950.

Standardization for type of structure increased the 1950 level of
homeownership in the late-consolidation tracts as a group from 14.0
to 17.1 per cent. The standardization increased the level of ownership in Zones 2-3 and 4-5 as well but had virtually no effect in Zone
6-14. However, the upward zonal gradient in homeownership remains
after standardization, as indicated by the following standardized percentages: Zone 2-3, 11.3 per cent; Zone 4-5, 16.4 per cent; and Zone
6-14, 22.6 per cent.

Table 40.—Summary of Regression Analysis for Housing Characteristics: Late-Consolidation Tracts, by Zone

Characteristic and Zone	Mean 1950 M_Y	Mean 1940 M_X	Regression Constants*		
			Intercept a	Slope b	Correlation r
Homeownership (per cent of occupied dwelling units owner-occupied):					
All tracts (28)	14.0	13.8	5.1	0.65	.86
Zone 2-3 (8 tracts)	5.7	5.0	1.0	0.94	.86
Zone 4-5 (10 tracts)	12.2	8.4	0.0	1.44	.86
Zone 6-14 (10 tracts)	22.5	26.2	7.0	0.59	.82
Rent (median contract monthly rent, tenant-occupied dwelling units, dollars):					
All tracts	36.84	22.57	18.49	0.81	.71
Zone 2-3	31.72	17.66	19.42	0.70	.53
Zone 4-5	34.07	21.03	5.70	1.35	.86
Zone 6-14	43.72	28.04	32.56	0.40	.44
Equipment:					
Per cent of dwelling units with central heating†					
All tracts	63.3	51.2	22.5	0.80	.94
Zone 2-3	49.0	31.8	27.5	0.67	.85
Zone 4-5	59.6	48.6	17.1	0.87	.98
Zone 6-14	78.4	69.4	21.2	0.82	.92
Per cent of dwelling units with mechanical refrigeration†					
All tracts	68.5	29.6	49.0	0.66	.75
Zone 2-3	54.5	12.6	45.9	0.68	.49
Zone 4-5	66.2	22.0	40.1	1.18	.83
Zone 6-14	82.1	50.8	56.6	0.50	.60

*For regression equation, $Y = a + bX$; all data are for combined white and non-white population in each tract; tracts not weighted by size.

†Percentages based on dwelling units reporting on this equipment item.

The average standardized percentage of owners in the late-consolidation tracts, 17.1, was below the standardized percentage for non-whites in the city as a whole, 21.8, although the crude percentage of 14.0 in the late-consolidation tracts was above the crude percentage of 12.1 for non-whites in the city as a whole.

Restricting the regression analysis to the non-white population, moderate stability in the ranking of tracts with respect to percentage of owners is observed—correlation coefficient of .84—over the 28 late-consolidation tracts; the correlation of 1950 with 1940 level of ownership for non-whites alone was somewhat higher than that for total population in Zone 2-3, somewhat lower in Zone 4-5, and about the same in Zone 6-14. A correlation of only .48 is observed between 1950 and 1940 level of ownership for whites, indicating little stability in the ranking of tracts.

There is evidence of an upward zonal gradient in homeownership for both non-whites and whites in both years; however, the gradient was somewhat steeper for non-whites. The average percentage of owners in the late-consolidation tracts was consistently lower among non-whites than among whites; but there was a tendency toward convergence during the decade. In 1940 the average percentage of owners was 12.1 among non-whites, as compared with 33.1 for whites; the percentages for the respective groups were 13.7 and 22.4 in 1950. Furthermore, on the basis of percentages standardized for type of structure, homeownership was more frequent among non-whites than among whites in 1950 not only for the late-consolidation tracts as a group but within each zone as well. The standardized percentage of owners was 17.3 among non-whites but only 15.1 among whites.

Median contract rent for tenant-occupied units increased in all 28 late-consolidation tracts between 1940 and 1950. The average median rent in 1950 was about $14 greater than that in 1940 for the group of tracts as a whole and for each zone as well.

However, there was only a moderate stability in the pattern of tract-by-tract variation in rent over the 28 tracts, as indicated by the correlation of .71. The stability in the ranking of tracts in Zone 4-5 with respect to median rent was somewhat greater, as shown by

the correlation of .86, and the absolute increases in rental during
the decade tended to be largest in tracts with a high rent level in
1940. But in Zones 2-3 and 6-14, median rent in 1950 was largely
independent of the 1940 level, with correlations of only .53 and .44
observed within the respective zones.

Tract 685, the most deviant of the late-consolidation tracts,
falls into Zone 6-14. Tenant-occupied units in the tract increased
from 97 to 934 between 1940 and 1950. The 1940 rent level was well
below average for a late-consolidation tract, but the rental units
created during the decade commanded rents nearly $10 higher than
units in any other late-consolidation tract. However, there are a
number of other tracts which deviate markedly from the average
tendency in which no special changes are evident.

In both 1940 and 1950 there was a strong upward gradient in
median rent, with a range from $18 in Zone 2-3 to $28 in Zone 6-14
in the former year and from $32 in Zone 2-3 to $44 in Zone 6-14 in
the latter year.

The results of the regression analysis for non-whites separately
were similar to those of the analysis for total population, a correlation of .76 and slope of 0.86 for non-whites as compared with a correlation of .71 and slope of 0.81 for total. Median rent for white households in 1950 was largely independent of the 1940 median rent for
white households, as indicated by the correlation of only .38.

The average median rent for the 28 late-consolidation tracts
was slightly higher for non-white than for white households in 1940
and substantially higher in 1950: $22 and $21 for the respective
groups in 1940 and $37 and $34 in 1950. However, within Zones 2-3
and 4-5, the median rent for non-whites appears to have been slightly
lower than for whites in 1940. Rents graded upward with distance
from the city's center for both non-white and white households in
both years, but the upward gradient was somewhat sharper in 1950,
because the largest absolute increases in rent occurred in Zone 6-
14.

Increases in the percentage of dwelling units with central heating and with mechanical refrigeration were observed in all the late-
consolidation tracts. However, the pattern of variation among tracts

was more stable during the decade with respect to central heating than with respect to mechanical refrigeration, as is shown by the correlations of .94 and .75 for the respective characteristics over all 28 tracts.

As in the case of the piling-up tracts, the pattern of changes in the proportion of units with central heating reflects the variation in proportion of units with central heating at the beginning of the decade. Over 75 per cent of the dwelling units in 10 of the late-consolidation tracts were centrally heated in 1940; absolute increases in percentage centrally heated ranged from 0.3 to 8.2 points among these tracts. At the other extreme were 8 tracts in which less than 25 per cent of the units were centrally heated in 1940; absolute increases in percentage with central heating ranged from 2.4 to 49.2 percentage points among these tracts. Within each zone as well, tracts in which the proportion of units with central heating was high at the beginning of the decade changed relatively little during the decade; tracts in which the proportion centrally heated was low at the beginning of the decade tended to experience substantial increases during the decade, although there was marked variation in the absolute size of the increases. Hence within each zone as well as for the entire group of tracts, high correlations and slopes somewhat under unity are observed.

The average percentage of units with central heating for the 28 tracts increased from 51.2 to 63.3 per cent during the decade. In both 1940 and 1950 an upward zonal gradient in percentage centrally heated is evident, although the steepness of the gradient diminished somewhat during the decade. The absolute increase in the average percentage of units with central heating was largest in Zone 2-3, in which the percentage of units with central heating was lowest at the beginning of the decade, and was smallest in Zone 6-14, in which the initial percentage centrally heated was highest.

In 1940 the average percentage of dwelling units with mechanical refrigeration for the 28 late-consolidation tracts was only 29.6; ten years later, 68.5 per cent of the units had mechanical refrigeration. An upward zonal gradient was evident at both the beginning and the end of the decade, although differences among zones were somewhat reduced between 1940 and 1950. There was a tendency for the tracts with an initially low percentage of units with mechanical refrigeration to experience the largest absolute increases during the decade; this holds both on a tract-by-tract basis and with respect to the zonal means.

In Zone 2-3, a correlation of only .49 was observed between the 1950 and 1940 percentages of units with mechanical refrigeration. The most marked shift in rank occurred for tract 434, in which slum housing was replaced by the Chicago Housing Authority's Brooks project during the decade. Tracts in Zone 4-5 were fairly stable in their relative positions, as indicated by the correlation of .83. There was a slight tendency for tracts with initially high percentages of units with mechanical refrigeration to experience the greatest absolute increase during the decade. Considerable shifting in rank with respect to percentage with mechanical refrigeration occurred among tracts in Zone 6-14, where the correlation was .60. The most marked shifts in rank occurred for tracts 683 and 685, in which a large volume of new construction took place during the decade. The apparent tendency for tracts with an initially low percentage of units with mechanical refrigeration to experience the largest absolute increase during the decade results primarily from these tracts in which new construction occurred.

In both 1940 and 1950 there was evidence of a strong upward zonal gradient. In the former year only 12.6 per cent of the units in Zone 2-3, but 50.8 per cent of those in Zone 6-14, had mechanical refrigeration; 54.5 per cent of the units in Zone 2-3 as compared with 82.1 per cent of the units in Zone 6-14 had mechanical refrigeration in 1950.

Consolidation

Changes in population and dwelling units.—The total population of the 35 consolidation tracts increased from 113,000 in 1940 to 138,000 in 1950. The decline in the white population in these tracts, from 83,000 to 51,000, was more than offset by the increase in non-white population from 30,000 to 87,000 between 1940 and 1950. At the beginning of the decade 26.7 per cent of the population was non-white, as compared with 63.2 per cent at the end of the decade.

The increase in gross population density from 21,900 to 26,900 persons per square mile between 1940 and 1950, though substantial, was undoubtedly less than the increase in net density. This can be inferred from the fact that the population increased more rapidly than did the supply of dwelling units and the bulk of the latter increase resulted from conversion rather than new construction. Population increased by 22.8 per cent over the decade, as compared with an increase of only 13.6 per cent in the total number of dwelling units and 18.8 per cent in the number of occupied dwelling units. In absolute terms, there were 4,394 more dwelling units in the consolidation tracts in 1950 than in 1940, but only 1,260 of the units enumerated in 1950 had been constructed since 1940. The difference (3,134 units) somewhat understates the amount of conversion, because in some tracts there was evidently demolition of old units to make way for the newly constructed ones.

Density and crowding.—In only 2 of the 35 consolidation tracts did gross population density decrease between 1940 and 1950. These were adjacent West Side tracts (397 and 402) in which roughly one-third of the area reverted from residential to non-residential uses during the decade; probably no decrease in net residential density occurred.

The pattern of tract-to-tract variation was fairly stable over the 35 tracts, as indicated by the correlation of .88 between 1950 and 1940 densities. The slope is only slightly above unity, 1.08, which suggests a general tendency for tract densities to increase by a constant amount, irrespective of the initial density. However, the two tracts in which an actual decrease in density occurred during the decade had densities well above the average for consolidation tracts in 1940; disregarding these tracts, there is evidence of larger absolute increases in density occurring in tracts with an initially high density.

Correlations of over .9 are observed between 1950 and 1940 densities within the North Side and the South Side groups of tracts; there was a strong tendency within the North Side group and a slight tendency within the South Side group for density to increase most in tracts with a high initial density. A correlation of only .68 and a slope somewhat below unity are observed within the West Side group of tracts, which includes tracts 397 and 402.

Both in 1940 and in 1950, average density was highest for North Side tracts, intermediate for West Side tracts, and lowest for South Side tracts. This is evident either from the unweighted averages of tract densities in Table 41 or from the weighted averages below (hundreds of persons per square mile):

	1950	1940
All tracts	269	219
North Side	426	354
West Side	324	276
South Side	209	163

In so far as the North Side tracts are located within 2 miles of the city's center, the West Side tracts from 1 to 4 miles from the center, and the South Side tracts from 2 to 14 miles from the city's center, the ordering implies a downward zonal gradient with respect to gross population density. The absolute increase in density was markedly higher for the North Side group, which had the highest initial density, than for the West Side or South Side groups.

Between 1940 and 1950 there was an increase in the proportion of two-or-more-person households living in crowded dwelling units in all but one of the consolidation tracts. The average increase was 13.5 percentage points, from 8.2 per cent in 1940 to 21.7 in 1950. However, this average increase is somewhat misleading, because, on the whole, only small increases occurred in tracts with comparatively low proportions of crowding in 1940, while there were large increases in the tracts with initially high proportions. All the within-area regression slopes, as well as that of the total group of tracts, were over 2.5, and the general consistency of the tendency is indicated by the correlations exceeding .8 in the total and West and South Side groups. Moreover, the crowding proportion increased less in the North Side tracts than in the West and South Side tracts, which had

Table 41.—Summary of Regression Analysis for Density and Crowding: Consolidation Tracts, by Area

Characteristic and Area	Regression Constants*				
	Mean 1950 M_Y	Mean 1940 M_X	Inter- cept a	Slope b	Corre- lation r
Density (population, in hundreds, per square mile of gross land area):					
All tracts (35)................	378	301	52.7	1.08	.88
North Side (6 tracts).........	553	443	-29.8	1.32	.94
West Side (14 tracts).........	390	330	111.6	0.84	.68
South Side (15 tracts)........	296	218	58.6	1.09	.92
Crowding (per cent of dwelling units with 1.51 or more persons per room):†					
All tracts....................	21.7	8.2	- 0.7	2.74	.84
North Side...................	14.3	5.0	1.6	2.53	.55
West Side....................	23.6	8.8	1.2	2.55	.89
South Side...................	22.9	8.8	- 3.3	2.96	.83

*For regression equation, $Y = a + bX$; all data are for combined white and non-white population in each tract; tracts not weighted by size.

†Based on dwelling units occupied by two or more persons.

somewhat higher proportions in 1940 than did the North Side.

In Table 42 the analysis of changes in crowding is broken down by color. In these data one may observe striking differences between whites and non-whites in the kinds of change taking place over the decade. In interpreting these changes one must bear in mind the type of population shift that occurred. In most tracts (31 of the 35) the white population decreased, and the non-white increased, between 1940 and 1950. Thus the 1950 white population consisted of persons slow to move out under pressure of non-white consolidation, where- as the 1950 non-white population consisted of survivors of non-whites who invaded the tracts before 1940 plus the new residents whose in- movement after 1940 constituted the consolidation. No data exist to demonstrate the point, but it seems very likely that a much larger proportion of the 1950 white population was living in the same tract in 1940 than was true of the non-white population.

Although the proportion of multiperson households living in crowded units increased for both whites and non-whites, the change was much greater for the latter. In 1940 the average tract percentage of crowded units was somewhat higher for non-whites than for whites, but in 11 of the 35 tracts the difference was in the opposite direction. By 1950 the average non-white percentage crowded was twice as large as the white percentage, and in 32 of the 35 tracts non-whites had the higher proportion of crowded units. Thus the changes over the decade served to make the color differential much more pro- nounced. The correlations between 1950 and 1940 percentages of crowded units were lower for both whites and non-whites than for the total population over all 35 tracts and within areas (compare Tables 41 and 42). The correlations for whites were, however, uni- formly higher than for non-whites, indicating a greater stability of the pattern of differences among tracts for whites than for non-whites.

Socioeconomic characteristics.—Despite the displacement of white by non-white population, the level of educational attainment in the consolidation tracts rose substantially over the 1940-50 decade (Table 43). There were considerable increases in both the over-all mean percentage of persons with one year or more of high school and in the means for the three areas. Moreover, all tracts but one

Table 42.—Summary of Regression Analysis for Crowding, by Color: Consolidation Tracts, by Area

Color and Area	Mean 1950 M_Y	Mean 1940 M_X	Regression Constants*		
			Intercept a	Slope b	Correlation r
White:					
All tracts (35)	12.5	7.3	2.7	1.34	.64
North Side (6 tracts)	8.6	4.6	1.4	1.55	.49
West Side (14 tracts)	14.6	10.0	1.5	1.31	.60
South Side (15 tracts)	12.0	5.8	2.0	1.75	.72
Non-white:					
All tracts	25.6	9.5	16.2	0.99	.42
North Side	19.0	6.2	15.3	0.61	.24
West Side	29.1	7.2	22.6	0.91	.14
South Side	25.0	13.0	6.8	1.39	.62

*For regression equation, $\underline{Y} = \underline{a} + \underline{b}\underline{X}$; tracts not weighted by size. Crowding is measured by the per cent of dwelling units with 1.51 or more persons per room, based on dwelling units occupied by two or more persons.

178

Table 43.—Summary of Regression Analysis for Socioeconomic Characteristics: Consolidation Tracts, by Area

Characteristic and Area	Mean 1950 $\underline{M}_Y$	Mean 1940 $\underline{M}_X$	Regression Constants*		Correlation $\underline{r}$
			Intercept $\underline{a}$	Slope $\underline{b}$	
Education:					
Per cent completed 1 year of high school or more†					
All tracts (35)	38.9	25.1	17.1	0.87	.75
North Side (6 tracts)	41.0	22.5	30.1	0.48	.43
West Side (14 tracts)	32.8	20.1	15.1	0.88	.62
South Side (15 tracts)	43.7	30.8	15.0	0.93	.82
Per cent completed 1 year of high school or more, standardized for age†					
All tracts	35.2	25.2	11.8	0.93	.82
North Side	37.0	22.4	20.4	0.74	.63
West Side	28.6	19.8	13.0	0.79	.63
South Side	40.7	31.4	9.8	0.98	.87
Unemployment (per cent of male labor force unemployed):‡					
All tracts	11.4	33.1	1.9	0.29	.70
North Side	10.2	33.8	-2.6	0.38	.69
West Side	13.0	37.4	2.0	0.29	.64
South Side	10.4	28.9	2.6	0.27	.75
White-collar employment (per cent of male employed labor force in white-collar occupations):					
All tracts	19.2	24.9	-0.2	0.78	.73
North Side	23.6	26.9	-4.0	1.03	.87
West Side	15.6	22.4	4.7	0.48	.34
South Side	20.8	26.4	2.1	0.71	.74

*For regression equation, $\underline{Y} = \underline{a} + \underline{b}\underline{X}$; all data are for combined white and non-white population in each tract; tracts not weighted by size.

†For persons twenty-five years old and over.

‡Unemployed includes persons on public emergency work in 1940.

showed an increase in terms of the crude percentage, and all but two in terms of the percentage standardized for age. The standardized percentage, in general, registered a somewhat smaller change than the crude percentage, but, even so, only a minor part of the change in the latter can be attributed to shifts in age distribution. The pattern of intertract differences in educational attainment was somewhat more stable over the decade when measured by the standardized percentage than when measured by the crude percentage. In both 1940 and 1950 the South Side tracts had a higher average percentage than the North and West Side tracts; but the differences among areas were somewhat less at the end than at the beginning of the ten-year period.

The marked decline in the unemployment rate between 1940 and 1950 brought the greatest changes, in absolute terms, in the tracts with initially high rates. This is evident from the regression slopes of about 0.3. Nonetheless, there was some similarity in the ranking of tracts at the beginning and the end of the decade, since the total and within-area correlations all exceed .60. The West Side tracts had the highest average unemployment rates in both years, but the North and South Side averages differed little in 1950 despite the more favorable record of the latter in 1940.

Population turnover in the consolidation tracts was generally accompanied by a decrease in the proportion of male white-collar workers, as would be expected from the low occupational status of Negroes in comparison with whites. In 1940 the (unweighted) average proportion of white-collar workers in the 35 tracts was 24.9 per cent, as compared with 19.2 per cent in 1950. Decreases of the same order of magnitude occurred in each of the three areas. However, 6 of the 35 tracts showed a change in the opposite direction. The pattern of intertract differences showed moderate stability in the North and South Side tracts and in the total 35 tracts, but the correlation between the 1940 and 1950 percentages of white-collar workers was low for the West Side tracts.

Table 44 gives a summary of the separate regression analyses for whites and non-whites on two socioeconomic characteristics— the age-standardized percentage with one year or more of high school

Table 44.—Summary of Regression Analysis for Education and Unemployment, by Color: Consolidation Tracts, by Area

Characteristic, Color, and Area	Mean 1950 M_Y	Mean 1940 M_X	Regression Constants* Intercept a	Slope b	Correlation r
Education (per cent completed 1 year of high school or more, standardized for age):†					
White					
All tracts (35)	40.3	27.8	17.3	0.83	.55
North Side (6 tracts)	40.6	23.3	25.2	0.66	.64
West Side (14 tracts)	31.3	23.7	17.1	0.60	.52
South Side (15 tracts)	48.7	33.5	22.6	0.78	.48
Non-white					
All tracts	31.7	21.6	12.7	0.88	.77
North Side	31.6	16.7	18.6	0.78	.41
West Side	24.8	15.8	17.1	0.49	.28
South Side	38.2	29.0	11.2	0.93	.89
Unemployment (per cent of male labor force unemployed):†					
White					
All tracts	7.8	26.4	3.2	0.18	.36
North Side	7.0	31.0	2.8	0.13	.33
West Side	9.4	31.7	5.8	0.11	.29
South Side	6.8	19.5	0.4	0.32	.41
Non-white					
All tracts	13.1	44.4	3.8	0.21	.65
North Side	13.1	48.1	12.6	0.01	.04
West Side	14.7	48.2	2.4	0.26	.64
South Side	11.7	39.4	3.2	0.22	.78

* For regression equation, $\underline{Y} = \underline{a} + \underline{bX}$; tracts not weighted by size.

† For persons twenty-five years old and over.

‡ Unemployed includes persons on public emergency work in 1940.

and the unemployment rate. The general superiority of white educational attainment is evident from the over-all and within-area means. However, in both 1940 and 1950 there were 9 tracts in which non-whites had the larger proportions of adults with at least some high-school education. The changes of the decade, on the whole, slightly widened the difference between white and non-white levels of educational attainment. Over the entire 35 consolidation tracts there was a higher correlation between 1950 and 1940 percentages with one year or more of high school for non-whites than for whites. However, the difference between the correlations was in the opposite direction within the North and West Sides.

In the consolidation tracts, as in the city as a whole, non-white unemployment rates were generally much higher than white unemployment rates in both 1940 and 1950. Nevertheless, in both 1940 and 1950 there were 4 tracts that furnished exceptions to this rule. The 1950 unemployment rates were lower than the 1940 rates in every tract but one for both whites and non-whites. Despite the marked decline in the level of unemployment rates, there was some similarity, for non-whites, between the 1940 and 1950 ranking of tracts, except among the North Side tracts. For whites, however, all the correlations between 1940 and 1950 rates were low. It is perhaps significant that the stability of socioeconomic characteristics was, if anything, greater for non-whites than for whites, whereas the reverse was true for crowding.

No regression analysis is shown for white-collar employment, since a color breakdown is not available for 1940. One may note, however, that the 1950 non-white percentage of white-collar workers was lower, and the 1950 white percentage was higher, than the 1940 percentage for both groups combined. This is true of the grand average, the area averages, and 21 of the 35 tracts. There were, however, 12 tracts in which the 1950 white percentage was lower than the 1940 percentage for combined whites and non-whites. It may be inferred, though somewhat conjecturally, that there was some tendency for disproportionate losses of white-collar workers to accompany the decline in white population in these tracts. Still, in 1950, there were only 2 tracts in which the proportion of white-collar workers was lower for whites than for non-whites. The correlation between the 1950 proportion of white-collar workers for whites and the 1940 proportion for total employed persons was only .47; the correlation between the 1950 non-white proportion white-collar and the 1940 proportion for all employed persons was even lower, .31. One can only surmise that there was a somewhat greater stability in the pattern of tract rankings for whites than for non-whites.

One summary conclusion of considerable importance may be noted here. It is quite possible for social changes affecting the community at large to nullify the anticipated concomitants or consequences of succession. Knowing that Negroes have a much lower socioeconomic status than whites, one would predict that in an area undergoing succession a rapid turnover in population would lead to declines in average level of educational attainment and in the proportions of white-collar workers and to an increase in the rate of unemployment. But from the evidence given in this section one can see that only one of these inferences is correct, the decline in proportion of white-collar workers. The fact that levels of educational attainment rose and unemployment rates declined for both the non-white and the white population generally meant that, despite the rapid turnover of population in the consolidation tracts, their status with respect to these two indicators did not deteriorate but, on the contrary, improved. This is not to deny the possibility that in-movement of Negroes retarded the potential improvement in educational level and employment conditions. But the significant point is that the supposed effects of succession may be counteracted by powerful general tendencies of socioeconomic change.

Housing characteristics.—Table 45 summarizes the regression analysis for four housing characteristics. On the whole, the picture is one of moderate to high stability in the relative positions of the 35 consolidation tracts with respect to housing characteristics, despite the turnover of population. This is indicated by correlations between 1950 and 1940 indexes of .74 and .78 for per cent with mechanical refrigeration and median rent, respectively, and .88 and .94 for per cent with central heating and homeownership.

On the average, there was a small increase in homeownership

Table 45.—Summary of Regression Analysis for Housing Characteristics: Consolidation Tracts, by Area

Characteristic and Area	Mean 1950 $\underline{M}_Y$	Mean 1940 $\underline{M}_X$	Regression Constants* Intercept $\underline{a}$	Slope $\underline{b}$	Correlation $\underline{r}$
Homeownership (per cent of occupied dwelling units owner-occupied):					
All tracts (35)............	16.6	15.3	-2.0	1.21	.94
North Side (6 tracts).......	7.9	10.5	7.8	0.01	.01
West Side (14 tracts).......	11.8	11.1	3.0	0.79	.85
South Side (15 tracts)......	24.6	21.1	-2.2	1.26	.97
Rent (median contract monthly rent, tenant-occupied dwelling units, dollars):					
All tracts.................	34.17	18.90	15.16	1.01	.78
North Side................	29.18	15.58	34.39	-0.33	-.16
West Side.................	31.54	16.46	5.20	1.60	.76
South Side................	38.61	22.49	19.79	0.84	.85
Equipment:					
Per cent of dwelling units with central heating†					
All tracts.................	50.3	38.1	17.2	0.87	.88
North Side................	38.2	19.1	33.5	0.25	.18
West Side.................	42.9	34.5	8.7	0.99	.92
South Side................	62.1	49.0	21.7	0.82	.91
Per cent of dwelling units with mechanical refrigeration†					
All tracts.................	69.0	30.6	48.6	0.67	.74
North Side................	73.9	25.3	63.0	0.43	.34
West Side.................	62.0	23.4	37.0	1.07	.89
South Side................	73.7	39.5	49.0	0.62	.76

*For regression equation, $\underline{Y} = \underline{a} + \underline{bX}$; all data are for combined white and non-white population in each tract; tracts not weighted by size.

†Percentage based on dwelling units reporting on this equipment item.

in the consolidation tracts over the 1940-50 decade. However, decreases occurred in 12 tracts scattered among the three areas, the
most important instance being in tract 133 on the North Side, where
a public housing project of rental units replaced some formerly
owner-occupied units. In both 1940 and 1950 there was a wide range
of variation from tract to tract in the percentage of homeownership,
and, except on the North Side, the relative positions of the tracts
were largely maintained. In both years the proportion of homeowners
in the South Side tracts was about double that in the West Side tracts
and exceeded the North Side's average proportion by an even greater
margin. The principal instances of large increases in homeownership over the decade occurred on the South Side.

The median rental for tenant-occupied dwelling units increased
in all tracts between 1940 and 1950, with the average for all tracts
and for each of the three areas in 1950 being nearly twice as large
as in 1940. Despite this drastic change, there was some stability in
the comparative levels of the individual tracts, except on the North
Side, with a correlation of .78 for all tracts, and correlations of .76
and .85 for West and South Side tracts, respectively. On the North
Side the tract in which public housing was constructed during the
decade had the lowest median rent in 1940 but the highest in 1950.
For the entire set of tracts the average tendency was for tracts to
increase their median rent by a constant amount, irrespective of the
1940 value, as is shown by the slope approximating unity. However,
the within-area regressions varied widely from this tendency.

The percentage of dwelling units with central heating actually
decreased between 1940 and 1950 in 5 of the 35 consolidation tracts,
despite the substantial increase from 38.1 to 50.3 in the average percentage of units with central heating.

The relative positions of tracts with respect to percentage of
units with central heating were quite stable, as indicated by the correlation of .88 for the 35 consolidation tracts. The most deviant
tracts were 133 on the North Side, in which slum housing was de-
molished and Chicago Housing Authority's Cabrini project was constructed during the decade, and 534 on the South Side, in which Chicago Housing Authority's Wentworth project was constructed on land

primarily in non-residential use in 1940. In both tracts, as would
be expected, the percentage of units with central heating increased
markedly between 1940 and 1950. On the average, tracts in which
the percentage centrally heated was lowest in 1940 experienced the
greatest absolute increase during the decade; this tendency was
reinforced, but not accounted for, by the two tracts in which housing
projects were constructed during the decade.

Within the North Side group of tracts, the 1950 percentage of
units with central heating was largely independent of the 1940 percentage centrally heated, with a correlation of only .18 observed between the 1950 and 1940 percentages. Tracts in this group varied
relatively little with respect to central heating in 1940, and 1 of the
6 tracts is the deviant 133. However, within the West Side and South
Side groups of tracts, correlations of above .9 are observed, indicating considerable stability in the ranking of tracts with respect to
central heating.

The average percentage of units with central heat was lowest
for North Side tracts and highest for South Side tracts at both the beginning and the end of the decade. However, the largest absolute increase occurred for North Side tracts between 1940 and 1950, and,
as a result, differences among groups were somewhat reduced during the decade.

The percentage of units with mechanical refrigeration increased
in each of the 35 consolidation tracts; the average tract percentage
rose from 30.6 in 1940 to 69.0 in 1950. However, there was substantial shifting in the relative positions of tracts, with a correlation of
only .74 observed over the 35 tracts. On the average, tracts with a
low percentage of units with mechanical refrigeration in 1940 tended
to experience the largest absolute increases during the decade.

Within the North Side group of tracts, the 1950 percentage of
units with mechanical refrigeration appears largely independent of
the 1940 percentage, as indicated by a correlation of only .34. However, the correlation would be substantially increased, were tract
133, in which the Cabrini housing project is located, excluded; only
16 per cent of the units in the tract had mechanical refrigeration at
the beginning of the decade, but 99 per cent of the units had mechani-

cal refrigeration at the end of the decade. On the other hand, within the West Side group, considerable stability in the relative positions of tracts is evident, as shown by the correlation of .89, and the average tendency was for tracts to experience about the same increase in percentage with mechanical refrigeration during the decade, irrespective of the initial percentage. There was substantial shifting in the relative positions of tracts within the South Side group, as indicated by the correlation of .76; the slope of 0.62 indicates an average tendency for tracts with a low initial percentage to experience the greatest absolute increase during the decade. Over 90 per cent of the units in three South Side tracts had mechanical refrigeration in 1940, and increases in percentage with mechanical refrigeration between 1940 and 1950 were, of course, negligible in these three tracts.

Differences among areas with respect to percentage with mechanical refrigeration were reduced between 1940 and 1950, and the relative positions of the areas changed. At the beginning of the decade the average percentage with mechanical refrigeration was substantially higher for South Side tracts than for North or West Side tracts—39.5, 25.3, and 23.4 per cent for the respective areas; however, in 1950 the difference in average percentage with mechanical refrigeration between South Side and North Side tracts had disappeared, with percentages of 73.7 and 73.9 observed for the respective areas, and the average percentage for West Side tracts had increased to 62.0.

Table 46 shows separate regression analyses by color for the two characteristics—homeownership and rent—for which the necessary information is available. During the 1940-50 decade the percentage of homeowners increased in 34 of the 35 consolidation tracts for non-whites, but in only 18 tracts for whites. Consequently, the difference between the white and non-white percentages diminished considerably. Whereas in 1940 the non-white exceeded the white percentage in only 3 tracts, there were 9 tracts where this was the case in 1950. The convergence is evident, as well, from the averages for all tracts and for the three areas. Although the non-white averages remained lower in 1950 than the white, the two were much closer together than in 1940. It may be noted that the white and non-white percent-

Table 46.—Summary of Regression Analysis for Homeownership and Rent, by Color: Consolidation Tracts, by Area

Characteristic, Color, and Area	Mean 1950 $\underline{M}\,\underline{Y}$	Mean 1940 $\underline{M}\,\underline{X}$	Regression Constants*		
			Inter-cept $\underline{a}$	Slope $\underline{b}$	Corre-lation $\underline{r}$
Homeownership (per cent of occupied dwelling units owner-occupied):					
White					
All tracts (35)	20.8	20.3	- 6.8	1.36	.83
North Side (6 tracts)	10.4	13.3	13.8	-0.26	-.26
West Side (14 tracts)	15.6	16.3	- 1.6	1.06	.75
South Side (15 tracts)	29.7	26.8	-10.6	1.50	.83
Non-white					
All tracts	14.8	7.9	7.0	0.99	.95
North Side	5.8	1.0	3.9	1.87	.88
West Side	9.6	2.0	7.6	1.00	.47
South Side	23.3	16.1	7.6	0.97	.97
Rent (median contract monthly rent, tenant-occupied dwelling units, dollars):					
White					
All tracts	30.43	19.77	8.92	1.09	.82
North Side	26.90	15.82	27.71	-0.05	-.02
West Side	27.45	17.33	8.22	1.11	.82
South Side	34.63	23.63	8.17	1.12	.85
Non-white					
All tracts	35.66	17.67	9.27	1.49	.75
North Side	30.06	14.69	23.96	0.42	.16
West Side	33.92	17.15	4.25	1.73	.86
South Side	39.53	19.36	16.69	1.18	.66

*For regression equation, $\underline{Y} = \underline{a} + \underline{b}\underline{X}$; tracts not weighted by size.

ages, when standardized for type of structure, differed only slightly, despite the substantial difference in the observed percentages, as may be seen from the means for all tracts in 1950:

	White.	Non-white
Observed	20.8	14.8
Standardized	17.4	16.4

Evidently, the higher observed percentages for whites are in good part attributable to their larger proportions residing in single-family structures.

The correlations between 1950 and 1940 percentages of home-ownership were higher for non-whites than for whites over all tracts and within the North and South Sides. For whites a regression slope of 1.36 for all tracts was produced by tendencies toward an increase in homeownership in tracts where the percentage was initially high and a decrease in tracts where it was low in 1940. For non-whites, however, the average tendency was for homeownership to increase by a constant number of percentage points, irrespective of the 1940 percentage. However, for both whites and non-whites the within-area regression slopes deviated considerably from the total regression slope.

For both whites and non-whites in both years the percentage of homeownership was much higher in the South Side tracts, on the average, than in the other two areas, and the North Side had the lowest percentage. Inasmuch as the South Side tracts are, in general, farthest from the center of the city and the North Side tracts nearest, there is evidence of an upward zonal gradient in homeownership. This gradient persists under standardization for type of structure for both whites and non-whites, although the variation by area is considerably reduced by the standardization. The mean standardized percentages for 1950 are as follows:

	White	Non-white
All tracts	17.4	16.4
North Side.	15.5	10.5
West Side	16.7	13.7
South Side	18.8	21.3

It may be noted that the standardization for type of structure re-verses the direction of the white-non-white difference for the South Side tracts, though not for the other two areas or for all tracts as a group.

The color breakdown on rent reveals a significant shift. Where-as in 1940, on the average, white rents were slightly higher than non-white, in 1950 rentals paid by non-whites considerably exceeded those paid by whites. Thus in 1940 the white and non-white averages over all tracts were about $20 and $18, respectively, but in 1950 the cor-responding figures were $30 and $36. White rents were higher than non-white rents in 22 of the 35 consolidation tracts in 1940, but in only 6 tracts in 1950. Although both non-white and white median rent increased in every tract between 1940 and 1950, the non-white in-creases were evidently larger, on the average.

Despite the shifts in the relative positions of whites and non-whites and the increases in rent in all tracts, an upward zonal gradi-ent in median rent appeared for both whites and non-whites in both years.

The correlation of 1950 with 1940 rent was low for both whites and non-whites in the North Side tracts, where the construction of a housing project in tract 133 produced a large increase in median rent. In the other two areas the correlations were higher for both groups, with the West Side correlation being slightly higher for non-whites than for whites, and the South Side correlation markedly higher for whites than for non-whites. Over the entire set of tracts the white correlation of .82 exceeded by an appreciable margin the non-white correlation of .75. For both groups, on the whole, the largest in-creases in rent occurred in the tracts with relatively high rents at the beginning of the decade. However, the comparison of regression slopes for whites and non-whites within areas is not consistent enough to warrant a summary conclusion.

A review of Tables 42, 44, and 46 reveals that the stability of intertract differences, as measured by the correlation between the 1950 and 1940 index values, was higher for whites than for non-whites with respect to crowding and rent; the non-white correlation was the higher for education (standardized), unemployment, and homeownership. Thus one can make no general summary statement as to which of the two color groups showed greater stability in residential characteristics. If it is true, as was suggested above, that a larger proportion of the non-whites than of the whites residing in the consolidation tracts in 1950 were relative newcomers to the area, then it is significant that stability was greater for non-whites for any characteristic. One must conclude from this finding that the succession process, despite the rapidity of population turnover which it may entail, is highly selective. In-movers are sorted into different areas according to their socioeconomic characteristics, and there is a strong tendency for areas to maintain their differential characteristics under an influx of population.

Early Consolidation

Changes in population and dwelling units.—A population of 58,000 resided in the early-consolidation tracts in 1940; ten years later, there were 74,000 residents. The white population in the early-consolidation tracts decreased by 11,000 during the decade, from 55,000 in 1940 to 44,000 in 1950; but the non-white population increased by 26,000 in the ten-year period, from 3,000 in 1940 to 29,000 in 1950. Non-whites, who had made up only 5 per cent of the total population in 1940, constituted two-fifths of the 1950 population.

In all but one of the 26 early-consolidation tracts, the white population decreased between 1940 and 1950; but in 23 of these tracts, the influx of non-white population exceeded the out-movement of white population and resulted in a net increase in total population. In the other two tracts, the out-movement of white population exceeded the influx of non-white population and resulted in a net decrease in total population.

The single tract (416) in which both the white and the non-white population increased during the decade is part of the "Skid Row" area. In both 1940 and 1950 the bulk of the white population consisted of males, forty years of age and over, living outside regular households. The number of dwelling units occupied by whites dropped by nearly a third, despite the slight increase in white population during the decade; on the other hand, there were about seven times as many units occupied by non-whites in 1950 as in 1940.

Gross population density in the early-consolidation tracts was lower than in the groups of tracts in later stages of the succession process, but the absolute increase in density between 1940 and 1950 was of about the same magnitude as in the consolidation tracts. At the beginning of the decade, there were 16,900 persons per square mile of gross land area in the early-consolidation tracts; by the end of the decade, gross population density had increased to 21,300 per square mile.

There was virtually no new construction in the early-consolidation tracts during the decade. Only 110 units were reported as located in structures built between 1940 and 1950; 70 of these units represent temporary units erected by the University of Chicago. But at least 3,440 units were added to the housing supply through conversion in structures existing in 1940.

Occupied dwelling units increased at about the same rate as population during the decade. Units increased by 12.5 per cent during the decade, whereas population increased by 12.6 per cent. Nonetheless, room crowding increased substantially in the ten-year period. The unweighted mean proportion of households comprising two members or more with 1.51 or more persons per room for the 26 early-consolidation tracts was only 12.0 per cent in 1940 as compared with 26.4 per cent in 1950.

In general, it seems evident that population congestion and intensity of residential land use increased between 1940 and 1950.

Density and crowding.—During the decade, gross residential density increased in 24 of the 26 census tracts in the early-consolidation stage of the succession process. Early-consolidation tracts were quite stable in their ranking with respect to density over the decade, as indicated by the correlation of .89 over the 26 tracts. Tracts with a high initial density tended to experience the greatest absolute increase in density over the ten-year period; hence intertract variation with respect to density increased. The regression analysis, summarized in Table 47, shows that among North and West Side tracts and among South Side tracts there was considerable stability in the relative positions of tracts with respect to density and an average tendency for tracts with a high initial density to experience the greatest absolute increase in density during the decade.

The difference between the North and West Side group of tracts and the South Side group with respect to gross population density also increased between 1940 and 1950. This is evident from either the unweighted averages of tract densities, shown in Table 47, or from the weighted averages below (hundreds of persons per square mile).

	1950	1940
All tracts	213	169
North and West Side	277	217
South Side	161	131

In 24 of the 26 early-consolidation tracts, the proportion of crowded dwelling units or households increased during the decade. Over the 26 tracts, there was some shifting in relative positions with respect to crowding, as indicated by the correlation of .75 between 1950 and 1940 proportions crowded. However, of the 17 tracts with proportions crowded below the average for early-consolidation tracts in 1940, 15 had 1950 proportions crowded below the 1950 average for the early-consolidation tracts; of the 9 tracts with 1940 proportions above the 1940 average for early-consolidation tracts, all had 1950 proportions above the 1950 average. The average tendency was for tracts with a high 1940 proportion crowded to experience the greatest absolute increase in crowding during the decade.

Among the North and West Side tracts, there was some stability in the relative positions of tracts, as indicated by the correlation of .75, and an average tendency for tracts to experience the same in-

Table 47.—Summary of Regression Analysis for Density and Crowding: Early-Consolidation Tracts, by Area

Characteristic and Area	Mean 1950 M_Y	Mean 1940 M_X	Regression Constants*		Correlation r
			Intercept a	Slope b	
Density (population, in hundreds per square mile of gross land area):					
All tracts (26)	336	252	- 2.0	1.34	.89
North and West Side (14 tracts)	404	294	19.2	1.31	.88
South Side (12 tracts)	257	203	-11.8	1.32	.90
Crowding (per cent of dwelling units with 1.51 or more persons per room):†					
All tracts	26.4	12.0	11.8	1.22	.75
North and West Side	28.4	12.8	15.8	0.98	.75
South Side	24.0	11.1	4.3	1.79	.81

*For regression equation, $Y = a + bX$; all data are for combined white and non-white population in each tract; tracts not weighted by size.

†Based on dwelling units occupied by two or more persons.

crease in crowding, irrespective of level of crowding in 1940. Tracts
were fairly stable in their ranking with respect to room crowding
among the South Side group, as shown by the correlation of .81; but,
on the average, the greatest absolute increases in crowding occurred
in tracts with a high level of crowding in 1940.

Examination of the unweighted averages of tract proportions
crowded, shown in Table 47, indicates that, between 1940 and 1950,
crowding increased slightly more for the North and West Side tracts
than for the South Side tracts—15.6 and 12.9 percentage points for the
respective groups of tracts. In so far as North and West Side tracts
were, on the average, more crowded in 1940, the difference between
the North and West Side group and the South Side group sharpened during the decade.

In summary, moderate to strong relationships obtain between the
1950 and 1940 densities and between the 1950 and 1940 proportions
crowded over the early-consolidation tracts as a group and within the
North and West Side and the South Side groups of tracts. Population
congestion, as measured by density, and intensity of residential use,
as measured by room crowding, increased considerably both for the
entire group of tracts and for the North and West Side and South Side
groupings; further, the greatest absolute increases occurred among
North and West Side tracts, which were initially most densely populated and crowded, and, as a result, differences between the North
and West Side and South Side groups of tracts were sharpened. In
general, intertract variation with respect to congestion and crowding
also increased during the decade.

The regression analysis of 1950 proportion crowded for whites
and for non-whites separately on the 1940 proportion crowded for
all households is summarized in Table 48. There are difficulties in
interpreting the findings which can be outlined quickly. In 1940 there
were fewer than 250 non-white residents in each of the early-consolidation tracts; but the proportion of the total population composed of
non-whites ranged from 2.1 to 59.5 per cent among the 26 tracts. It
is clear that in some tracts the 1940 population represented an essentially all-white population; in other tracts the 1940 total population
included more non-whites than whites. Hence it cannot be inferred

Table 48.—Summary of Regression Analysis for Crowding, with Classification by Color in 1950: Early-Consolidation Tracts, by Area

Color (in 1950) and Area	Regression Constants*				
	Mean 1950 M_Y	Mean 1940 M_X	Intercept a	Slope b	Correlation r
White, 1950 (Y) on Total, 1940 (X):					
All tracts (26)	16.6	12.0	6.0	0.89	.68
North and West Side (14 tracts)	21.5	12.8	10.1	0.89	.73
South Side (12 tracts)	11.0	11.1	2.5	0.77	.63
Non-white, 1950 (Y) on Total, 1940 (X):					
All tracts	33.6	12.0	19.0	1.22	.72
North and West Side	36.0	12.8	25.1	0.86	.72
South Side	30.8	11.1	7.5	2.11	.83

*For regression equation, $Y = a + bX$; tracts not weighted by size. Per cent of dwelling units with 1.51 or more persons per room (based on dwelling units occupied by two or more persons).

from the fact that the 1950 value for whites is higher than the 1940 value for total that the 1950 value for whites is higher than the 1940 value for whites; similarly, it cannot be inferred that the 1950 value for non-whites is lower than the 1940 value for non-whites from the fact that the 1950 value for non-whites is lower than the 1940 value for total.

However, it is evident from the analysis summarized in Table 48 that the 1940 proportion crowded for all households was a fairly important determinant of the 1950 proportion crowded for both white and non-white households, within areas as well as over the 26 tracts as a group.

In most cases, intertract variation with respect to room crowding and household size was less for white households and for non-white households in 1950 than for all households in 1940. The major exception is with respect to room crowding among South Side tracts; the increase in non-white crowding in 1950 over total crowding in 1940 was greatest in tracts with a high level of crowding in 1940.

In 16 of the 26 early-consolidation tracts the 1950 proportion crowded for white households was greater than the 1940 proportion crowded for all households. In 10 of the tracts, the 1950 proportion crowded for white households was lower than the 1940 proportion for all households; it is possible that the 1950 proportion for white households was also lower than the 1940 proportion for white households in the majority of these tracts, for in 7 of the 10 tracts non-whites comprised less than 5 per cent of the 1940 total population.

In 25 of the 26 early-consolidation tracts the 1950 proportion crowded for non-white households was greater than the 1940 proportion crowded for all households. It seems likely, but cannot be demonstrated, that in most tracts the 1950 proportion for non-whites was also greater than the 1940 proportion for non-whites.

For the 26 tracts as a group, the mean proportion crowded in 1950 for both whites and non-whites was higher than the mean proportion crowded in 1940 for all households—1950 proportions of 16.6 per cent for whites and 33.6 per cent for non-whites as compared with a 1940 proportion of 12.0 per cent for all households. For the North and West Side group of tracts, mean proportions crowded of 21.5 per cent for whites in 1950, 36.0 per cent for non-whites in 1950, and 12.8 per cent for total in 1940 are observed; for the South Side group, mean proportions crowded for 11.0 per cent for whites in 1950, 30.8 per cent for non-whites in 1950, and 11.1 per cent for total in 1940 are observed. The 1950 white-non-white differential with respect to room crowding was somewhat less sharp for the North and West Side tracts than for the South Side tracts. It appears that, on the South Side, whites remaining in or entering the area after the succession process was under way maintained their previous room densities; but on the North and West Side, whites remaining in or entering the area lived at higher room densities than had been the case before the succession process was well under way. In both areas, non-whites entering the area apparently utilized their living space much more intensively than had the previous residents.

Socioeconomic characteristics. —The socioeconomic level of the population residing in early-consolidation tracts improved during the decade, despite the changing racial composition. The percentage of the population twenty-five years of age or older having completed at least one year of high school increased in 24 of the 26 early-consolidation tracts; the percentage with some high school, standardized for age, increased in 21 tracts.

The mean percentage with some high-school education for the 26 tracts increased by 11.2 points on an unstandardized basis and by 7.7 points on a standardized basis. The pattern of tract-to-tract variation with respect to educational level remained fairly stable over the decade, as indicated by correlations of .88 between 1950 and 1940 percentages with some high school and .80 between the 1950 and 1940 percentages standardized for age. The slopes are somewhat below unity, indicating an average tendency for educational level to increase most in tracts with a low initial educational level (see Table 49).

Correlations of .7 to .8 obtain within the North and West Side group and the South Side group between 1950 and 1940 crude and standardized percentages with some high-school education; as for all tracts, an average tendency is evident for the educational level to increase most in tracts with a low initial educational level.

Table 49.—Summary of Regression Analysis for Socioeconomic Characteristics: Early-Consolidation Tracts, by Area

Characteristic and Area	Mean 1950 M_Y	Mean 1940 M_X	Regression Constants*		Correlation r
			Intercept a	Slope b	
Education:					
Per cent completed 1 year of high school or more†					
All tracts (26)	38.7	27.5	14.5	0.88	.88
North and West Side (14 tracts)	31.5	21.7	12.2	0.89	.85
South Side (12 tracts)	47.0	34.3	21.4	0.74	.84
Per cent completed 1 year of high school or more, standardized for age†					
All tracts	35.4	27.7	15.2	0.73	.80
North and West Side	29.0	21.7	14.2	0.68	.78
South Side	42.8	34.7	21.3	0.62	.72
Unemployment (per cent of male labor force unemployed):‡					
All tracts	9.0	27.9	4.2	0.17	.42
North and West Side	9.1	33.2	3.2	0.18	.34
South Side	8.8	21.6	3.1	0.26	.72
White-collar employment (per cent of male employed labor force in white-collar occupations):					
All tracts	20.8	27.4	- 5.2	0.95	.92
North and West Side	17.7	24.9	- 2.0	0.63	.81
South Side	24.6	30.4	- 3.0	0.91	.89

*For regression equation, $\underline{Y} = \underline{a} + \underline{b}X$; all data are for combined white and non-white population in each tract; tracts not weighted by size.

†For persons twenty-five years old and over.

‡Unemployed includes persons on public emergency work in 1940.

However, the difference in educational attainment between the North and West Side group of tracts and the South Side group was not lessened during the decade. After controlling age composition, the educational attainment of the South Side population remained substantially higher than that of the North and West Side population in both 1940 and 1950. The mean percentage with some high school was 13.0 points higher for the South Side in 1940 and 13.8 points higher in 1950.

The unemployment rate for males dropped substantially in all but one of the 26 early-consolidation tracts during the decade 1940-50. The single exception (tract 897) had a lower proportion of unemployed males than any other tract in 1940, 6.8 per cent; in 1950, 7.1 per cent of the males were unemployed.

However, on a tract-by-tract basis, there was little relationship between the 1950 and 1940 unemployment rates, as indicated by the correlation of .42 over the 26 tracts. The correlation of .3 indicates that among the North and West Side group of tracts the level of unemployment in 1950 was largely independent of the 1940 unemployment level; but there is a moderately strong relationship between 1950 and 1940 unemployment levels for the South Side group, as indicated by the correlation of .7. Among the North and West Side group the greatest shift with respect to unemployment level occurred for tract 443, which ranked highest in 1940 but was tenth of 14 in 1950; this instability may arise in part from the small numbers of males in the labor force—81 in 1940 and 174 in 1950.

In 1940 the average unemployment rate for the 26 early-consolidation tracts was 27.9 per cent, with individual tracts ranging from 6.8 to 54.3 per cent; in 1950 the mean percentage unemployed was 9.0 per cent, with individual tracts ranging from 1.7 to 21.0 per cent.

The differential with respect to unemployment between the North and West Side and the South Side groups of tracts virtually disappeared during the decade. At the beginning of the decade, 33.2 per cent of the males were unemployed for the North and West Side group as compared with only 21.6 per cent for the South Side group; at the end of the decade, the percentages were 9.1 and 8.8 for the respective areas.

White-collar workers decreased as a proportion of all employed males in 22 of the 26 early-consolidation tracts between 1940 and 1950. But the ranking of tracts with respect to proportion white-collar was much the same in both years, as indicated by the correlation of .92 between 1950 and 1940 proportions. Within areas as well, a fairly strong relationship between 1950 and 1940 proportions white-collar obtained—correlations of .81 for the North and West Side group of tracts and .89 for the South Side group.

The average of the tract white-collar proportions dropped from 27.4 per cent in 1940 to 20.8 per cent in 1950 for the 26 early-consolidation tracts. The mean proportion of white-collar workers decreased during the decade for both the North and West Side and the South Side groups of tracts—by 7.2 and 5.8 points for the respective areas. In both 1940 and 1950 the mean proportion of white-collar workers was somewhat lower for the North and West Side group than for the South Side group. In the former year, 24.9 per cent of the North and West Side workers as compared with 30.4 per cent of the South Side workers, and, in the latter year, 17.7 per cent as compared with 24.6 per cent, were white-collar workers. This differential with respect to white-collar workers remains, although it is lessened when tract 617, adjacent to the University of Chicago campus, is excluded from the South Side group of tracts.

In summary, the socioeconomic level of tracts in 1940 was a fairly important determinant of their 1950 socioeconomic level. The educational attainment of the population increased and the unemployment rate decreased between 1940 and 1950, whereas the proportion of white-collar workers decreased during the decade; but the relative positions of the early-consolidation tracts with respect to these characteristics showed considerable stability over the ten-year period. However, intertract variation with respect to socioeconomic level diminished between 1940 and 1950.

At the beginning and end of the decade the socioeconomic level of the North and West Side group of tracts was somewhat lower than that of the South Side group. This may in part reflect the zonal gradient with respect to socioeconomic status obtaining in the city; 12 of the 14 tracts in the North and West Side group are located within 3 miles

202 / The Negro Population of Chicago

of the city's center, but only 2 of the 12 tracts in the South Side group are located so close to the center.

As Table 50 shows, the 1950 educational attainment of both the white and the non-white population in the early-consolidation tracts was higher than that of the total population in 1940. The mean proportion of whites with some high-school education was 40.4 per cent and that of non-whites 36.9 per cent in 1950, as compared with the mean proportion of 27.5 per cent observed for the total population in 1940. After standardization for age, the mean proportion of whites with some high school was 42.5 per cent and that of non-whites 31.0 per cent, as compared with the mean proportion of 27.7 per cent for the combined groups in 1940. It is evident that the age composition of the non-white population was relatively more favorable to high educational attainment than that of the white population, for standardization tends to reduce the educational level for non-whites but to increase it for whites.

Tracts in which the 1940 educational level was high tended to manifest the highest educational attainment for both white and non-white residents in 1950. The relationship between 1950 educational attainment of white residents and 1940 educational attainment of all residents was, however, stronger than that between 1950 educational attainment for non-white residents and the 1940 educational level. The most deviant tracts, i.e., those which shifted most in relative position with respect to educational level, had exceptionally small populations. Only 15 whites reported educational attainment in tract 443 and only 45 in tract 897 in 1950; only 170 non-whites reported educational attainment in tract 858 in 1950. Tract 443 falls far below the regression line; tracts 897 and 858 fall far above it.

The extent to which the educational attainment of the white population in 1950 exceeded that of the total population in 1940 tended to be constant, irrespective of the 1940 educational level. But the 1950 educational attainment of the non-white population tended to exceed that of the 1940 total population more in tracts with a low 1940 educational level than in tracts with a high 1940 educational level.

The unemployment rates for both whites and non-whites in 1950 were substantially lower than the rate for total population in 1940.

Table 50.—Summary of Regression Analysis for Education, with Classification by Color in 1950: Early-Consolidation Tracts, by Area

Color (in 1950), Characteristic, and Area	Mean 1950 M_Y	Mean 1940 M_X	Regression Constants*		Correlation r
			Intercept a	Slope b	
White, 1950 (Y) on total, 1940 (X):					
Per cent completed 1 year of high school or more†					
All tracts (26)	40.4	27.5	12.8	1.00	.86
North and West Side (14 tracts)	32.5	21.7	10.3	1.02	.68
South Side (12 tracts)	49.6	34.3	19.9	0.87	.90
Per cent completed 1 year of high school or more, standardized for age†					
All tracts	42.5	27.7	14.8	1.00	.76
North and West Side	32.6	21.7	14.6	0.83	.62
South Side	54.1	34.7	25.6	0.82	.70
Non-white, 1950 (Y) on total, 1940 (X):					
Per cent completed 1 year of high school or more†					
All tracts	36.9	27.5	17.2	0.72	.70
North and West Side	30.4	21.7	13.3	0.79	.70
South Side	44.4	34.3	25.6	0.55	.57
Per cent completed 1 year of high school or more, standardized for age†					
All tracts	31.0	27.7	16.3	0.53	.55
North and West Side	25.5	21.7	13.6	0.55	.68
South Side	37.4	34.7	24.4	0.38	.37

*For regression equation, $Y = a + bX$; tracts not weighted by size.

†For persons twenty-five years and over.

Whereas 27.9 per cent of the males were unemployed in 1940, the mean proportion unemployed in 1950 was only 6.7 per cent for whites and 11.4 per cent for non-whites in the 26 early-consolidation tracts. The 1950 unemployment rates for both whites and non-whites were largely independent of the 1940 unemployment rates for total population, as indicated by the correlations of .4 and .3 between 1950 and 1940 rates (see Table 51).

The 1950 proportion of white workers in white-collar occupations was lower than the 1940 proportion white-collar for all workers in 15 of the 26 early-consolidation tracts; the average of the tract proportions of white-collar workers for whites in 1950 was only 0.2 percentage points lower than the mean proportion for total workers in 1940. But it is very likely that if the 1950 proportion white-collar for white workers were compared with the 1940 proportion white-collar for white workers, a much larger number of tracts would show a decrease. The proportion of non-white workers in white-collar occupations in 1950 was lower than the 1940 proportion for all workers in each of the 26 early-consolidation tracts, and the average of the tract proportions of white-collar workers for non-whites in 1950 was 6.6 percentage points lower than the mean proportion for total workers in 1940.

The 1950 proportion white-collar for white workers was not independent of the 1940 proportion white-collar for all workers; but there was considerable shifting in the relative positions of tracts, as indicated by the correlation of only .70. The same may be said of the relationship between proportion white-collar for non-white workers in 1950 and the 1940 proportion white-collar for all workers—a correlation of .67 obtains between the 1950 and 1940 proportions.

Within the South Side group of tracts the relationships are slightly stronger; but within the North and West Side group the 1950 proportions white-collar for both white and non-white workers are largely independent of the 1940 proportion white-collar, as indicated by correlations of only .4 and .2.

In 1950 the mean proportions white-collar for both whites and non-whites were lower for the North and West Side tracts than for the South Side tracts. A similar differential between the North and

Table 51.—Summary of Regression Analysis for Unemployment and White-Collar Employment, with Classification by Color in 1950: Early-Consolidation Tracts, by Area

Color (in 1950), Characteristic, and Area	Mean 1950 M_Y	Mean 1940 M_X	Regression Constants*		Correlation r
			Intercept a	Slope b	
White, 1950 (Y) on total, 1940 (X):					
Unemployment (per cent of male labor force unemployed)†					
All tracts (26)	6.7	27.9	2.0	0.17	.41
North and West Side (14 tracts)	7.1	33.2	0.9	0.18	.35
South Side (12 tracts)	6.3	21.6	1.5	0.22	.56
White-collar employment (per cent of male employed labor force in white-collar occupations)					
All tracts	27.2	27.4	2.8	0.89	.70
North and West Side	23.6	24.9	12.8	0.44	.40
South Side	31.4	30.4	4.5	0.88	.72
Non-white, 1950 (Y) on total, 1940 (X):					
Unemployment (per cent of male labor force unemployed)†					
All tracts	11.4	27.9	6.8	0.17	.31
North and West Side	10.6	33.2	2.1	0.26	.36
South Side	12.3	21.6	6.4	0.27	.63
White-collar employment (per cent of male employed labor force in white-collar occupations)					
All tracts	13.4	27.4	- 1.1	0.53	.67
North and West Side	10.5	24.9	8.7	0.07	.16
South Side	16.9	30.4	- 0.3	0.56	.72

*For regression equation, $Y = a + bX$; tracts not weighted by size.

†Unemployed includes persons on public emergency work in 1940.

West Side and the South Side tracts is evident with respect to educational attainment; and unemployment rates on the South Side were lower than those on the North and West Side, on the average. It is, then, evident that for the white and non-white populations separately, as well as for the total population, the socioeconomic level of the South Side population is, on the average, higher than that of the North and West Side population.

In general, tracts in the early-consolidation stage of the succession process evidence a selectivity for persons resembling their previous residents in socioeonomic status. This selectivity is manifest for non-whites entering the tract as well as for whites remaining in or entering the tract after the succession process is under way.

Housing characteristics.—Homeownership became more frequent in 16 of the 26 early-consolidation tracts between 1940 and 1950; the average of the tract proportions of owner-occupants was 16.6 per cent in 1950, as compared with 15.2 per cent in 1940 (see Table 52).

There was considerable stability in the relative positions of tracts with respect to homeownership over the ten-year period, as indicated by the correlation of .93 between 1950 and 1940 proportions owner-occupied. The 14 North and West Side tracts were fairly stable in their ranking with respect to homeownership during the decade; and there was virtually no shifting in rank among the 12 South Side tracts. Frequency of homeownership in South Side tracts tended to increase by a constant amount, irrespective of 1940 level of ownership; but among North and West Side tracts there was an average tendency for the increase in ownership between 1940 and 1950 to vary inversely with the 1940 level of ownership. Over all 26 tracts, there was a very slight tendency for tracts with a low level of ownership in 1940 to experience greater absolute increases in homeownership during the decade than tracts with a high level of ownership in 1940.

At the beginning of the decade, the mean proportion of owner-occupied units was only 12.9 per cent for North and West Side tracts, as compared with 18.0 per cent for South Side tracts. The differential sharpened during the decade; by 1950, an average of 13.8 per cent of the units for North and West Side tracts, as compared with 19.8 per

Table 52.—Summary of Regression Analysis for Housing Characteristics: Early-Consolidation Tracts, by Area

Characteristic and Area	Regression Constants*				
	Mean 1950 M_Y	Mean 1940 M_X	Inter-cept a	Slope b	Corre-lation r
Homeownership (per cent of occupied dwelling units owner-occupied):					
All tracts (26)	16.6	15.2	2.1	0.95	.93
North and West Side (14 tracts) ...	13.8	12.9	4.0	0.75	.83
South Side (12 tracts)	19.8	18.0	2.1	0.99	.96
Rent (median contract monthly rent, tenant-occupied dwelling units, dollars):					
All tracts	36.76	20.35	17.02	0.97	.78
North and West Side	34.92	17.75	13.30	1.22	.71
South Side	38.90	23.37	17.42	0.92	.85
Equipment:					
Per cent of dwelling units with central heating†					
All tracts	61.8	56.6	11.0	0.90	.97
North and West Side	55.9	49.8	10.8	0.90	.98
South Side	68.7	64.4	11.2	0.89	.95
Per cent of dwelling units with mechanical refrigeration†					
All tracts	66.8	32.6	44.4	0.69	.69
North and West Side	63.1	24.5	43.1	0.82	.61
South Side	71.1	42.1	41.3	0.71	.75

*For regression equation, $Y = a + bX$; all data are for combined white and non-white population in each tract; tracts not weighted by size.

†Percentages based on dwelling units reporting on this equipment item.

cent of the units for the South Side tracts, were owner-occupied.

The 1950 proportion of owner-occupied units, standardized for type of structure, was greater than the unstandardized 1950 proportion in 20 of the 26 early-consolidation tracts. The average of the unstandardized tract proportions of homeowners in 1950 was 16.6 per cent; but the average of the standardized tract proportions of homeowners in 1950 was 20.6 per cent for the early-consolidation tracts. When type of structure is taken into account, the difference between the North and West Side and the South Side groups of tracts is reduced; the average proportion of homeowners, standardized for type of structure, was 19.1 per cent for the 14 North and West Side tracts, as compared with 22.5 per cent for the 12 South Side tracts.

The 1950 median rental for tenant-occupied units was substantially higher than the 1940 median rental in each of the 26 early-consolidation tracts. The average of the tract medians was $37 in 1950 as compared with only $20 in 1940. Nonetheless, the relative positions of tracts with respect to rental were somewhat similar at the beginning and end of the decade, as indicated by the correlation of .78 between 1950 and 1940 medians. The average tendency was for rentals to increase by a constant amount between 1940 and 1950, irrespective of the 1940 rent level.

On the average, rentals increased only slightly more among North and West Side tracts than among South Side tracts. For the former group of tracts, the average of the tract medians was $35 in 1950 as compared with $18 in 1940; for the latter group, the average of the tract medians was $39 in 1950 as compared with $23 in 1940. North and West Side tracts were somewhat less stable in their ranking with respect to rent over the ten-year period than were South Side tracts, as indicated by correlations of .71 and .85 for the respective areas. Furthermore, among North and West Side tracts the average tendency was for the increase in rental to vary inversely with the 1940 rent level.

A larger proportion of the units in the early-consolidation tracts were equipped with central heating and mechanical refrigeration in 1950 than in 1940. The mean of the tract proportions with central heating increased from 56.6 to 61.8 per cent in the ten-year period; the mean of the tract proportions with mechanical refrigeration increased from 32.6 to 66.8 per cent during the decade.

Tracts with a low proportion of centrally heated units in 1940 had low proportions centrally heated in 1950; tracts with a high proportion of centrally heated units in 1940 had high proportions centrally heated in 1950. In both years there was a wide range among the 26 tracts with respect to proportion of units with central heating—from 3.6 to 100.0 per cent in 1940 and from 8.8 to 99.0 per cent in 1950.

In 15 tracts the proportion of units centrally heated was above 60 per cent in 1940 and above 75 per cent in 1950. Within this group of tracts, there was a fair amount of shifting in rank with respect to frequency of central heating. But over the 26 tracts a correlation of .97 between the 1950 and 1940 proportions with central heating obtains. Equally high correlations between the 1950 and 1940 proportions of centrally heated units obtain among the North and West Side and the South Side groups of tracts. In each case the slope is somewhat below unity, indicating an average tendency for the absolute increase in proportion centrally heated during the decade to vary inversely with the 1940 proportion centrally heated.

The difference between the North and West and the South Side groups of tracts decreased somewhat between 1940 and 1950; however, in both years central heating was more frequent among South Side than among North and West Side units. In 1940 the mean of the tract proportions with central heating for the 12 South Side tracts was 64.4 per cent, whereas for the 14 North and West Side tracts it was only 49.8; however, the mean proportion for South Side tracts in 1950 was 68.7 per cent as compared with 55.9 per cent for North and West Side tracts.

In each of the early-consolidation tracts, mechanical refrigeration became more frequent during the decade. The mean of the tract percentages of units with mechanical refrigeration for the 26 tracts increased by 34.2 percentage points in the ten-year period. The mean of the tract percentages of units with mechanical refrigeration for the 14 North and West Side tracts increased by 38.6 points—from 24.5 to 63.1 per cent; and the mean of the tract percentages for the 12 South

Side tracts increased by 29.0 points—from 42.1 to 71.1 per cent.

The difference between the North and West Side and the South Side groups of tracts with respect to prevalence of mechanical refrigeration dropped substantially during the decade; and intertract variation decreased as well, as indicated by the fact that the slopes of the regression equations in Table 52 are well below unity. The relationships between 1950 and 1940 percentages of units with mechanical refrigeration are only moderately strong—correlations of .69 over the 26 tracts, .61 for the 14 North and West Side tracts, and .75 for the 12 South Side tracts.

Despite more intense residential use, high rates of conversion, and a high rate of population turnover, the early-consolidation tracts maintained their relative positions with respect to housing characteristics during the decade; however, in general, variation among tracts with respect to these characteristics decreased somewhat. The level of homeownership, rents, and the proportion of units equipped with central heating and/or mechanical refrigeration, on the average, increased in early-consolidation tracts. In both 1940 and 1950, homeownership was more frequent, rents were higher, and central heating and mechanical refrigeration were more prevalent among South Side tracts than among North and West Side tracts.

Homeownership became more frequent among both whites and non-whites during the decade. The mean of the tract proportions of owner-occupants among whites increased from 17.1 per cent in 1940 to 19.2 per cent in 1950; the mean of the tract proportions of owner-occupants among non-whites increased from 7.6 per cent in 1940 to 15.4 per cent in 1950 (see Table 53).

In 7 of the early-consolidation tracts the absolute number of units owned and occupied by whites, as well as the proportion of owner-occupants among whites, increased during the decade; at least in these tracts, it is evident that whites were purchasing and occupying homes despite the changing racial composition of the tract's population. In the remaining tracts it is not clear whether whites were purchasing and occupying homes during the decade or whether white owners simply were more likely to remain in the area than were white tenants.

Table 53.—Summary of Regression Analysis for Homeownership, by Color: Early-Consolidation Tracts, by Area

Color and Area	Mean 1950 $\underline{M}_Y$	Mean 1940 $\underline{M}_X$	Regression Constants*		
			Inter-cept $\underline{a}$	Slope $\underline{b}$	Corre-lation $\underline{r}$
White, 1950 (Y) on white, 1940 (X):					
All tracts (26)................	19.2	17.1	1.1	1.06	.91
North and West Side (14 tracts).....	16.9	15.4	3.4	0.87	.93
South Side (12 tracts).............	22.0	19.0	0.0	1.16	.91
Non-white, 1950 (Y) on non-white, 1940 (X):					
All tracts.................	15.4	7.6	11.7	0.48	.61
North and West Side........	12.2	3.4	11.2	0.31	.20
South Side	19.1	12.4	13.3	0.47	.64

*For regression equation, $\underline{Y} = \underline{a} + \underline{b}\underline{X}$; tracts not weighted by size.

In 1950, homeownership among whites was high in tracts in which homeownership among whites had been high in 1940 and was low in tracts in which homeownership among whites had been low in 1940. A correlation of .91 is observed between 1950 and 1940 proportions of owner-occupants for whites. Equally high correlations are observed among the North and West Side tracts and among the South Side tracts. For all 26 tracts and for the 14 North and West Side tracts there is a slight average tendency for the increase in homeownership during the decade to vary inversely with 1940 level of homeownership; but for the 12 South Side tracts there is a slight average tendency for the increase in ownership during the decade to vary directly with 1940 level of ownership.

The mean of the tract proportions of owner-occupants among whites was higher for the South Side than for the North and West Side tracts in both 1940 and 1950; and the difference was sharpened during the decade—the mean for the South Side tracts increased by 3.0 points, whereas the mean for the North and West Side tracts increased by only 1.5 points. Standardization for type of structure reduces the difference between the South Side and the North and West Side groups of tracts. In 1950 the means of the unstandardized percentages of owner-occupants among whites were 22.2 for the South Side and 16.9 for the North and West Side; the means of the standardized percentages were 19.5 for the South Side and 19.1 for the North and West Side.

During the decade there was considerable shifting among tracts in their relative positions with respect to the proportion of owner-occupants among non-whites. In 1940 there were 12 tracts in which there were no non-white owner-occupants; in 1950 the proportion of owner-occupants among non-whites for these 12 tracts ranged from 0.9 to 25.0 per cent. The moderate correlation over all 26 tracts is accounted for primarily by the fact that two South Side tracts (858 and 897) had proportions of owner-occupants among non-whites in both 1940 and 1950 substantially greater than those observed in any other early-consolidation tract. Among North and West Side tracts the proportion of owner-occupants among non-whites in 1950 is largely independent of the 1940 proportion of owner-occupants among non-whites.

The proportion of owner-occupants among non-whites increased substantially for both North and West Side and South Side tracts. The mean of the tract percentages of owner-occupants for all early-consolidation tracts increased by 7.8 points during the decade, the mean for the 14 North and West Side tracts increased by 8.8 points, and that for the 12 South Side tracts increased by 6.7 points. Among nonwhites, as among whites, the percentage of owner-occupants was higher for South Side than for North and West Side tracts.

When type of structure is controlled, the 1950 proportion of homeownership among non-whites was higher than that among whites in 14 of the 26 early-consolidation tracts. The mean of the standardized tract proportions of owners was 20.4 per cent among non-whites as compared with 19.3 per cent among whites. The mean of the standardized tract proportions of owners was 22.5 per cent among non-whites as compared with 19.5 per cent among whites for the 12 South Side tracts and 18.7 per cent as compared with 19.1 per cent for the 14 North and West Side tracts. Controlling type of structure reduces the white-non-white differential in homeownership as well as the difference between the South Side and North and West Side groups of tracts.

The 1950 median rent for units occupied by whites was higher than the 1940 median rent for all units in 25 of the 26 early-consolidation tracts, and the 1950 median rent for units occupied by nonwhites was higher than the 1940 median in all tracts. However, the average of the 1950 tract medians was substantially higher for nonwhites than for whites—$40.59 and $33.56 for the respective groups. These can be compared with the average of the 1940 tract medians of $20.35 for all units (see Table 54).

Despite the marked increase in rent level during the decade, there was moderate stability in the ranking of tracts with respect to rent. The correlations between 1950 median rent for whites and 1940 median rent were .7 over all 26 tracts, .6 for the North and West Side tracts, and .9 for the South Side tracts. The correlations between 1950 median rent for non-whites and 1940 median rent were .7 for all 26 tracts, .6 for the North and West Side, and .8 for the South Side. However, 1950 median rent for whites was highest in

Table 54.—Summary of Regression Analysis for Rent, with Classification by Color in 1950: Early-Consolidation Tracts, by Area

Color (in 1950) and Area	Mean 1950 M_Y	Mean 1940 M_X	Regression Constants*			Correlation r
			Intercept a	Slope b		
White, 1950 (Y) on total, 1940 (X):						
All tracts (26).	33.56	20.35	12.19	1.05		.70
North and West Side (14 tracts)	33.70	17.75	13.41	1.14		.61
South Side (12 tracts)	33.39	23.37	3.03	1.30		.88
Non-white, 1950 (Y) on total, 1940 (X)						
All tracts.	40.59	20.35	25.83	0.72		.73
North and West Side.	38.87	17.75	24.99	0.78		.61
South Side	42.59	23.37	25.92	0.71		.80

*For regression equation, $\underline{Y} = \underline{a} + b\underline{X}$; tracts not weighted by size. Median contract monthly rent, tenant-occupied dwelling units (dollars).

comparison to 1940 median rent in tracts with a high 1940 rent level; 1950 median rent for non-whites was highest in comparison to 1940 median rent in tracts with a low 1940 rent level. With respect to rent, intertract variation among whites in 1950 was slightly greater than among total in 1940, whereas intertract variation among non-whites in 1950 was less than among total in 1940.

The mean of the tract median rentals for whites in 1950 for the 12 South Side tracts was about the same as that for the 14 North and West Side tracts; but the mean of the tract median rentals for non-whites in 1950 for the 12 South Side tracts was $3.72 higher than that for the 14 North and West Side tracts.

Invasion

Changes in population and dwelling units.—At the invasion stage, as at later stages of the succession process, tracts typically experienced a net increase in population—the influx of non-whites more than offset the out-movement of whites. At the beginning of the decade, 153,000 whites and 1,000 non-whites resided in the invasion tracts; by the end of the decade, there were 122,000 white and 51,000 non-white residents. The net result was an increase of 19,000 persons during the ten-year period—from 154,000 to 173,000.

In 29 of the 33 invasion tracts, the white population decreased and the non-white population increased between 1940 and 1950. The rate of turnover, however, varied from tract to tract. For example, in tract 624 there were 3,279 white and 5 non-white residents at the beginning of the decade; in 1950, 69 whites and 4,261 non-whites resided in the tract. On the other hand, there were 5,670 white and 81 non-white residents in tract 299 in 1940; at the end of the decade, there were 5,585 white and 264 non-white residents.

In the other four of the 33 invasion tracts, both the white and the non-white population increased during the decade. Two of these tracts, 418 and 419, are part of the "Skid Row" area; and a substantial proportion of the white population is composed of older males living outside regular households. In another of the tracts, 671, the increase in number of persons born in Mexico is sufficient to account for the observed increase in white population. In the final tract, 596, the absolute increase in white population was only 19 persons.

In 28 of the 33 invasion tracts, a net increase in total population occurred between 1940 and 1950. For the group of tracts as a whole, the increase in occupied dwelling units between 1940 and 1950 slightly exceeded the increase in population—occupied units increased by 13.3 per cent and population increased by 12.4 per cent during the decade. But, whereas about 50 dwelling units were added to the housing supply in the invasion tracts through new construction, not less than 5,100 units were added through conversion.

Further evidence of increasing population congestion is the fact that the unweighted mean of the tract proportions of crowded dwelling units increased from 8.9 per cent in 1940 to 16.6 per cent in 1950. There were 34,200 residents per square mile of gross land area in the invasion tracts in 1940, and by 1950 the gross population density had risen to 38,500 persons per square mile.

The general patterns of population change occurring in the invasion tracts during the decade are similar to those taking place in tracts further along in the succession process.

Density and crowding.—It has already been observed that an increase in population occurred in 28 of the 33 invasion tracts during the decade, and, of course, gross population density also increased in these tracts. The average tendency was for tracts to experience about the same absolute increase in density during the ten-year period, irrespective of their density at the beginning of the decade; and a strong relationship between 1950 and 1940 gross population densities is evident over the 33 invasion tracts, as indicated by the correlation of .96 between 1950 and 1940 densities. The same can be said for the 17 West Side tracts and the 16 South Side tracts.

Both the unweighted averages of the tract densities shown in Table 55 and the weighted averages shown below (in hundreds of persons per square mile) indicate that, on the average, gross population density was considerably higher for West Side than for South Side tracts. Inasmuch as the West Side invasion tracts are all between 1 and 4 miles from the center of the city and the South Side tracts between 4 and 12 miles, the figures imply a downward zonal gradient in population density in both years.

	1950	1940
All tracts	385	342
West Side	412	373
South Side	358	312

Crowded households were also more frequent among the West Side than among the South Side tracts, and the between-area difference became greater during the decade. In 1940 the unweighted mean of the tract proportions crowded was 8.9 per cent for the 33 invasion tracts—10.7 per cent for the 17 West Side tracts and 7.1 per cent for the 16 South Side tracts; in 1950 the unweighted mean of the tract proportions crowded was 16.6 per cent for the 33 invasion tracts— 20.9 per cent for the West Side and 12.0 per cent for the South Side.

Moderately strong relationships obtained between 1950 and 1940 proportions crowded over the 33 invasion tracts and over the 17 West Side and 16 South Side tracts, as indicated by correlations of .8 or more. The average tendency was for the increase in crowding during the ten-year period to vary directly with the level of crowding in 1940; hence intertract variation, as well as the between-area difference, increased between 1940 and 1950.

The 1940 total population in the invasion tracts was composed almost entirely of whites; non-whites numbered less than 250 and made up less than 2 per cent of the population in each of the 33 invasion tracts. Hence comparisons between the 1950 white population and the 1940 total population are essentially comparisons between the whites who have remained in or entered the area during the invasion stage and the whites who were living in the area immediately before invasion; comparisons between the 1950 non-white population and the 1940 total population are essentially comparisons between the non-whites who entered the area during the invasion stage and the whites who were living in the area immediately before invasion.

Figure 16 shows the regression of per cent crowding in 1950, broken down by color, on per cent crowding for the total population (essentially white) in 1940. The constants of the regression lines are

Table 55.—Summary of Regression Analysis for Density and Crowding: Invasion Tracts, by Area

Characteristic and Area	Mean 1950 $\underline{M}\underline{y}$	Mean 1940 $\underline{M}\underline{x}$	Regression Constants*		Correlation $\underline{r}$
			Intercept $\underline{a}$	Slope $\underline{b}$	
Density (population, in hundreds, per square mile of gross land area):					
All tracts (33)	410	357	43.7	1.03	.96
West Side (17 tracts)	444	387	48.4	1.02	.95
South Side (16 tracts)	374	326	42.6	1.02	.96
Crowding (per cent of dwelling units with 1.51 or more persons per room):†					
All tracts	16.6	8.9	5.3	1.26	.86
West Side	20.9	10.7	7.7	1.23	.88
South Side	12.0	7.1	4.0	1.12	.78

*For regression equation, $\underline{Y} = \underline{a} + \underline{bX}$: all data are for combined white and non-white population in each tract; tracts not weighted by size.

†Based on dwelling units occupied by two or more persons.

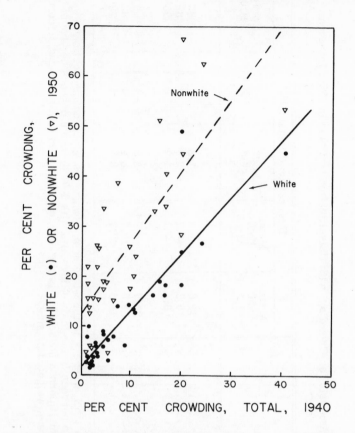

Fig. 16.—Regression of 1950 Crowding, by Color, on 1940 Crowding: Invasion Tracts.

given in Table 56. From these data a number of significant conclusions may be drawn: (1) As non-whites invaded these tracts, they came in at higher levels of crowding than the population they displaced. Thus non-white crowding in 1950 was greater than white (i.e., total) crowding in 1940 in 32 of the 33 invasion tracts. In absolute terms the greatest discrepancy between non-white crowding in 1950 and white (i.e., total) crowding in 1940 was in the tracts which already had relatively high levels of crowding in 1940. This is indicated by the regression slopes considerably exceeding unity and by the fact that the greatest increase in crowding, on the average, was

Table 56.—Summary of Regression Analysis for Crowding, with Classification by Color in 1950: Invasion Tracts, by Area

Color (in 1950) and Area	Mean 1950 M_y	Mean 1940 M_x	Regression Constants*			Correlation r
			Intercept a	Slope b		
White, 1950 (Y) on total, 1940 (X):						
All tracts (33)	12.0	8.9	1.8	1.14		.89
West Side (17 tracts)	15.3	10.7	2.9	1.16		.89
South Side (16 tracts)	8.4	7.1	1.9	0.91		.90
Non-white, 1950 (Y) on total, 1940 (X):						
All tracts	25.7	8.9	12.8	1.44		.79
West Side	32.5	10.7	18.4	1.31		.80
South Side	18.6	7.1	8.6	1.40		.78

*For regression equation, $Y = a + bX$, where Y is the white or non-white (as specified) proportion of households consisting of two or more persons living in dwelling units with 1.51 or more persons per room in 1950, and X is the proportion of all multiperson households (white and non-white combined) crowded, according to this definition, in 1940; tracts not weighted by size.

in the West Side tracts, whose crowding was greater than that of the South Side tracts to begin with. (2) Despite the fact that invasion entailed a much higher average level of crowding than prevailed before invasion, the proportion of crowded units among non-white households entering these tracts during the decade was substantially related to the proportion of crowded units among white households living in the tracts at the beginning of the decade. This is indicated by the correlations of about .8 between 1950 non-white crowding and 1940 crowding for the total (essentially white) population. (3) Increases in crowding were due not only to the high levels of crowding of the invading population but also to increases in crowding in the white population already living in the invasion tracts in 1940 or entering them subsequent to 1940. This change was not entirely uniform, inasmuch as the proportion of crowded units for whites in 1950 was lower than for whites (i.e., total) in 1940 in 1 of the 17 West Side tracts and in 4 of the 16 South Side tracts. There was, nonetheless, a clear increase in the mean proportion of white households in crowded units in both areas, as well as in the 33 invasion tracts as a group. The increase in crowding for white households was not systematically related to the level of crowding in 1940. (4) There was considerable stability in the ranking of tracts according to the proportion of crowded units, as indicated by correlations of .9 between white crowding in 1950 and white (i.e., total) crowding in 1940. (5) Non-white crowding exceeded white crowding in 1950 by a substantial margin, the respective averages being roughly in a ratio of 2 to 1. In Figure 16 the non-white regression line lies well above the white regression line, and non-white was higher than white crowding in every tract in 1950.

Socioeconomic characteristics.—The regressions of 1950 on 1940 levels of education, unemployment, and white-collar employment for the total population in the 33 invasion tracts are shown in Table 57. There was a substantial rise in the level of educational attainment in these tracts between 1940 and 1950, as shown by the mean percentages of adults with one year or more of high school; the increase amounted to 12 percentage points in the observed proportion with some high school and 9 percentage points in the proportion standardized for age. The former index registered an increase in each of

Table 57.—Summary of Regression Analysis for Socioeconomic Characteristics: Invasion Tracts, by Area

Characteristic and Area	Mean 1950 M_Y	Mean 1940 M_X	Regression Constants*		Correlation r
			Intercept a	Slope b	
Education:					
Per cent completed 1 year of high school or more†					
All tracts (33)	48.7	36.7	19.0	0.81	.94
West Side (17 tracts)	41.0	28.4	20.2	0.73	.82
South Side (16 tracts)	56.9	45.4	23.2	0.74	.93
Per cent completed 1 year of high school or more, standardized for age†					
All tracts	46.3	37.2	18.4	0.75	.89
West Side	38.7	29.0	22.1	0.57	.63
South Side	54.5	45.9	24.1	0.66	.87
Unemployment (per cent of male labor force unemployed):‡					
All tracts	8.1	20.0	2.0	0.31	.76
West Side	9.2	24.5	0.5	0.36	.72
South Side	7.0	15.2	2.6	0.28	.79
White-collar employment (per cent of male employed labor force in white-collar occupations):					
All tracts	29.0	37.8	− 3.7	0.86	.92
West Side	22.9	32.9	− 1.6	0.75	.89
South Side	35.4	43.1	− 0.9	0.84	.93

*For regression equation, $Y = a + bX$; all data are for combined white and non-white population in each tract; tracts not weighted by size.

†For persons twenty-five years of age and over.

‡Unemployed includes persons on public emergency work in 1940.

the 33 invasion tracts, and the latter in all but 4 tracts. In general, the absolute increase, in percentage points, was somewhat greater in tracts with initially low educational levels, as indicated by the regression slopes well below unity. Over the entire set of tracts the ranking on educational level was rather stable over the decade, as indicated by the correlation of about .9 between 1950 and 1940 values of the index of educational attainment. There was somewhat less stability within areas, particularly for the West Side tracts. The correlations for the observed percentages were a little higher than for the standardized percentages. In both 1940 and 1950 the educational level of the South Side tracts was substantially higher than that of the West Side tracts, and there was little change in the difference between the area means. Hence the zonal pattern of educational level was relatively stable, despite the turnover of population involved in invasion.

The rate of unemployment dropped in all tracts but one between 1940 and 1950, in most cases by a substantial amount. On the whole, the absolute percentage-point decreases were greatest in tracts with initially high unemployment rates, as indicated by the low regression slopes. Consistent with this tendency was a marked diminution in the difference between the West and South Side tracts. However, at the end of the decade, as at the beginning, there was less unemployment in the South Side than in the West Side tracts. The moderately high correlations between 1950 and 1940 unemployment rates are interpreted to mean that there was some stability in the pattern of differences among tracts despite the drastic change in the average level of the unemployment rate and the turnover of population.

There was a considerable decline in the average proportion of male white-collar workers, from about 38 to 29 per cent, between 1940 and 1950. Decreases occurred in 31 of the 33 invasion tracts; on the whole, they were somewhat larger in absolute terms in the tracts with initially high white-collar percentages. However, the decrease was slightly greater in the West Side tracts, on the average, than in the South Side tracts; hence the interarea difference, in favor of the South Side tracts, widened somewhat over the decade. The total and within-area correlations of about .9 indicate considerable stability in the ranking of tracts, despite the change in average level of white-collar employment.

Tables 58 and 59 summarize the regression analyses relating the socioeconomic characteristics of the white and non-white populations, respectively, in 1950 to those of the total—essentially white —population in 1940. Figure 17 presents a graphic representation of the regressions for one characteristic, the proportion of white-collar workers. From this chart it is evident immediately that non-whites in the invasion tracts in 1950 had lower proportions of white-collar workers than did whites, this being true in all but one of the 33 tracts. The mean tract percentage of white-collar workers was 33.9 for whites and 17.4 for non-whites in 1950. Both figures are below that

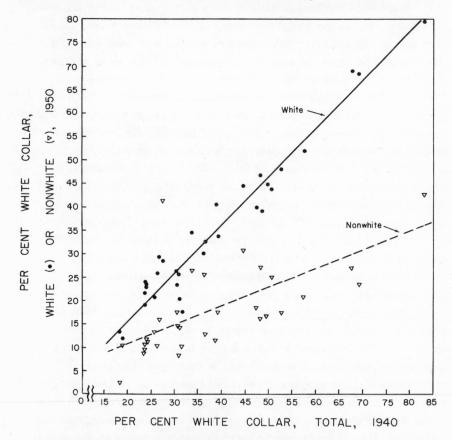

Fig. 17.—Regression of 1950 Percentage White Collar, by Color, on 1940 Percentage White Collar: Invasion Tracts.

for the total (essentially white) population in 1940, 37.8 per cent. Thus invasion involved a decline in the proportion of white-collar workers, not only because the invading population was one of low socioeconomic status compared to the 1940 residents, but also because of a selectivity in the population turnover among whites themselves. The latter effect may have involved one or both of two kinds of change: a disproportionate movement out of the invasion tracts of white workers employed in white-collar occupations or a disproportionate in-movement of white workers in manual occupations. It is significant, however, that the decrease in the proportion of whites in white-collar occupations occurred more or less uniformly, i.e., was of about the same amount irrespective of the 1940 proportion of white-collar workers. Thus the regression of the 1950 white on the 1940 total proportion of white-collar workers has a slope approximating unity, and the correlation is very high, .97. The regression of the 1950 non-white on the 1940 total proportion of white-collar workers has a much lower slope. The correlation of .65 is not high, but, nevertheless, over two-fifths of the variance in the 1950 tract proportions of white-collar workers for non-whites is accounted for by the 1940 proportions. This indicates that invasion was highly selective. Virtually all the non-whites in these tracts in 1950 had entered them after 1940, but in 1950 they were distributed among residential areas in such a way that the relative socioeconomic ranking of the tracts tended to be similar to that obtaining in 1940. The significant point of this analysis, then, is not that invasion entailed a decline in the proportion of workers in occupations of higher socioeconomic status—this would be expected simply on the grounds that non-whites have much lower socioeconomic status than whites. But, rather, the point to be stressed is that the change in racial composition of tracts did not entail random changes in socioeconomic characteristics. On the contrary, the turnover of population left the tracts in about the same rank order with respect to the proportion of white-collar workers in 1950 as was observed in 1940.

A comparison of Tables 58 and 59 shows that in all cases but one the correlation between 1950 white characteristics and 1940 total (essentially white) characteristics is higher than the corre-

Table 58.—Summary of Regression Analysis for Socioeconomic Characteristics of White Population in 1950 on Socioeconomic Characteristics of Total Population in 1940: Invasion Tracts, by Area

Characteristic and Area	Mean 1950 M_Y	Mean 1940 M_X	Regression Constants*			Correlation r
			Intercept a	Slope b		
Education:						
Per cent completed 1 year of high school or more†						
All tracts (33)	49.1	36.7	18.1	0.85		.95
West Side (17 tracts)	42.0	28.4	19.9	0.78		.77
South Side (16 tracts)	56.6	45.4	18.0	0.85		.96
Per cent completed 1 year of high school or more, standardized for age†						
All tracts	49.7	37.2	20.2	0.79		.90
West Side	42.6	29.0	18.8	0.82		.80
South Side	57.2	45.9	23.2	0.74		.87
Unemployment (per cent of male labor force unemployed):‡						
All tracts	7.0	20.0	1.0	0.30		.72
West Side	8.1	24.5	- 2.0	0.41		.74
South Side	5.9	15.2	3.0	0.19		.71
White-collar employment (per cent of male employed labor force in white-collar occupations):						
All tracts	33.9	37.8	- 5.1	1.03		.97
West Side	27.1	32.9	- 3.4	0.93		.94
South Side	41.3	43.1	- 1.0	0.98		.99

*For regression equation, $Y = a + bX$, where Y is the index value of the specified characteristic for the white population in 1950, and X is the index for the total population in 1940; tracts not weighted by size.

†For persons twenty-five years old and over.

‡Unemployed includes persons on public emergency work in 1940.

Table 59.—Summary of Regression Analysis for Socioeconomic Characteristics of Non-white Population in 1950 on Socioeconomic Characteristics of Total Population in 1940: Invasion Tracts, by Area

Characteristic and Area	Mean 1950 M_Y	Regression Constants*			
		Mean 1940 M_X	Intercept a	Slope b	Correlation r
Education:					
Per cent completed 1 year of high school or more†					
All tracts (33)	46.4	36.7	22.7	0.65	.64
West Side (17 tracts)	38.9	28.4	23.0	0.56	.44
South Side (16 tracts)	54.4	45.4	32.8	0.48	.47
Per cent completed 1 year of high school or more, standardized for age†					
All tracts	38.2	37.2	17.5	0.56	.59
West Side	30.6	29.0	22.1	0.29	.27
South Side	46.3	45.9	30.0	0.36	.38
Unemployment (per cent of male labor force unemployed):‡					
All tracts	10.2	20.0	6.3	0.20	.55
West Side	11.4	24.5	10.4	0.04	.14
South Side	9.0	15.2	3.3	0.37	.77
White-collar employment (per cent of male employed labor force in white-collar occupations):					
All tracts	17.4	37.8	2.8	0.40	.65
West Side	12.7	32.9	4.0	0.26	.73
South Side	22.5	43.1	8.2	0.33	.58

*For regression equation, $Y = a + bX$, where Y is the index value of the specified characteristic for the non-white population in 1950, and X is the index for the total population in 1940; tracts not weighted by size.

†For persons twenty-five years old and over.

‡Unemployed includes persons on public emergency work in 1940.

227

sponding correlation between 1950 non-white and 1940 total characteristics. The interpretation of this difference must be somewhat
speculative, but the following line of argument has plausibility. The
1950 white population consisted of whites who lived in the invasion
tracts in 1940 and remained there over the decade, plus those whites
who entered the tracts after 1940 and remained until 1950. There is
no way to be certain, but it seems likely that the former category—
the "old residents"—made up a large proportion of the 1950 white
population. If so, one would expect to find a measure of continuity in
tract characteristics in comparing the 1950 white population with
the 1940 total (essentially white), simply because the same individuals would appear in both terms of the comparison. There was, to be
sure, selectivity in the out-movement of whites from the invasion
tracts, as seems clearly to be indicated in the occupation data, and
there may well have been a socioeconomic selectivity of those whites
(whatever their number) who did move in during the decade. Moreover, the "old residents" themselves may have undergone social
mobility—i.e., a change of socioeconomic characteristics—without
changing their residence. Hence the continuity in tract characteristics provided by the core of residents present in both years would
only predispose the correlations between 1950 and 1940 socioeconomic characteristics to be positive; it would not necessitate that
they be high. But, by contrast, virtually all the 1950 non-white residents of the invasion tracts were "newcomers," i.e., they entered
these tracts after 1940. Hence any positive correlation on a tract-
by-tract basis between their characteristics and those of persons
residing there in 1940 would have to be explained by selectivity of
in-movement—no part of it is attributable to continuity of residence.
The correlations in Table 59 between 1950 non-white characteristics
and characteristics of the 1940 total population vary around .6 over
all 33 tracts for education, unemployment, and white-collar employment. These correlations, though not high, imply that the persons of
comparatively high socioeconomic status in the invading population
went, disproportionately, into tracts with relatively high socioeconomic status in 1940, while those of comparatively low status generally took up residences primarily in tracts ranking low in socioeconomic status at the beginning of the decade.

Aside from this general import of the data in Tables 58 and 59, there are some details worth noting. On the average, both the white and the non-white population in 1950 had higher levels of educational attainment than did the total (essentially white) population in 1940. The 1950 white level was above the 1940 level in all 33 invasion tracts on the basis of the observed percentage with at least some high-school education and in all tracts but 1 on the basis of the percentage standardized for age. The 1950 non-white level was higher than the 1940 level in 25 tracts on the basis of observed percentages and in 20 tracts on the basis of standardized percentages. The standardization for age does not greatly affect the 1940 percentages or the 1950 percentages for whites, but it substantially lowers the 1950 percentages for non-whites. This implies an age distribution among the invading non-whites favorable to high levels of educational attainment, i.e., a concentration in the younger adult age groups.

The white unemployment rate in 1950 was lower than that of the total (essentially white) population in 1940 in all but 1 of the 33 invasion tracts, and the 1950 non-white rate was lower than the 1940 rate for the total population in all but 3 tracts. Evidently, the general improvement in economic conditions was a powerful enough force to counteract any tendency, associated with invasion, for unemployment to rise in these tracts.

The data in Tables 58 and 59 indicate a considerable stability in the pattern of zonal differentiation of socioeconomic characteristics. In 1940 the West Side tracts, which are nearer the center of the city than the South Side tracts, had lower levels of educational attainment, higher proportions unemployed, and lower proportions of white-collar workers than did the South Side tracts. These same differences appeared in 1950 not only for the total population but also within the white and non-white populations examined separately.

Housing characteristics.—The characteristics covered in Table 60 show both substantial changes in levels of the indexes and moderate to high stability in the patterns of intertract variation over the 1940-50 decade. For all four characteristics the difference between West Side and South Side tracts observed in 1940 remained in 1950. Thus, in both years, West Side tracts had the lower percentages of

Table 60.—Summary of Regression Analysis for Housing Characteristics: Invasion Tracts, by Area

Characteristic and Area	Mean 1950 $\underline{M_Y}$	Mean 1940 $\underline{M_X}$	Regression Constants* Intercept $\underline{a}$	Slope $\underline{b}$	Correlation $\underline{r}$
Homeownership (per cent of occupied dwelling units owner-occupied):					
All tracts (33)	17.9	14.4	1.8	1.11	.97
West Side (17 tracts)	14.0	10.9	3.4	0.97	.90
South Side (16 tracts)	22.0	18.2	1.1	1.15	.98
Rent (median contract monthly rent, tenant-occupied dwelling units, dollars):					
All tracts.	44.53	28.30	23.59	0.74	.86
West Side.	40.64	22.55	24.51	0.72	.70
South Side.	48.67	34.40	21.70	0.78	.89
Equipment:					
Per cent of dwelling units with central heating†					
All tracts	80.0	75.7	19.4	0.80	.93
West Side	76.7	72.1	16.4	0.84	.92
South Side	83.4	79.5	22.5	0.77	.95
Per cent of dwelling units with mechanical refrigeration†					
All tracts	83.9	53.6	60.2	0.44	.80
West Side	77.4	37.1	51.8	0.69	.77
South Side	90.9	71.2	68.3	0.32	.89

*For regression equation, $\underline{Y} = \underline{a} + b\underline{X}$; all data are for combined white and non-white population in each tract; tracts not weighted by size.

†Percentages based on dwelling units reporting on this equipment item.

homeownership, median rentals, and percentages of dwelling units with central heating and mechanical refrigeration. Each of the four correlations between 1950 and 1940 housing characteristics was somewhat higher for the South Side tracts than for the West Side tracts, indicating a greater stability in the relative positions of tracts within the former area.

Homeownership increased in 30 of the 33 invasion tracts between 1940 and 1950, the increase in percentage points being about the same, irrespective of the 1940 percentage. The correlation of .97 indicates a high degree of stability in the ranking of tracts with respect to homeownership.

The general increase in rent levels between 1940 and 1950 was reflected in a change from a tract average of about $28 in 1940 to about $45 in 1950. The median rent was higher in every tract in 1950 than in 1940, the absolute dollar amounts of the increase being somewhat greater, on the average, in tracts with initially low rents. Despite the marked change in rent level, the ranking of the tracts by rent was not greatly disturbed, as is shown by the correlation of .86 between 1950 and 1940 median rent.

In general, there was an increase in the proportion of dwelling units with central heating between 1940 and 1950, raising the average proportion for the 33 invasion tracts from 76 to 80 per cent. There were actually 9 tracts in which the proportion decreased, but in most of these the 1940 proportion was very high, and the decrease was very small. On the other hand, substantial increases occurred in several tracts where the 1940 proportion was low. Nevertheless, the tracts did not change greatly in rank order with respect to proportion of units centrally heated; this is shown by the correlations exceeding .9 for all tracts and within areas.

An increase in the percentage of units with mechanical refrigeration occurred in all tracts over the 1940-50 decade. The increase was slight, of course, in those tracts that already had high percentages in 1940; but it was substantial in most of the tracts with initially low percentages. Consequently, the regression of 1950 on 1940 tract percentages has a slope well below unity. Moderate stability in the ranking of tracts is to be inferred from the correlation of .8.

Table 61 shows the regressions of 1950 on 1940 homeownership and rent, with a breakdown by color for 1950. The correlations for whites are uniformly higher than for non-whites. The probable explanation of this difference (continuity of residence for whites, but not non-whites) was discussed in the section on socioeconomic characteristics of the invasion tracts.

Figure 18 shows the regression of white and non-white homeownership percentages, respectively, in 1950 on the percentage of homeownership in 1940 for all (essentially white-occupied) units. Both the white and the non-white mean proportions of owner-occupied units in 1950 were higher than the proportion for all units in 1940.

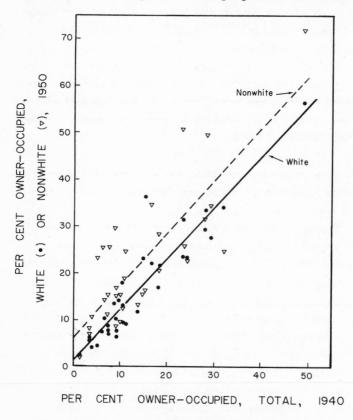

Fig. 18.—Regression of 1950 Percentage of Homeownership, by Color, on 1940 Percentage of Homeownership: Invasion Tracts.

Table 61.—Summary of Regression Analysis for Housing Characteristics, with Classification by Color in 1950: Invasion Tracts, by Area

Characteristic, Color (in 1950), Year, and Area	Regression Constants*				Correlation r
	Mean 1950 My	Mean 1940 Mx	Intercept a	Slope b	
Homeownership (per cent of occupied dwelling units owner-occupied):					
White, 1950 (Y) on total, 1940 (X)					
All tracts (33)	16.9	14.4	1.1	1.09	.93
West Side (17 tracts)......	12.9	10.9	2.1	0.98	.90
South Side (16 tracts)......	21.2	18.2	1.0	1.11	.92
Non-white, 1950 (Y) on total, 1940 (X)					
All tracts	22.2	14.4	6.2	1.11	.81
West Side	17.0	10.9	6.2	0.98	.68
South Side	27.8	18.2	8.3	1.07	.81
Rent (median contract monthly rent, tenant-occupied dwelling units, dollars):					
White, 1950 (Y) on total, 1940 (X)					
All tracts	41.84	28.30	15.87	0.92	.90
West Side	37.83	22.55	19.38	0.82	.73
South Side	46.12	34.40	9.18	1.07	.97
Non-white, 1950 (Y) on total, 1940 (X)					
All tracts	51.85	28.30	36.00	0.56	.72
West Side	48.92	22.55	33.50	0.68	.68
South Side	54.96	34.40	36.59	0.53	.69

*For regression equation, $\underline{Y} = \underline{a} + \underline{b}\underline{X}$, where $\underline{Y}$ is the index for white- or non-white-occupied dwelling units (as specified) in 1950, and $\underline{X}$ is the index for all occupied units in 1940; tracts not weighted by size.

However, the non-white proportion was substantially higher than the white. The two regression lines have very similar slopes, with the non-white line lying above the white throughout the range of the data. One might suppose that the difference between whites and non-whites in respect to homeownership could be explained by a tendency for the invading population to seek out single-family residences or their handicap in finding quarters in apartment buildings. However, the difference does not disappear under standardization for type of structure. In fact, the standardization increases the absolute difference between white and non-white homeownership percentages. The following are the means of the standardized percentages for 1950:

	White	Non-white
All tracts	20.8	31.4
West Side	19.2	28.7
South Side	22.6	34.2

The evidence seems rather clear, then, that invasion, during the 1940-50 decade, was accomplished by, or accompanied with, the acquisition of residential property by non-white households to a much greater extent than could be anticipated from a knowledge of the characteristics of the areas invaded or of the city-wide residential arrangements of non-whites. It may well be that non-whites experienced difficulty in finding suitable rental units, as is suggested by the fact that they paid higher rents in the invasion tracts in 1950 than did whites. But, even with allowances for differences between whites and non-whites in occupancy of single- and multiple-family structures, the non-whites had the greater proportions of homeownership.

Figure 19 shows the regression of median rent in 1950 for white and non-white tenant-occupied units, respectively, on the 1940 median rent for all tenant-occupied units. The general rise in rent levels is, of course, reflected in these data. But more significant is the fact that non-whites paid higher rents than whites in 1950 in all but four

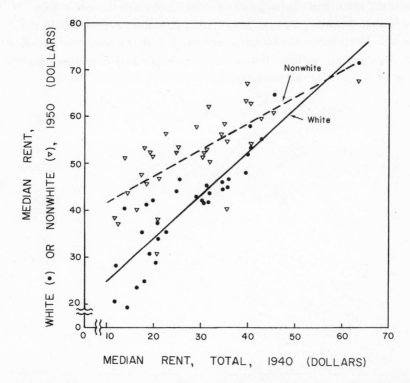

Fig. 19.—Regression of 1950 Median Rent, by Color, on 1940 Median
Rent: Invasion Tracts.

of the invasion tracts, three of the exceptional tracts being ones with
very high rents, relatively speaking, in 1940. The regression slope
of 1950 white on 1940 total (essentially white) median rent is not far
from unity; but the slope for 1950 non-white on 1940 total median
rent is well below unity. The two regression lines cross at the upper
end of the rent scale, suggesting that the white-non-white differential
is inoperative there; however, the data are too scanty to permit confidence in this inference. It is clear, though, that non-whites paid
much higher rents than whites in 1950 in those tracts that had low
rents in 1940.

Keeping in mind that non-white-occupied units had a much higher proportion crowded than did white-occupied units in the invasion

tracts in 1950, one can make the rather important inference that non-whites invading an area must pay a premium rental, which they are able to finance only by using residential space very intensively, e.g., by doubling up families in the household or by including relatives or lodgers in the household.

Chapter VIII

Residential Succession and the
Differentiation of Negro Residential Areas

A very large part of the area in Chicago now inhabited by Negroes
was formerly occupied by whites; only in isolated instances are
areas to be found in which Negroes were the original settlers. It follows, then, that the present residential patterning of the Negro community is the product of a long process of succession from white to
Negro occupancy, as modified by changes occurring within the Negro
community subsequent to succession. In this final chapter of the
study, therefore, the discussion of changes in characteristics of residential areas associated with succession is coupled with a description of some of the major kinds of variation among areas observed
in the Negro community as of 1950. Much of the material in the first
part of the chapter consists of a summary of data presented in more
extended form in chapter vii. The analysis here is based on systematic comparisons of the five sets of areas classified according to
stage of succession and of the subareas into which these were divided
for analytical purposes; such comparisons were introduced only incidentally in the exposition of findings in chapter vii.

Changes Accompanying Succession

The most general finding of the succession analysis is the conclusion that the same kinds of changes in population and housing characteristics occurred at each stage of succession over the decade
1940-50. There were, of course, individual tracts with changes unlike
the modal ones, and the degree of change and its incidence upon the
white and Negro population varied among areas. But every broad state-

237

ment about the changes occurring at one stage of succession will be found to hold for all other stages. A summary of these changes follows.

At each stage of succession there was an increase in gross population density. Since the areas were the same in 1950 as in 1940, this is, of course, tantamount to saying that population increased in each of the five groups of tracts. This bare statement, not surprising in itself, gains great significance in the light of two other facts. First, population growth, or increase in density, by no means characterized all parts of the city. In fact, the majority of the census tracts within a 7-mile radius of the center of the city, excluding those undergoing racial succession, experienced decreases, rather than increases, of population. Only on the periphery of the city, where vacant land was more generally available, was population increase typical of tracts not in process of white-to-Negro succession. The inner zones of the city, by and large, experienced a decrease in white population.[1] This was likewise true in the tracts undergoing succession; but in each of the five sets of tracts, considered as an aggregate, the increase in non-white population more than compensated for the decrease in white population. Second, the increase in gross population density was not accompanied by any material increase in available living space. In each of the five sets of tracts the population expanded more rapidly than did the number of dwelling units. Moreover, such increases in number of dwelling units as did occur were not, on the whole, the result of new housing construction during the decade but rather of conversion of non-residential structures to residential use, of transient or lodging quarters to dwelling units, or of large to small units. Thus not only was there an increase in gross population density, but there must have been an increase in net density as well, although the latter has not been measured directly. It can be shown, however, that room crowding of dwelling units increased considerably at each stage of succession. Table 62 shows that the described

---

1.   For more complete analysis see Beverly Duncan, Growth and Redistribution of the Resident Population in the Chicago Standard Metropolitan Area (Chicago: Chicago Plan Commission, 1954).

Table 62.—Percentage of Census Tracts with Indicated Changes in Population and Housing Characteristics, 1940–50, by Stage of Succession

Type of Change	Stage of Succession and Color								
	Piling Up	Late Consolidation	Consolidation			Early Consolidation	Invasion		
			Total	White	Non-white		Total	White*	Non-white†
Number of census tracts . . .	32	28	35	35	35	26	33	33	33
Increase in gross population density	91	96	94	. . .†	. . .†	92	85	. . .†	. . .†
More dwelling units added by conversion than by new construction§	96	85	87	. . .†	. . .†	100	100	. . .†	. . .†
Increase in room crowding .	66	93	97	69	91	92	94	85	97
Increase in educational level‖	97	100	94	86	94	81	88	97	61
Decrease in unemployment . .	100	100	97	97	97	96	97	97	91
Decrease in white-collar employment	50	61	80	. . .†	. . .†	85	94	82	97
Increase in homeownership .	91	79	63	51	97	62	91	67	85
Increase in rent	100	100	100	100	100	100	100	100	100
Increase in proportion of dwelling units with									
Central heating	72	100	86	. . .†	. . .†	73	73	. . .†	. . .†
Mechanical refrigeration .	97	100	100	. . .‡	. . .‡	100	100	. . .‡	. . .‡

*Change as indicated by comparison of white population in 1950 with total population in 1940.

†Change as indicated by comparison of non-white population in 1950 with total population in 1940.

‡Category not applicable or data not available.

§Based on census tracts in which number of dwelling units increased.

‖Based on standardized percentage with 1 year or more of high school.

changes in intensiveness of residential land uses characterized not only each of the five aggregates of tracts but most of the individual tracts in each of the five sets. It is evident that "piling up" was a typical concomitant of succession at all stages and was not confined to the piling-up tracts, where it occurred in the absence of further change in the racial composition of the population.

Evidence covering a large number of American cities over a period of several decades has shown that the usual pattern of expansion of the urban community is that of radial growth, involving substantial increases in population at the periphery and lesser increases or actual decreases in population in the central portions of the city.[2] This has been the experience of Chicago as well in earlier decades, and the deviation from this pattern afforded by the tracts undergoing racial succession between 1940 and 1950 calls for explanation. Special circumstances of the 1940-50 period may be relevant. Residential construction was held back by shortages of labor and materials during the war, and it may be that the rent-control regulations in force during the decade made the population somewhat less mobile than it otherwise would have been. Neither of these factors, however, accounts for the localization of the deviant growth pattern in the area subject to succession. The growth of the city's population over the decade was largely a function of Negro in-migration. The migrants did not find residences in all parts of the city but only in areas already inhabited by Negroes or in process of succession to Negro occupancy. Entering Negro residential areas, the migrant population generated a pressure for living space which was expressed by an expansion of the area of Negro residence. But this process did not overcome completely the "inertia" of the pattern of Negro residential segregation, and therefore the succession which occurred was unevenly distributed over the city and insufficient to prevent a differential rate of growth as between areas of Negro residence and comparable non-Negro areas.

---

2. Richard W. Redick, "Population Growth and Distribution in Central Cities, 1940-1950," American Sociological Review, XXI (February, 1956), 38-43.

Given the well-known fact of the Negroes' inferiority to whites in regard to all aspects of socioeconomic status which have been measured, one would expect to find that an area undergoing succession would also experience a decline in the over-all level of socioeconomic status of its population. Such an expectation, however, rests on the assumption of essentially static social conditions. In point of fact, areas in which succession occurred during the decade 1940-50 exhibited simultaneous rises in some aspects of socioeconomic status and declines in others. In the background of these changes are the cyclical improvement of business conditions between 1930-40 and 1940-50 and the secular, or long-term, rise in the level of living of the population of the United States. Both types of change have affected Negroes as well as whites, though doubtless in different ways and in varying degrees.

An excellent example is available in the changes in educational status. In each of the five sets of tracts, except the piling-up tracts, there was a considerable increase in the proportion of Negroes in the population between 1940 and 1950. Yet at all five stages of succession there was an improvement in educational status, as indexed by the proportion of adults with at least some high-school education. This happened despite the fact that the educational attainment of Negroes was substantially below that of whites both in 1950 and in 1940. The general rise in educational level in the population as a whole was more than sufficient to counterbalance the presumably depressing effect of population turnover on the educational level of tracts undergoing succession.

A similar observation can be made regarding unemployment. Despite the pronounced differential between races in unemployment rates, there were fewer unemployed persons at the end than at the beginning of the decade in the tracts where succession took place. The general improvement of business conditions outweighed the influence of the racial differential in determining the direction of change in these tracts.

In contrast to these findings is the observation that an occupational indicator generally registered a decrease in socioeconomic status in the areas under examination. The proportion of male white-collar workers declined in each of the five sets of tracts considered as an aggregate, though exceptions to this change were fairly numerous among individual tracts at the piling-up and late-consolidation stages (see Table 62).

In view of the contrary changes noted, one is unable to make a summary generalization about changes in socioeconomic status accompanying succession. Indeed, it seems best to regard the term "socioeconomic status" as simply a convenient label for a number of variables which are positively intercorrelated but each of which has a specific meaning as well as elements in common with the others.

Turning to housing characteristics, the situation again is one in which general tendencies of social and economic change appear to outweigh the hypothesized effects of residential succession. Thus in every tract included in the succession analysis there was an increase in median rent of tenant-occupied dwelling units over the decade. But this change occurred, as well, all over the city in tracts where no succession took place, along with the general rise in the level of consumer prices. The only basis for inferring an effect of succession on rent levels is the variation among stages of succession and between white and non-white rents, discussed later.

The general increase in proportions of homeownership, though not so widespread as the rent increase, is no doubt related to the same changes in economic conditions. Increases in consumer income presumably enhanced the effective demand for housing, while the housing shortage led some households, who might otherwise have remained tenants, into purchases of homes. Again, any inference as to the specific effect of succession must be based on comparisons among component areas or population groups rather than on the common tendency for increases in homeownership in tracts where succession occurred.

Data on housing equipment are not available for whites and non-whites separately, but it seems likely that in the city as a whole proportionately more white than non-white households have central heating and mechanical refrigeration in their dwelling units. If such be the case, then the changes in proportions of units with these items were generally in the opposite direction from what would be expected solely on the basis of changes in population composition by race. In nearly every tract the proportion of units with mechanical refrigeration increased, and in the great majority of tracts there were increases, as well, in the proportion with central heating (Table 62). Evidently, certain forces were at work to improve these aspects of housing conditions despite the presumable tendency toward deterioration associated with crowding and conversion of units. One caution should be remembered with regard to central heating. It seems likely that conversion was more frequent in large structures than in small ones and that the former would be more likely to be centrally heated than would the latter. A subdivision of units in a structure with central heating multiplies the number of dwelling units with central heating without, of course, actually increasing the amount of living space with this facility.

In summary, a review of the changes in population and housing characteristics occurring along with racial succession discloses no evidence that any given type of change is unique to a particular stage of succession. Moreover, it demonstrates that changes which presumably would accompany succession in an otherwise static situation may not be evidenced because of the quantitatively greater effect of social and economic changes that are essentially independent of succession. This finding has both theoretical and practical importance. It emphasizes the fact that for any study of, or social action with respect to, modifications of residential patterns to be realistic or effective, it must take account of the dynamic social setting of these modifications. A fair summary of findings must, of course, take note of the exceptions to generally prevailing changes. Table 62 shows that there were several individual tracts whose changes did not parallel those of the aggregate, though they were distinctly in the minority in most cases. A thorough understanding of these deviant tendencies could be reached only by meticulous investigation of each case, probably involving the analysis of types of data not available in the sources used in this study. However, several cases seem explicable on the basis of changes associated with public housing and urban redevelopment projects, and it will be recalled that a few tracts with atypical

succession patterns attributable to such factors were excluded from
the succession analysis. One has the general impression that centralized planning and governmental housing programs have not yet had a
major impact on the over-all pattern of racial succession in Chicago
or on the changes associated with succession. However, a great expansion of such activity might conceivably set in motion forces other
than those which have hithertc been the principal determinants of
residential patterns and changes therein.[3]

As has been indicated, one cannot infer consequences of succession merely from the direction of changes in average values of population and housing characteristics. Rather, such inferences must
rest on comparisons of the amounts of change among stages of succession, since the direction of change was uniform for all stages. If
it could be shown that the change in a given characteristic involved
a large magnitude at the early stages of succession but only a small
magnitude at the late stages, there would be some basis for inferring
that this type of change is characteristic of invasion and the beginning of consolidation, but less so of the terminal phase of succession.
The comparison of changes, however, should take account of two conditions: first, that an area with a high (low) average is not so likely,
other things being equal, to experience a large increase (decrease)
in the index of a characteristic as is an area with a low (high) average; second, that 1950 indexes of tract characteristics are, on the
whole, moderately to highly correlated with the corresponding 1940
indexes. In other words, changes should be "adjusted" for initial
level, making use of the available information about the relationship
between initial level and terminal level.

The procedure for adjusting changes was as follows: The "average within-stage regression coefficient" was calculated from the
pooled sums of squares and products obtained in computing the indi-

---

3. A vigorous, if somewhat controversial, discussion of policy
implications of residential succession for city planning is given in
David A. Wallace, "Residential Concentration of Negroes in Chicago"
(unpublished Ph.D. dissertation, Harvard University, 1953). An
evaulation of the issues in this discussion is beyond the scope of the
present study.

vidual within-stage regressions described in chapter vii. This coefficient was multiplied by the deviation of the mean for each stage in
1940 from the grand mean over all stages in 1940, and the resulting
quantity was subtracted from the corresponding mean for each stage
in 1950 to obtain the "adjusted 1950 mean." The "adjusted change"
was then secured by subtracting the 1940 grand mean from each
1950 adjusted mean.[4]

Comparative data on changes by stage of succession are shown
in Figures 20 and 21 and in Tables 63 and 64. The 1950 adjusted
means are shown on the charts as deviations from the 1940 grand
mean for all stages; the deviation is, of course, the adjusted change.
In the tables both actual changes and adjusted changes are shown.
It should be understood that the changes shown for the total population are not sums of the changes for whites and non-whites, because
the regression coefficients and adjusted means were computed
separately for total, white, and non-white population. The color
breakdown is shown for only those variables and stages for which
requisite data are available. Comments will be made on each of the
characteristics in turn, with reference to the color classification
where appropriate.

The most striking feature of the data on gross population density is the comparatively small increase in the invasion tracts; the
four later stages all had rather larger increases but differed little
among themselves. The importance of the adjustment of the 1950
mean for 1940 level is seen in the fact that the invasion tracts had
the lowest adjusted mean density, though their actual density level
was second only to that of the piling-up tracts in both 1940 and 1950
(Appendix Table I-1). Inspection of the changes indicates that, al-

---

4. Statisticians will recognize this procedure as one step in
the conventional analysis of covariance. For the reasons outlined
in Appendix H, the additional steps involving tests of significance
of changes and of the homogeneity of the individual within-stage regressions were not taken. The results, accordingly, require qualification, and conclusions as to their significance must involve a considerable element of judgment. Particular caution is required in
instances where the individual within-stage regression coefficients
differ widely among themselves (see Appendix Table I-5).

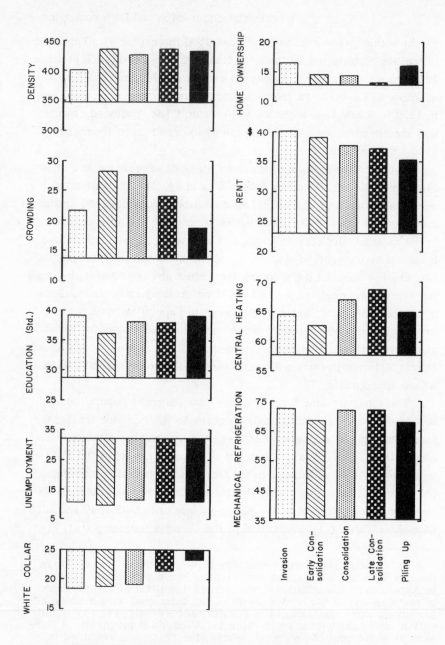

Fig. 20.—Adjusted 1950 Means of Census-Tract Characteristics, by
Stage of Succession. (Base line: 1940 grand mean over all stages.)

246

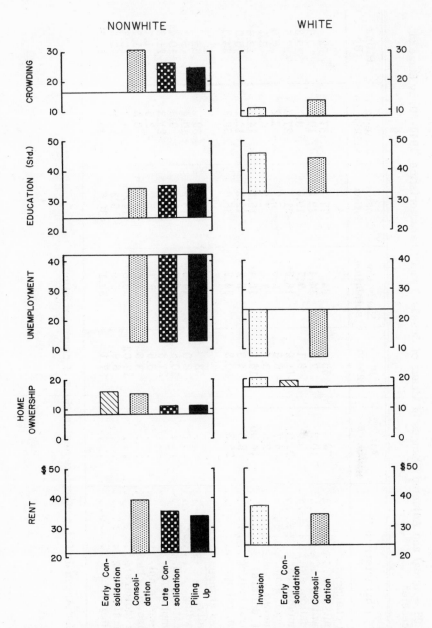

Fig. 21.—Adjusted 1950 Means of Census-Tract Characteristics, by Stage of Succession and Color. (Base line: 1940 grand mean for all stages represented.)

Table 63.—Actual and Adjusted Changes in Means of Census-Tract Characteristics, 1940-50, by Stage of Succession

Characteristic*	All Stages	In-vasion	Early Con-solidation	Consoli-dation	Late Con-solidation	Piling Up
Actual change:						
Density.	78	53	84	77	87	92
Crowding.	10.2	7.7	14.4	13.5	10.4	5.9
Education, std. . . .	9.6	9.1	7.7	10.0	9.7	10.8
Unemployment . . .	-21.3	-11.9	-18.9	-21.7	-27.0	-27.5
Wh.-col. empl. . . .	- 4.7	- 8.8	- 6.6	- 5.7	- 2.2	0.0
Homeown., obs. . .	2.0	3.5	1.4	1.3	0.2	3.7
Rent (dollars). . . .	14.90	16.23	16.41	15.27	14.27	12.44
Central heating. . .	8.0	4.3	5.2	12.2	12.1	5.9
Mech. refrig.	35.3	30.3	34.2	38.4	38.9	34.6
Adjusted change:						
Density.	. . .	53	88	79	89	85
Crowding.	. . .	8.0	14.5	13.9	10.4	5.1
Education, std. . . .	. . .	10.5	7.5	9.4	9.3	10.4
Unemployment . . .	. . .	-21.3	-22.1	-20.8	-21.3	-21.2
Wh.-col. empl. . . .	. . .	- 6.5	- 6.1	- 5.7	- 3.5	- 1.7
Homeown., obs. . .	. . .	3.6	1.6	1.5	0.3	3.2
Rent (dollars). . . .	. . .	17.02	16.00	14.65	14.20	12.70
Central heating. . .	. . .	6.9	5.0	9.3	11.1	7.3
Mech. refrig.	. . .	37.1	33.1	36.6	36.7	32.4

*See Appendix G for complete designations of characteristics.

248

Table 64.—Actual and Adjusted Changes in Means of Census-Tract Characteristics, 1940-50, by Stage of Succession and Color

Characteristic* and Color	All Stages†	Invasion	Early Consolidation	Consolidation	Late Consolidation	Piling Up
WHITE						
Actual change:						
Crowding	4.1	3.1	...	5.2	...	...
Education, std.	12.5	12.5	...	12.5	...	...
Unemployment	-15.8	-13.0	...	-18.6	...	...
Homeown., obs.	1.7	2.5	2.1	0.5	...	...
Rent (dollars)	12.06	13.54	...	10.66	...	...
Adjusted change:						
Crowding	...	2.9	...	5.4	...	...
Education, std.	...	13.4	...	11.6	...	...
Unemployment	...	-15.6	...	-16.2	...	...
Homeown., obs.	...	3.1	2.1	-0.1	...	...
Rent (dollars)	...	13.66	...	10.54	...	...
NON-WHITE						
Actual change:						
Crowding	10.9	...	...	16.1	10.2	5.9
Education, std.	10.5	...	...	10.1	10.7	10.8
Unemployment	-29.3	...	...	-31.3	-28.9	-27.5
Homeown., obs.	5.0	...	7.8	6.9	1.6	3.7
Rent (dollars)	15.02	...	...	17.99	14.25	12.44
Adjusted change:						
Crowding	...	...	...	14.3	9.8	8.2
Education, std.	...	...	...	9.8	10.8	11.0
Unemployment	...	...	...	-29.3	-29.4	-29.1
Homeown., obs.	...	...	7.6	6.8	2.7	3.0
Rent (dollars)	...	...	...	18.04	14.23	12.40

*See Appendix G for complete designations of characteristics.

†Refers to grand mean for all stages represented in succeeding columns.

though invasion entails increasing density, the increase is less rapid than at subsequent stages of succession.

The adjusted changes for crowding differ little from the actual changes. Both sets of data indicate that the increase in crowding is most severe in the middle stages of succession. Apparently, by the time tracts reach the piling-up stage, they are nearing a "saturation" point, where additional crowding becomes less probable, while at the beginning of succession increases in crowding occur but not so rapidly as at a subsequent period. This conclusion must be qualified because of the considerable differences among stages in their individual within-stage regression coefficients (see Appendix Table I-5). The conclusion is supported, however, by the data for white and non-white population analyzed separately.

The adjusted changes in educational level (standardized for age) show a comparatively large increase for the invasion tracts and a small increase for the early-consolidation tracts, with the magnitude of the increase rising thereafter until that of the piling-up tracts is as great as that of the invasion tracts. The separate data for whites show that the invasion tracts had a larger increase than the consolidation tracts; and the non-white data show the same gradient over the last three stages as the data for the total population. Apparently, the selective population shifts occurring in the intermediate stages of succession are unfavorable with respect to educational level. It is difficult to suggest a clear-cut rationalization of this finding.

Unemployment data demonstrate again the importance of adjusting the changes for initial differences. Although the actual changes vary somewhat from stage to stage, the adjusted changes exhibit no significant variation, either for the total population or for whites and non-whites separately. There is, then, no evidence for selectivity of the succession process, per se, for employment status, despite the fact that mean unemployment rates differ considerably by stage of succession.

Both the adjusted and the actual changes in proportion of white-collar workers fall into a gradient pattern by stage of succession, with a large decrease at the invasion stage and a small decrease (or no change, for the observed data) at the piling-up stage. Unfortu-

nately, no data are available by color, but it may be noted that the
pattern of changes is somewhat like what one would anticipate on
the basis of changes in color composition. From Table 32, chapter
vi, it may be ascertained that the changes in the proportion of Negroes between 1940 and 1950, by stage, were as follows:

Piling up.	0.3
Late consolidation	6.3
Consolidation.	35.9
Early consolidation	34.6
Invasion	28.1

If the change in white-collar proportion were a function solely of a
fixed color difference in proportion of white-collar workers and a
variable change in color composition, then the changes in the white-
collar proportion would be linearly related to the change in proportion non-white. The decrease in white-collar proportion in the invasion tracts is, however, too large to be accounted for on this simple
hypothesis. Apparently, a selective factor was at work, in addition
to population turnover, to produce the change, though the degree of
selectivity was probably slight. A slightly disproportionate out-movement of white males in white-collar occupations would have been sufficient to produce the result described; but the data do not, of course,
establish definitely that this occurred. Such a selection would seem
somewhat inconsistent with the adjusted change in educational level.
It may be, then, that the Negro in-movement involved a disproportionately small number of white-collar workers. Clearly, the findings
can be given only a speculative interpretation, and it must be borne
in mind that the data pertain to residuals or changes. In both 1940
and 1950 the invasion tracts ranked as the highest stage on proportion of white-collar workers in the total population, and the same
was true of the white and non-white population separately in 1950
(see Appendix Tables I-1 and I-2).

The adjusted changes in homeownership for the total population,
like the actual changes, fall into a downward-sloping gradient pattern
from the invasion tracts through the late-consolidation tracts; but
the increase in homeownership was as great in the piling-up tracts

as in the invasion tracts. Separate data for non-whites show, however, that the adjusted change in the piling-up tracts was only slightly above that in the late-consolidation tracts and below those of the other two stages. Recalling the finding in chapter vii that non-white homeowner- ship in the invasion tracts in 1950 considerably exceeded white home- ownership, one feels fairly secure in inferring that an increase in homeownership is a distinctive concomitant of the early phases of succession but is unimportant in the later phases.

The rent data present an exceptionally clear-cut finding. Both the adjusted and the actual changes in rent level for whites and non- whites separately, as well as for the total population, were greatest in the invasion tracts and diminished regularly to a relatively low figure in the piling-up tracts. The finding can be explained on the sup- position that competition between whites and non-whites for rental units pushes up their price in the initial stages of succession but has less effect as succession proceeds. This interpretation cannot, how- ever, be demonstrated with the data at hand.

Neither of the housing-equipment items—central heating and mechanical refrigeration—shows a pattern of changes that is readily interpreted. It is noteworthy, however, that the variation among stages in the magnitude of the adjusted changes is considerably less than in the actual changes. It is perhaps significant, too, that the rent changes do not parallel those in the equipment items; this at least suggests that the rent changes are not attributable to differential changes in housing quality.

Cross-sectional Comparisons of Stages

Turning from the analysis of changes accompanying succession, the next problem to be considered is the relation between succession and the differentiation of Negro residential areas. Various hypotheses about such a relationship may be entertained on the basis of knowledge and conjecture about the way in which succession takes place. Con- sider the following two simplified models of the manner in which the expansion of the Negro community took place.

1. Assume that during the period before the Negro population be- gan to increase rapidly as a proportion of the total population of the

city there was a "core" settlement of Negroes, i.e., an area of predominantly, though not exclusively, Negro residences. With the beginning of large-scale Negro in-migration, migrants began to take
the places of whites remaining in the "core," and the "consolidation"
of the "core" was accomplished rapidly, with the ultimate result
that pressure of the Negro population on available living space in
the "core" became so great that some of the residents were com-
pelled to find residences elsewhere. Their movement out of the
"core" amounted to an "invasion" of other areas. With the continuing
pressure of Negro population, invasion areas would become consolidation areas, and new invasion areas would appear. The areal expansion, however, would not take place rapidly enough to prevent a
rising density of population in older areas of Negro residence.
Finally, assume that in-migrants would continue throughout this
period to make the old "core" their "port of entry" and that the invasion of new areas and the early phases of their consolidation
would be accomplished by older residents of the city. The latter,
having lived in Chicago for a longer time, would be more "assimilated" than the recent arrivals and would have risen to higher levels
of socioeconomic status.

If the process just described had gone on for a number of years
and an investigator were to study the changes during a recent period,
he might classify as "invasion" tracts those invaded during the period of his study; as "consolidation" tracts, those invaded prior to the
period of his study but not yet exclusively Negro areas; and as "piling-up" tracts, those that were inhabited exclusively by Negroes before the period covered by his study began. The "piling-up" tracts
would, of course, include the old "core" as well as such other tracts
as were fully consolidated before the period under investigation.

Under the conditions described and with the type of selectivity
assumed, a cross-sectional comparison of tracts grouped by "stage
of succession" as of the end of the period under study would reveal
a gradient pattern. With respect to population density and indicators
of housing congestion, the "piling-up" tracts would have high indexes,
the "consolidation" tracts indexes of intermediate value, and the
"invasion" tracts low indexes. Indicators of socioeconomic status

would show a gradient in the opposite direction, i.e., low values for
the "piling-up" tracts, intermediate values for the "consolidation"
tracts, and high values for the "invasion" tracts. Characteristics
other than those mentioned would also be expected to exhibit gradient
patterns, if they were correlated with density and congestion and/or
socioeconomic status. Moreover, the gradient observed on a cross-
sectional basis could validly be reinterpreted as an indication of the
type of change in area characteristics as succession occurs, i.e.,
an increase in congestion ("piling-up") and a decline in socioeconomic levels.

2. The second model is not necessarily inconsistent with the
first but brings in an additional element, that of the spatial orienta-
tion of succession. Assume that the old "core" was located near the
center of the city and that the spatial expansion of the Negro community, by invasion and consolidation, took place along a radial axis
away from the center of the city. Assume, too, that radial growth of
the city had, before the expansion of Negro population occurred, resulted in a zonation or gradient pattern such that the inner zones
were characterized by high residential density and low socioeconomic
status and the outer zones by low density and high socioeconomic
status, with intervening zones being of an intermediate character.[5]
Finally, assume that the succession process was a selective one, in
that Negroes entering a formerly all-white area tended to resemble
in their socioeconomic characteristics the whites whom they displaced.

Under these conditions a study design like the one described
would again discover a gradient pattern by "stage of succession,"
but the gradient by stages would also be a spatial gradient, since
the "piling-up" tracts would be located near the center of the city
and the invasion tracts would be farther from the city center than
other areas of Negro residence.

It is worth noting that if the second model held precisely, there
would be no possibility of isolating effects of racial succession as

---

5. Cf. E. W. Burgess, "The Growth of the City," in R. E. Park,
E. W. Burgess, and R. D. McKenzie, The City (Chicago: University
of Chicago Press, 1925).

such, for racial succession would simply be part and parcel of the "normal" processes of urban community expansion.

It scarcely needs to be pointed out that both these models are highly idealized and that neither can be considered a close description of what actually occurred. Yet, because many of the findings of the study lend some plausibility to the assumptions on which these models are based, it is worth pointing out some of the major ways in which they fail to accommodate the facts.

As an example, consider the following mean density figures for 1950 and 1940 (in hundreds of persons per square mile, weighted averages):

Stage	1950	1940
Piling up	540	467
Late consolidation	332	248
Consolidation	236	193
Early consolidation.	213	169
Invasion	385	342

The hypothesized gradient appears over four of the stages, but the invasion tracts in both 1940 and 1950 had the second highest, rather than the lowest, density. The high density of the invasion tracts is evidently not a function of racial succession, since it appeared in 1940, before these tracts had any sizable number of Negroes. The cross-sectional comparison is clearly a misleading basis for inferring sequential changes, in so far as it suggests a lowering of density after invasion occurs. Unfortunately, figures on net residential density are not available, and the high gross density of the invasion tracts may simply reflect a comparatively low proportion of land in non-residential use.

As is true of density, the patterns of means by stage of succession in. Appendix Tables I-1 and I-2 for most characteristics fail to show a regular gradient of the kind expected from the simplified models described above, either in 1940 or in 1950. It is possible that a careful analysis of some of these data would disclose what

factors disturb the hypothesized gradient pattern. Consider two
characteristics for which the departure from a gradient is quite evident—central heating and rent. (The central-heating data are not
available by color, but the pattern of interstage differences in rent
is similar for whites and non-whites, despite the disparity in absolute level.)

The rent data used throughout this study are for contract rent,
which includes rent paid for furniture and utilities when these are
furnished to the tenant and billed to him as part of his rent. For
1940, data are available on gross rent, i.e., the estimated rent of
the dwelling unit without furniture, plus the monthly cost to the tenant of water, electricity, gas, and other fuel. Thus variations among
areas in rents due to differing practices with respect to the inclusion
of heat, utilities, and furniture in the contract rent are eliminated
from the gross-rent figures. The following is a tabulation of the unweighted means of the census-tract medians of contract and gross
monthly rent (for total renter-occupied units) by stage of succession,
in 1940:

Stage	Contract Rent	Gross Rent
Invasion	$28.30	$31.67
Early consolidation . . .	20.35	23.56
Consolidation	18.90	25.10
Late consolidation	22.57	27.91
Piling up.	24.79	27.63

Evidently, the differences by stage of succession do not fall in quite
the same pattern on the two bases of measuring rent. However, the
means for gross rent, like those for contract rent, fail to show a
monotonic gradient by stage of succession. In both sets of data the
invasion tracts have a conspicuously high value, and the early-consolidation and consolidation tracts conspicuously low values. Inspection of the gross-rent figures does not, therefore, greatly clarify
the interpretation of differences among stages of succession in average rent levels.

Looking next at the data for central heating, Appendix Table I-1 shows that the regression of the mean tract percentage of units with central heating on stage of succession was U-shaped in both 1940 and 1950; i.e., markedly high percentages were observed for the invasion and piling-up tracts and markedly low percentages for the consolidation tracts. But central heating is known to vary with type of structure. For example, in Chicago in 1950, 94 per cent of the units in structures consisting of ten or more dwelling units were centrally heated, as compared with only 56 per cent of the units in structures consisting of three or four dwelling units. Thus, if there is variation by stage of succession in the proportional distribution of units by type of structure, this would be expected to produce variation in the average proportion of units with central heating. To check this possibility, the proportion of units with central heating in 1950 was standardized, by the indirect method, for type of structure; the following (unweighted) mean percentages by stage of succession were obtained:

Stage	Observed	Standardized
Invasion	73.1	77.1
Early consolidation.	63.3	65.5
Consolidation	50.3	53.1
Late consolidation	61.8	64.0
Piling up.	80.0	81.8

Although the absolute level of the percentages is somewhat modified by the standardization, this calculation does not yield a comparison by stage of succession much different from that presented by the observed percentages. Hence the relationship of central heating to stage of succession cannot be explained by interstage differences in type of structure.

A third consideration with regard to rent and central heating is the likelihood that the interstage differentials in the two characteristics are related. In Chicago in 1950, units with central heating had a median rent of about $49, as compared with only $24 for units with-

out central heating. This suggests that the variations among stages
of succession in average rent level may be at least partially explained by variations in the prevalence of central heating. The tract
data on contract rent may be standardized, by the indirect method,
for the proportion of units with central heating, with the following
results for 1950:

Stage	Median Contract Rent		Per Cent Stand-ard Units
	Observed	Standardized	
Invasion	$44.53	$43.22	64.3
Early consolidation .	36.76	40.41	44.0
Consolidation.	34.17	43.04	48.7
Late consolidation . .	36.84	40.02	44.0
Piling up.	37.23	37.56	37.1

Allowance for the effect of central heating on rent considerably modi-
fies the comparison among stages of succession. The $10 difference
between the (unweighted) means of the median rentals in the invasion
and the consolidation tracts disappears under standardization, and the
standardized figures place the piling-up tracts lowest, in place of
second highest among the five sets. Also included in the foregoing
tabulation is a set of (unweighted) means of tract proportions of standard dwelling units in 1950, i.e., units with private bath and not dilapidated. These data are included as an indicator of the quality of housing to help explain the residual variation in rentals after the effect
of central heating is removed. Disregarding the invasion tracts, the
rent averages, standardized for central heating, do appear to be
closely related to the proportion of standard dwelling units. However,
the rent average for the invasion tracts is lower than would be expected if the proportion of standard units were the only determinant
of rent levels other than central heating. These data strongly suggest
that the principal explanation for rent differentials by stage of succession is that the areas classified into the five categories differ
with regard to the quality of the housing available in them. This is
not a firm conclusion, to be sure, because not all the major aspects
of quality have been considered; average size of units has been ig-

nored; and only rough comparisons are possible between the rent data based on tenant-occupied units and the data on heating equipment, condition, and plumbing based on all units. Nonetheless, the provisional conclusion is that at least one major determinant of rent variation by stage of succession is the factor of housing quality operating independently of the racial composition of the population or changes therein.

From the foregoing it is evident that a full explanation of departures of the means of population and housing characteristics from a regular gradient pattern would entail an examination of a number of variables and relationships not thoroughly investigated in this study. But this is only another way of stating that the simple models of succession proposed above are inadequate. It means, as well, that a strictly cross-sectional comparison of areas classified by stage of succession cannot substitute for a study of actual changes as a basis for inferring concomitants and consequences of succession.

One need not, of course, investigate gradients of characteristics by stage to demonstrate that the simple spatial order of succession assumed in the second model is descriptively inadequate. As was observed in chapter v, the expansion of the Negro community in Chicago has been, generally, along radial lines. But it has not proceeded from a single core or along a single axis. Both southward and westward movements from the center are observable, but the westward movement came, on the whole, somewhat later and began at a point somewhat nearer the center of the city. Actually, both the West Side and the South Side Negro settlements have grown toward, as well as away from, the center of the city, though the latter movement has been more pronounced.

As a result of the complex fashion in which expansion took place, the classification by stage of succession as of 1950 is by no means equivalent to a zonal classification. This is brought out by the tabulation in Table 65, and by the figures below, showing mean and median radial distance (in miles) from the center of the city for the tracts in each of five stages:

	Mean	Median
Piling up.	4.56	4.45
Late consolidation . .	4.75	3.75
Consolidation.	3.78	2.75
Early consolidation. .	3.46	2.88
Invasion	4.92	4.50

Table 65.—Number of Census Tracts by Stage of Succession, Direction, and Distance from Center of City, Chicago, 1950

Direction and Distance from Center (Miles)	All Stages	Stage of Succession				
		Piling Up	Late Con-solidation	Consoli-dation	Early Con-solidation	In-vasion
North:						
0-2.	9	0	0	6	3	0
West:						
1-2.	10	0	1	4	2	3
2-3.	21	1	3	7	7	3
3-5.	18	0	2	3	2	11
South:						
1-3.	9	0	4	3	2	0
3-4.	21	10	6	3	2	0
4-5.	21	12*	2	1	3	3
5-6.	15	5	4	1	1	4
6-8.	22	4	3	4	4	7
9-15	8	0	3	3	0	2
All tracts	154	32	28	35	26	33

*Includes one tract counted as Zone 6 in succession analysis.

The failure of the early-consolidation tracts to fall into the gradient pattern could perhaps be explained by the fact that this category was distinguished from the others partly on the basis of the kind of data available for its tracts, rather than strictly according to the criteria of timing of succession. Yet, even with this category removed, the required gradient does not appear. It is clear, however, that the invasion tracts, on the average, are located at the greatest zonal distances. Moreover, if attention is confined to census tracts on the South Side and the early-consolidation tracts are ignored, there is a tendency for zonal distance to decrease with advancing stages of succession. Thus the median tract in the piling-up and late-consolidation stages is 4-5 miles from the center of the city; the median consolidation tract is 5-6 miles from the center; and the median invasion tract is 6-8 miles from the center. Yet there is much overlapping of the zonal distributions of the several stages. Inclusion of the North and West Side tracts with the South Side tracts destroys even this semblance of relationship between zonal location and stage of succession, since these two sectors have disproportionate numbers of tracts in the early stages of succession but are, on the whole, nearer the city center than the South Side Negro residential area.

A later section of this chapter shows that there are fairly clear zonal gradients for many characteristics of Negro residential areas. For the most part, it can be assumed, first, that these gradients for the Negro population have been present for some time[6] and, second, that similar gradients would appear in an analysis for the city as a whole.[7] To some extent, then, it is probably true that the zonal differentiation of the Negro community is due to forces not dependent on the processes of racial succession, per se, except for the fact that the succession process is a selective one in so far as Negro in-movers tend to resemble the population being displaced in socioeconomic characteristics. Some evidence for this type of selection has been vouchsafed in chapter vii; the whole trend of the data on stability of area characteristics—summarized later in this chapter—is to support this hypothesis.

There is one more point to be made about the cross-sectional comparison of stages of succession. Several of the characteristics covered in Appendix Tables I-1 and I-2 indicate a relatively favorable position for the invasion tracts. As compared with other stages, they

6. Cf. E. Franklin Frazier, The Negro Family in Chicago (Chicago: University of Chicago Press, 1932).

7. There has been a great deal of research on Chicago residential patterns confirming the presence of general zonal gradients.

show low unemployment rates, high proportions of white-collar employment, high educational levels, high proportions of homeownership, and high rent levels. It seems unlikely that this situation is explained solely by the recency of succession in these tracts, as would be suggested by the first simplified model described at the beginning of this section. Rather, it appears probable that these tracts, on the average, have enjoyed a relatively favorable status for a long time. Their invasion during the decade 1940-50, then, represents an expansion of the Negro community into comparatively desirable areas, perhaps made possible by the rising socioeconomic status of the Negro population under the favorable economic conditions of the decade.

Some fragmentary data are available for these tracts for periods antedating their invasion. Figures on occupational composition in 1920 can be compiled for the 24 consolidation tracts having less than 5 per cent Negro population in that year and for the 21 early-consolidation and 33 invasion tracts meeting the same criterion. The 1920 occupation classification is not comparable with that of 1940 and 1950, but the following figures on mean tract percentages of males in professional service and clerical occupations suggest that interstage differences in proportion of white-collar workers existed at that time:

Stage	Professional	Clerical
Consolidation.	3.3	10.1
Early consolidation . .	4.6	10.7
Invasion	5.6	13.1

In 1930 the average median rent in the invasion tracts was $48.01 per month, as compared with $37.60 for the 18 early-consolidation tracts then having less than 5 per cent Negro population. For the same groups of tracts, the proportion of persons eighteen years old and over having completed at least one year of high school was, in 1934, 38.0 per cent for the invasion tracts and 28.6 per cent for the early-consolidation tracts.

The data cannot definitely establish the point, but they are con-

sistent with the suggestion that the socioeconomic differences between the invasion, early-consolidation, and consolidation tracts existed for the white population living in them before succession com-
menced. If this is true, then factors other than succession are responsible for the differences observed in 1950, which reflect discrepancies in the timing of succession among the areas rather than reveal an effect of succession.

Stability of Area Characteristics

In chapter vii, the term "stability" was defined, for purposes of
this study, to refer to the maintenance of relative position in a comparison. Thus if 15 census tracts have the same rank order with respect to median rent in 1950 as in 1940, the characteristic, median
rent, would be said to be a stable one in this comparison, even if its
absolute average level had doubled over the decade. The indicator of
stability most frequently used in chapter vii was the coefficient of
correlation between 1950 and 1940 census-tract characteristics. In
this section the topic of stability is treated in summary fashion.

Appendix Table I-6 brings together the correlations between
1950 and 1940 census-tract characteristics for the total population
and for the white and non-white population separately, where the
latter are available. Considering, first, the correlations for total
population, there are five coefficients—one for each stage of succession—for each of ten characteristics. The coefficients range from
.42 (for unemployment in the early-consolidation tracts) to .98 (for
central heating in the piling-up tracts).

Disregarding the characteristic, observed education (since it
largely duplicates the information of the characteristic, standardized education), the first part of Table I-6 contains 45 correlation
coefficients. These may be arranged in a frequency distribution as
follows:

Correlation	Frequency
.93 to .98	8
.88 to .92	10
.80 to .87	8
.73 to .79	10
.42 to .71	9
Total	45

The median of these 45 coefficients is .82. Two-fifths of them exceed .87; i.e., in 40 per cent of the cases, over three-fourths of the variance in 1950 census-tract characteristics is explained by the 1940 values of respective characteristics. Four-fifths of the coefficients exceed .71, which means that in 80 per cent of the cases over half the 1950 variance is accounted for by the 1940 tract indexes. Altogether, despite some cases of rather low correlations, these results indicate a rather considerable stability in census-tract characteristics over the decade. This finding is significant primarily in light of the fact that these tracts were experiencing large-scale changes in population. It must be remembered that the increase in total population and the change in racial composition of the tracts undergoing succession indicate only net change. It doubtless required a large volume of both in- and out-movement of population to produce these net changes. But in the face of such movement the factors of density and crowding, socioeconomic status, and housing characteristics which differentiated these tracts at the beginning of the decade continued to do so, in much the same way, at the end of the decade.

Besides indicating an impressive degree of general stability in tract characteristics, the correlations in Appendix Table I-6 show, as well, that certain characteristics were considerably more stable than others. Thus, for example, all five correlations for central heating and all the density correlations are .88 or higher, whereas none of the unemployment correlations exceeds .76, and there is no correlation higher than .80 for mechanical refrigeration. An inspection of the five sets of correlations for the ten characteristics reveals that central heating and density fairly consistently rank high, with respect to their 1940-50 correlation, and unemployment, mechanical refrigeration, and crowding generally rank low, though not with entire uniformity. These results do not seem unreasonable. As was pointed out in chapter vii, central heating is a semipermanent attribute of residential structures, whose frequency would not be expected to change markedly or erratically in the absence of great change in the inventory of housing structures. Variations in gross population density reflect the intensity of residential land use, primarily determined by the prevailing type of residential structures and the incidence of non-residential uses; both these factors would ordinarily not be subject to large short-run fluctuating changes. In contrast, unemployment is, or may be, a quite transitory characteristic of a person, and its incidence in an area would be expected to respond to many short-run influences. The remarkable thing is that correlations as high as .42 to .76 are observed over a ten-year period with many such shifting influences at work during the decade under study. Similarly, mechanical refrigeration and crowding have no basis of permanence either in the characteristics of individuals or in the sheerly physical aspects of the dwellings and areas they occupy. Yet the correlations for these characteristics, though among the lowest of those observed, are by no means negligible in size.

Another way of looking at the correlations in the first part of Table I-6 concerns the differences among the five stages of succession. It may be seen that all but one of the correlations for characteristics of the invasion tracts are .80 or higher. On nine characteristics these tracts show either the first or the second highest correlation. There appears to be no consistent differentiation among the other four sets of tracts with respect to the magnitudes of the correlations on the ten characteristics. Two reasons for the apparently greater stability of the invasion tracts may be suggested. First, in net terms, there was less turnover of population in the invasion tracts than in the early-consolidation, consolidation, or late-consolidation tracts (see Table 32, chap. vi). Second, and probably more important, the invasion tracts are a spatially scattered and internally diversified set of tracts, whose initial heterogeneity would predispose them to the maintenance of their pattern of differentiation. The apparent high stability of characteristics of the invasion tracts is not, therefore, so significant in itself but rather because it re-emphasizes the observation that invasion occurred during 1940-50 in a wide variety of tracts and was not confined to tracts with special kinds of characteristics other than location near areas in which succession had occurred earlier.

The breakdown of the 1940-50 correlations by color, in Appendix Table I-6, is limited to areas and characteristics for which the requisite data are available. No substantive interpretation of the white-non-white differences for the late-consolidation tracts is warranted, because the number of whites in these tracts, particularly in 1950, was so small as virtually to preclude stability on statistical grounds alone. For the consolidation tracts, in which both whites and non-whites were represented in substantial numbers in both 1940 and 1950, there is no uniform difference by color. The 1940-50 correlations are higher for whites with respect to crowding and rent, but the difference is in the opposite direction with respect to education, unemployment, and homeownership. With but two exceptions, the correlations by color are lower than the corresponding coefficients for the total population. But this difference may merely reflect the larger numbers, and hence greater statistical stability, involved in the latter comparisons.

Appendix Table I-7 shows 1940-50 correlations for the 13 sets of tracts produced by the area classification within stage of succession. The frequency distribution of the correlation coefficients for nine characteristics (omitting observed education) is as follows:

Correlation	Frequency
.93 to .99	22
.87 to .92	25
.76 to .86	25
.61 to .75	23
-.34 to .60	22
Total	117

Three of the coefficients are negative, and the frequency distribution is skewed toward the low end. Nevertheless, the median coefficient, .83, is about the same as in the earlier tabulation. Two-fifths of the coefficients are as high as .87 (i.e., three-fourths or more of the 1950 variance accounted for by 1940 values), and seven-tenths are above .70 (i.e., half or more of the 1950 variance accounted for). Again, the general picture is one of moderate to high stability.

On the whole, it appears that stability was somewhat greater in the outer zones of the piling-up and late-consolidation tracts than in the zone nearest the center of the city. At the other stages, relatively high stability, on the average, characterized the South Side tracts in comparison with the North and West Side tracts. The former, it will be recalled, are for the most part at greater zonal distances from the city center than are the latter. These zonal comparisons, though not holding uniformly, are compatible with the usual characterization of the inner zones of the city as an "area in transition." Cursory inspection suggests that physical changes, such as demolition of residential structures and shifts in type of land use, are more frequent in these zones than in the outer zones.

As in the data previously described, density and central heating rank high in stability, among the ten characteristics, and unemployment and mechanical refrigeration rank low. Crowding, however, does not consistently rank low, as was true in the comparison over five sets of correlations.

Inspection of Appendix Table I-1 shows that there was a fair degree of stability in the mean differences among the five sets of tracts representing the five stages of succession. Table 66 summarizes an analysis of interarea stability, where the areal units are the 13 groupings of tracts obtained by subdividing the stages of succession by zone or area. The data entering this analysis are shown in Appendix Table I-3. Table 66 shows the regression of the 1950 area means on the corresponding 1940 area means. All but one of the correlations are .92 or higher, indicating a great deal of stability in the relative positions of the 13 areas over the 1940-50 decade, despite the differential changes taking place in population composition and the large shifts in absolute levels of most of the characteristics. The characteristic exhibiting only moderate stability is crowding, with a 1940-50 correlation of only .66 over the 13 areas. There is no apparent explanation for this low degree of stability. All but 1 of the 13 areas increased in mean level of crowding over the decade, with the exceptional one showing no change. Had these changes been more nearly uniform in amount, or systematically related to the level of crowding in 1940, the 1940-50 correlation would, of course, have been higher.

In summary, a rather extensive analysis of the stability of characteristics of residential areas indicates that any changes in these characteristics associated with succession amount to somewhat minor variations on a pattern of areal differentiation with considerable inertia or resistance to change. The implication is that succes-

Table 66.—Summary of Regression of 1950 on 1940 Area Means of
Population and Housing Characteristics

(For 13 Zones or Areas within Stages of Succession)

| Characteristic* | Regression Constants† | | | | |
	Mean 1950 $\underline{M}_Y$	Mean 1940 $\underline{M}_X$	Inter-cept a	Slope b	Corre-lation r
Density, weighted mean† . .	380	308	47.6	1.08	.92
Density, unweighted mean†.	436	355	91.9	0.97	.95
Crowding	24.3	14.1	15.0	0.66	.66
Education, observed	40.4	28.3	12.2	1.00	.96
Education, standardized. . .	37.8	28.0	9.6	1.01	.96
Unemployment	10.9	33.3	3.5	0.22	.93
White-collar employment .	19.5	23.6	3.4	0.69	.92
Homeownership, observed .	14.1	12.3	3.6	0.85	.92
Rent (dollars)	37:25	22.63	16.06	0.94	.94
Central heating	64.3	55.5	21.1	0.78	.98
Mechanical refrigeration. .	69.9	33.8	48.2	0.64	.92

*See Appendix G for complete designations of characteristics.

†For regression equation, $\underline{Y} = \underline{a} + \underline{bX}$, where $\underline{Y}$ is the mean of the 13 area means in 1950 and $\underline{X}$ is the corresponding figure for 1940; all data are for combined white and non-white population; areas not weighted for size.

‡In hundreds of persons per square mile of gross land area; all other characteristics, except rent, in percentage form.

sion is a selective process, inasmuch as the incoming population is sorted into residential areas in much the same way as these areas differentiated the outgoing population. Furthermore, the data are consistent with the supposition that differences among areas in different stages of succession can be accounted for largely in terms of forces producing areal differentiation in the community at large rather than factors specific to one or two stages of succession.

Relations between Non-white and White Characteristics

Because areas undergo succession at varying rates and at different times, there is, at any given time, a number of areas with a mixed residential population—both whites and Negroes being present in substantial proportions. It is of interest, for two reasons, to determine whether whites and Negroes living in the same tracts resemble each other. First, one may suppose that in a mixed tract the white residents represent the population being displaced, and the Negro residents the incoming population. This supposition is not necessarily correct, for there may be turnover within both the white and the Negro population. Nevertheless, it seems plausible that, on the average, in a tract which has recently experienced a loss of white population and a gain of non-white population the whites will have resided there longer than the non-whites. If this assumption is accepted, then cross-sectional comparisons of white and non-white characteristics have presumptive value for the analysis of changes accompanying succession. Second, even if the foregoing assumption is unacceptable, the comparisons are valuable for the information they yield about the nature of the processes involved in the differentiation of residential areas. If there is a high correlation between white and non-white characteristics over a given set of tracts, it may be reasoned that the forces producing differentiation of residential areas operate irrespective of the racial composition of the resident population. If, on the other hand, the correlation is essentially nil, it would be inferred that selective factors associated with race were as important in their effects as were those independent of race.

Figure 22 will serve as a graphic illustration of the mode of analysis employed here. On the horizontal axis is the scale for median rentals paid by whites in the consolidation tracts, and on the vertical axis is the scale for rentals of non-white-occupied dwelling units. Two sets of observations are shown in the diagram: those for 1950 and those for 1940. The two solid lines are the regressions, for 1950 and 1940, respectively, of non-white on white median rentals. The dashed line connects the means of the tract figures for the two dates. The shift of the means upward and to the right indicates that both non-white and white rentals increased during the decade. The two regressions, however, are similar. In both years, on the whole, non-white rentals were relatively high in those tracts in which whites were paying high rents, and low non-white rents were observed in

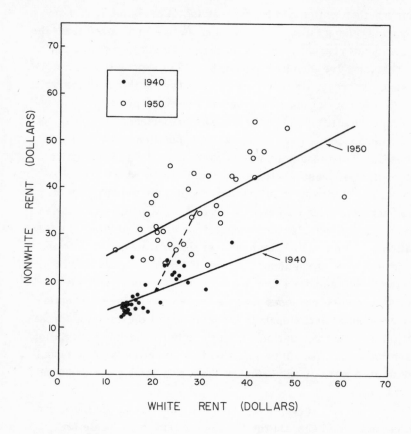

Fig. 22.—Regression of Non-white on White Median Monthly Rent: Consolidation Tracts, 1940 and 1950.

tracts with low white rents. There is, of course, considerable scatter of the points around the regression lines, showing that certain tracts provided exceptions to this general tendency. The degree of consistency of the relationship is indicated by the correlation of .67 observed in both 1940 and 1950 (Table 67). This correlation is not high, but it indicates that non-white and white rentals, on a tract-by-tract basis, are far from being unrelated. It is striking that the correlation did not change between 1940 and 1950, despite the general rise in rents

Table 67.—Summary of Regression Analysis of Non-white on White Population and Housing Characteristics, for Census Tracts in Three Stages of Succession, 1950 and 1940

Characteristic*	Regression Constants†					Regression Constants†				
	Mean, Non-white M_Y	Mean, White M_X	Inter-cept a	Slope b	Correlation r	Mean, Non-white M_Y	Mean, White M_X	Inter-cept a	Slope b	Correlation r
	Consolidation Tracts, 1950					Consolidation Tracts, 1940				
Crowding	25.6	12.5	14.4	0.90	.69	9.5	7.3	7.9	0.22	.19
Married couples w/o own hsld.	22.0	13.8	20.4	0.12	.20	...	...	...	...	...
Married females, spouse absent	22.6	14.8	21.0	0.11	.19	...	...	...	...	...
Per cent unrelated individuals	15.0	21.5	12.2	0.13	.51†	...	...	...	...	...
Education (standardized)	31.7	40.3	15.6	0.40	.61	21.6	27.8	7.0	0.52	.60
Unemployment	13.1	7.8	9.2	0.50	.56	44.4	26.4	24.5	0.75	.56
White-collar employment	13.4	28.1	13.6	0.00	-.02	...	...	...	...	...
Family income (dollars)	2,505	3,108	1,756	0.24	.38§	...	...	...	...	...
Homeownership (observed)	14.8	20.8	-0.7	0.74	.88	7.9	20.3	-11.4	0.95	.71
Homeownership (standardized)	16.4	17.4	11.4	0.29	.26	17.67	19.77	10.34	0.37	.67
Rent (dollars)	35.66	30.43	18.68	0.56	.67	...	...	...	...	...
Substandard dwelling units	58.9	40.7	25.3	0.82	.78	...	...	...	...	...
	Early-Consolidation Tracts, 1950					Invasion Tracts, 1950				
Crowding	33.6	16.6	17.0	1.00	.76	25.7	12.0	10.6	1.26	.88
Married couples w/o own hsld.	22.5	14.9	22.9	-0.02	-.02	20.4	8.9	21.2	-0.10	-.05
Married females, spouse absent	19.0	14.1	19.0	0.00	-.01	16.4	7.2	16.4	0.00	.00
Per cent unrelated individuals	17.4	26.8	12.7	0.18	.49†	15.1	18.6	13.8	0.07	.19
Education (standardized)	31.0	42.5	11.2	0.47	.65	38.2	49.7	3.3	0.70	.65
Unemployment	11.4	7.1	5.3	0.86	.66	10.2	7.0	8.8	0.21	.25
White-collar employment	13.4	27.2	5.3	0.30	.48	17.4	33.9	4.0	0.39	.69
Family income (dollars)	2,495	3,192	1,752	0.23	.30†	2,783	3,556	902	0.53	.82
Homeownership (observed)	15.4	19.2	4.1	0.59	.62	22.2	16.9	7.7	0.86	.74
Homeownership (standardized)	20.4	19.3	18.3	0.11	.08	31.4	20.8	20.9	0.50	.28
Rent (dollars)	40.59	33.56	28.40	0.36	.54	51.85	41.84	29.13	0.54	.71
Substandard dwelling units	66.9	44.8	36.8	0.67	.76	49.0	32.6	20.3	0.88	.78

*See Appendix G for complete designations of characteristics; all variables except income and rent in percentages; income and rent in dollars.

†For regression equation, $Y = a + bX$, where Y is the tract index for non-whites and X is the tract index for whites; tracts not weighted by size.

‡Two census tracts omitted, because of small number of cases.

§One Census tract omitted in computation of regression constants, because of small number of cases.

and the turnover of population, which reduced the average proportion of whites in the consolidation tracts from 73 per cent in 1950 to 37 per cent in 1940 and raised the non-white proportion from 27 to 63 per cent. Thus, both at a relatively early stage in the succession process and at a much later stage, the incoming population showed a significant tendency to be areally differentiated in the same manner as the population being superseded.

Analyses like the one just illustrated were carried out for five census-tract characteristics for the consolidation tracts in 1950 and 1940. Seven additional characteristics could be studied for 1950 only. The analysis was extended to the early-consolidation and invasion tracts, using data on all twelve characteristics in 1950. Tracts in these two stages did not, of course, meet the criterion of "mixed" populations in 1940, and, anyway, separate data for whites and non-whites in these tracts are not available for that year. Table 67 summarizes the regression analysis for the three sets of tracts.

Considering, first, the five characteristics for which both 1950 and 1940 regressions are available, it is possible to make certain summary statements: (1) In both years the five correlations were all positive. (2) The correlations for 1950 were either substantially the same as those for 1940, or else higher. Therefore, the progress of succession did not reduce the tendency for white and non-white characteristics to vary together on an area-by-area basis. (3) The means for non-white and white characteristics changed together over the decade. The percentages of crowding, persons with at least some high-school education, and homeownership, and the average rent went up for non-whites as for whites, while the percentage unemployed declined for both groups. (4) The difference between non-white and white means was in the same direction in both years for four characteristics, the exceptional characteristic being rent. However, the magnitude of the difference was reduced for two characteristics (unemployment and homeownership) but increased for three (crowding, education, and rent). Hence no general statement can be made to the effect that whites and non-whites became more (or less) alike during the ten-year period.

On the whole, one may perhaps conclude, the continuation of the

succession process in the consolidation tracts did not greatly alter
the comparison between whites and non-whites residing in them, the
most significant exception to this generalization being the reversal
of the sign of the difference between the two groups in average rent.
This is not to deny that changes occurred which are, in part, attributable to succession. But these changes were not unique to the non-
white population; rather, they tended to affect the characteristics
of both groups.

Disregarding the 1940 data in Table 67, there are three sets
of twelve regressions available for summary and comparison. The
twelve characteristics seem to fall into fairly clearly demarcated
groups on the basis of the magnitudes of the correlation coefficients.
The two variables with clearly the highest correlations are crowding and substandard dwelling units; a third variable with comparatively high correlations is homeownership. Now the correlations for
all three of these variables reflect the physical aspects of housing
in an area. This is evident with respect to substandard units, which
refers to the proportion of units lacking a private bath or in a dilapidated structure (or both). Crowding, likewise, is a physical concept,
the ratio of persons to rooms. Homeownership, per se, is a socioeconomic relationship of persons to real property, but variations in
homeownership by area apparently are strongly influenced by differences among areas in the distribution of units by type of structure,
essentially a physical concept. This is inferred from the fact that
the correlations of .6-.9 between white and non-white homeownership drop to .1-.3 when homeownership is standardized for type of
structure. The consistent appearance of moderate to high correlations between white and non-white values of these three variables,
then, suggests that racial groups respond similarly to the physical
characteristics of areas. This is not to overlook the existence of
differences by race within areas: crowding and occupancy of substandard units are much higher for non-whites than for whites in
all three sets of tracts, and there are differences by race in the percentage of homeowners, though not consistent as to direction among
the three sets of tracts. Nonetheless, the data strongly suggest the
conclusion that factors making for relatively high levels of crowding,

substandard units, and homeownership for whites work in about the same way for non-whites.[8]

A fourth variable, rent, shows correlations that are moderately high, .5-.7, with some consistency. One of the major determinants of rent is surely the size and quality of dwelling units. Thus non-whites tend to respond like whites to the physical aspects of housing in regard to their expenditures for housing, as well as with respect to their acquisition of property. Again, there are differences by race in the average levels of rent, and these are, significantly, in the opposite direction from what would be predicted on the basis of a crude indicator of quality. Although non-whites in these three sets of tracts occupied much the higher proportions of substandard units, they paid higher rents, on the average, than whites. It may be, however, that they did occupy somewhat larger units than whites. But, irrespective of these kinds of differences, it is true that white and non-white rents vary together to a more than negligible degree.

Inasmuch as there is an economic selection of the population on the basis of rents paid that operates similarly for whites and non-whites—apparently, via the physical aspects of housing—one would expect other aspects of what is conventionally termed "socioeconomic status" likewise to show similar patterns of areal differentiation for whites and non-whites. Four such characteristics are represented in ·Table 67—education, unemployment, white-collar employment, and family income. The correlations between white and non-white values

---

8. Some caution is required in interpreting the high correlation for percentage of substandard units. One component of this concept, dilapidation of structure, is strictly a matter of judgment on the part of the semiskilled census enumerators who worked with fairly concrete, but in part subjective, criteria of what constitutes dilapidation. Since each enumeration district was covered by one enumerator and census tracts are combinations of enumeration districts, variation in the proportion of dilapidated units among census tracts represents, in some unknown degree, simply variation among enumerators. It may well be, however, that the inflation of the correlation resulting from the systematic error of enumerator bias is compensated for by the attenuation of the correlation resulting from random unreliability of enumerators' estimates. In any case, these remarks apply only to the dilapidation aspect of substandard housing and not to the aspect of possession of specified plumbing facilities, which is susceptible of rather objective determination.

of these variables range over the extremes from -.02 for white-collar employment in the consolidation tracts to .82 for family income in the invasion tracts, with the remaining ten correlations falling between .25 and .7. Except for education, the correlations are somewhat erratic in the variation of their magnitudes among the three sets of tracts; the education variable, unlike the others, was standardized for age, and one source of variability was thus removed. Despite this somewhat mixed picture, it seems justifiable to conclude that the white-non-white correlations on the socioeconomic status variables run somewhat lower than the correlations on variables that reflect fairly directly the variations among areas in physical aspects of living conditions. There is, nonetheless, a discernible tendency for socioeconomic selection by area for non-whites to resemble that for whites, although, to be sure, whites have uniformly the higher average levels of socioeconomic status.

There remain three variables for discussion—the percentage of married couples living in households other than their own, the percentage of married females whose spouses were not living with them, and the percentage of all persons (except inmates of institutions) fourteen years old and over living as unrelated individuals rather than as members of families. The correlations for the first two characteristics are essentially zero. Two of the correlations for unrelated individuals are .5, the third (for the invasion tracts) being about .2, a negligible value in this situation. No doubt one reason for these low correlations is that the tract values from which they were computed were often based on small numbers of cases, especially since data on married couples were reported for only a 20 per cent sample. However, this factor is apparently of limited importance, in view of the following check. All the tracts in the three sets were aggregated into their respective community areas, and the correlations were recomputed for these 25 areas; a value of .23 was obtained for married couples without own household, and .17 for married females with spouse absent. The conclusion seems justifiable, therefore, that there is no important association between the white and the non-white patterns of areal differentiation of these two aspects of family structure. One cannot draw

276 / The Negro Population of Chicago

so strong a conclusion concerning the percentage of unrelated individuals, in view of the lack of consistency in the magnitude of the
correlation among the three sets of tracts; but certainly the relationship, if any, is not a pronounced one.

The difference between whites and non-whites in the average
level of the proportion of married couples without own household and
the proportion of married females with spouse absent is in the same
direction in the racially mixed tracts as in the city as a whole. However, a significant reversal occurs with respect to the percentage of
unrelated individuals. In Chicago in 1950, 18.8 per cent of the non-
white population fourteen years old and over were not living with
family members, as compared with 11.4 per cent of the white population. But in the aggregate of the consolidation, early-consolidation,
and invasion tracts the percentages were 16.3 for non-whites and
20.5 for whites. As Table 67 indicates, the latter difference occurs
in each of the three sets of tracts consistently.

The evidence seemingly warrants the conclusion that indicators
of family characteristics of whites and non-whites do not vary together on an area-by-area basis to any substantial degree, although
both groups manifest pronounced areal differentiation with respect
to these characteristics. The nature of the selective processes involved in this situation can only be surmised. The high proportion
of unrelated individuals among whites living in mixed tracts suggests
that in areas experiencing succession the outgoing white population
is selective of families, leaving behind disproportionate numbers of
unrelated individuals. The lack of relationship between the white and
non-white proportions of females with spouse absent may reflect a
basic difference in patterns of family organization. Among both white
and non-white females there is an apparent overreporting of the
number of females married, presumably accounted for in part by
unwed mothers reporting themselves as married with spouse absent.
Moreover, it is likely that separation rather than divorce is a more
common pattern of marital dissolution among non-whites than among
whites. Since the factors determining the status of married persons
with spouse absent appear to be somewhat different for non-whites
than for whites, no doubt the bases for areal differentiation of this

characteristic are different as well. In regard to the proportions of
married couples without own household, it seems likely that the
forms of doubling up represented by this condition are somewhat different for whites and non-whites. Although the information is not
available for Chicago, 1950 Census data for the urban and rural-non-
farm areas of the United States show that 57 per cent of the white
married couples without own household were living with parents of
one of the spouses, as compared with only 31 per cent of the corresponding non-white couples. On the other hand, 47 per cent of the
non-white couples without own household were either lodgers or
residents of quasi-households, as compared with only 20 per cent
of the white couples. Among whites, then, this condition appears to
represent a type of living arrangement that is entered into on the
basis of family relationships, whereas among non-whites it more
often reflects simply the unavailability of suitable separate dwelling
units for married couples' occupancy. This reasoning can, of course,
be applied to the situation in mixed residential tracts only by hypothesis. But at least the facts are consistent with the supposition
that the determinants of areal differentiation in frequency of married couples without own household are not entirely similar for
whites and non-whites.

The upshot of the analysis in this section seems to be somewhat
as follows. In the displacement of one population by another that
constitutes the process of residential succession, the incoming population does not distribute itself at random among the various areas
in which succession occurs. Rather the succession process is a selective one, in that the incoming population tends to be differentiated
according to residential areas, in many respects, in much the same
way as the population being displaced. This tendency is most pronounced with respect to the mode of adjustment to the physical char-
acteristics.of the available living space; it is somewhat attenuated
with respect to socioeconomic characteristics that are associated
somewhat indirectly with these adjustments; and it is scarcely in
evidence at all for characteristics reflecting family structure and
household arrangements, whose determinants appear to differ by
race.

Spatial Patterns of Negro Residential Areas

Areal differentiation of the Negro community in Chicago with respect to eleven characteristics is shown graphically by the series of
eleven maps, Figures 24-34. The 162 census tracts of the city in
which non-whites numbered 250 or more in 1950 and in which the non-
white population was predominantly Negro in 1950 make up the universe, excluding tracts whose non-white population lived in institutions. Tracts were arrayed from high to low with respect to each
characteristic and then divided into sextiles for mapping purposes.
Figure 23 is a reference map included to facilitate identification of
particular areas. It will be noted that the areas of Negro residence
which are spatially separated from the main concentrations of Negro
population are shown as insets on the map rather than in their actual
positions. In two cases—Morgan Park and South Chicago—the names
given these areas are those of the community areas in which they
are located. The term "Lilydale" is the name frequently used for the
Negro settlement, the bulk of which is in community area 49, but
which extends slightly into community area 44. The term "Altgeld
Gardens" refers to the public housing project in which live the bulk
of the Negroes residing in community area 54. In the case of the out-
lying areas the map is drawn to show, approximately, the actual area
of Negro settlement rather than to follow tract boundaries altogether.
It was not feasible to adjust all boundaries within the major area of
concentration in this fashion. However, some boundaries were re-
drawn in order not to show Washington Park (community area 40)
and Douglas Park (community area 29) as residential areas, and to
exclude portions of tracts 126 and 517 having no Negro residents in
1950.

Cursory inspection of the maps suggests that, on the average,
the ranking of tracts varies systematically with their location in
terms of distance and direction from the city's center. A somewhat
more systematic analysis of these differences in rank by distance
and direction from the city's core is summarized in Table 68. The
162 census tracts were divided into ten groups on the basis of their
location with respect to the center of Chicago. Within each of the ten
groups, census tracts falling in the upper three sextiles, or above

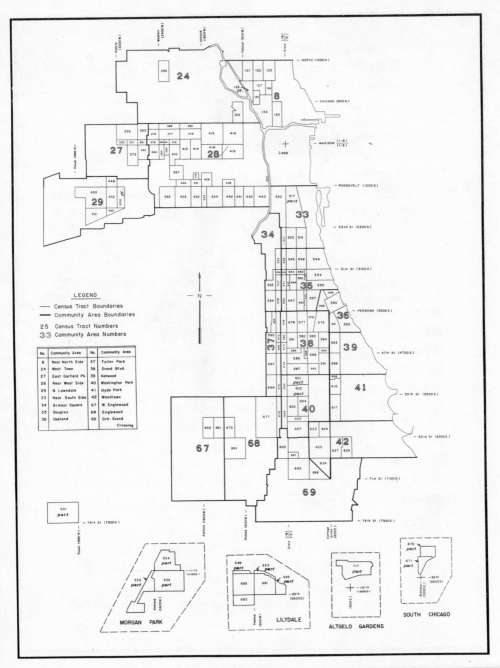

Fig. 23.—Negro Residential Areas, Chicago, 1950

279

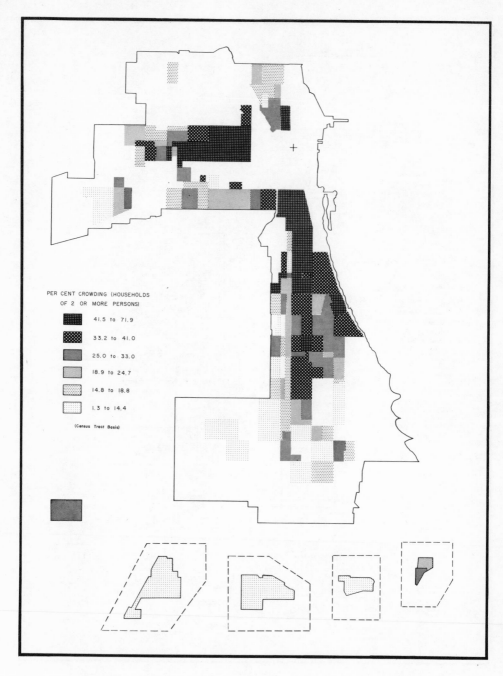

Fig. 24.—Crowding, Non-white Population, Chicago, 1950

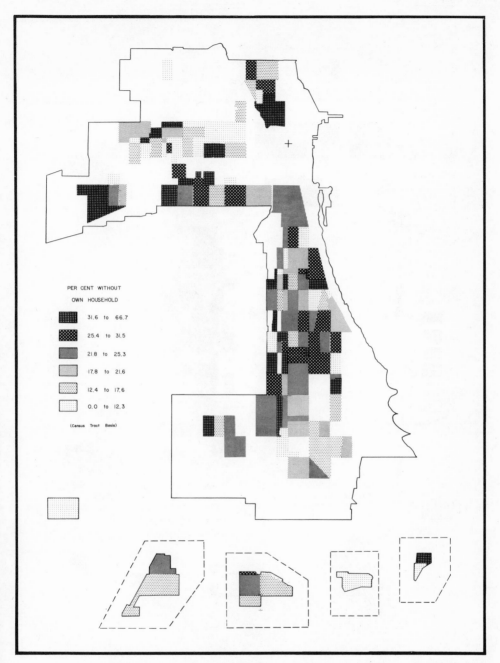

PER CENT WITHOUT

OWN HOUSEHOLD

31.6 to 66.7

25.4 to 31.5

21.8 to 25.3

17.8 to 21.6

12.4 to 17.6

0.0 to 12.3

(Census Tract Basis)

Fig. 25.—Married Couples without Own Household, Non-white Population, Chicago, 1950.

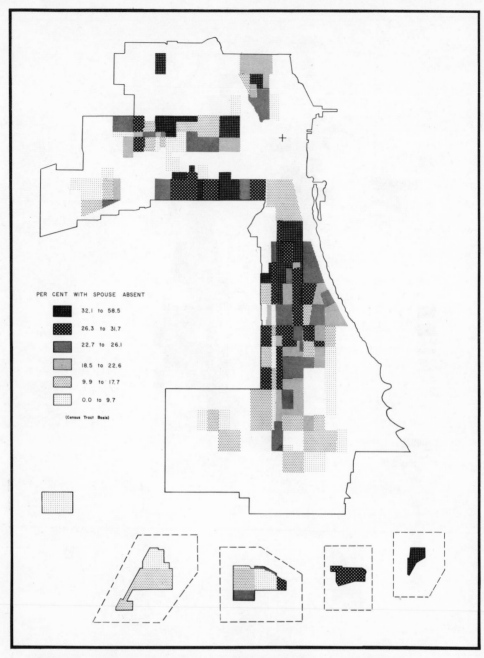

Fig. 26.—Married Females with Spouse Absent, Non-white Population, Chicago, 1950.

282

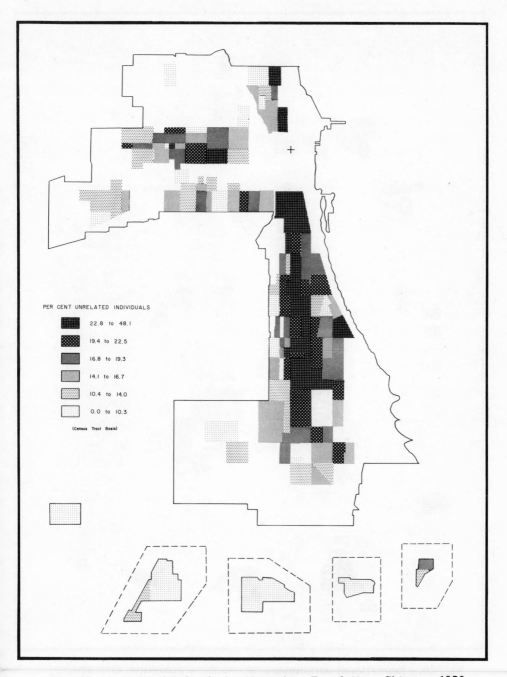

PER CENT UNRELATED INDIVIDUALS

22.8 to 48.1
19.4 to 22.5
16.8 to 19.3
14.1 to 16.7
10.4 to 14.0
0.0 to 10.3

(Census Tract Basis)

Fig. 27.—Unrelated Individuals, Non-white Population, Chicago, 1950

283

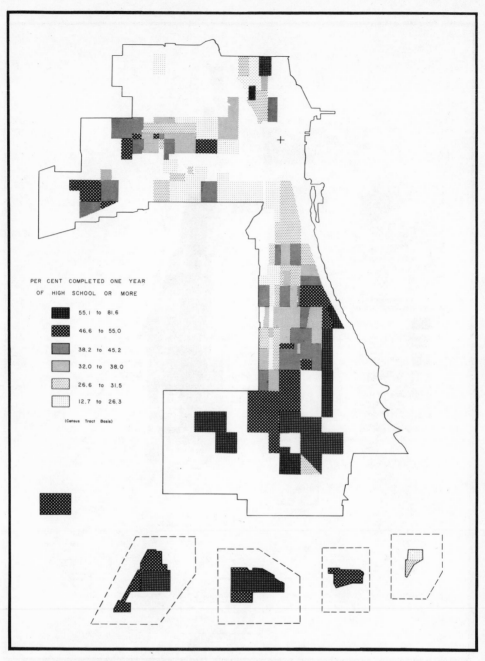

Fig. 28.—Educational Attainment, Non-white Population, Chicago, 1950.

284

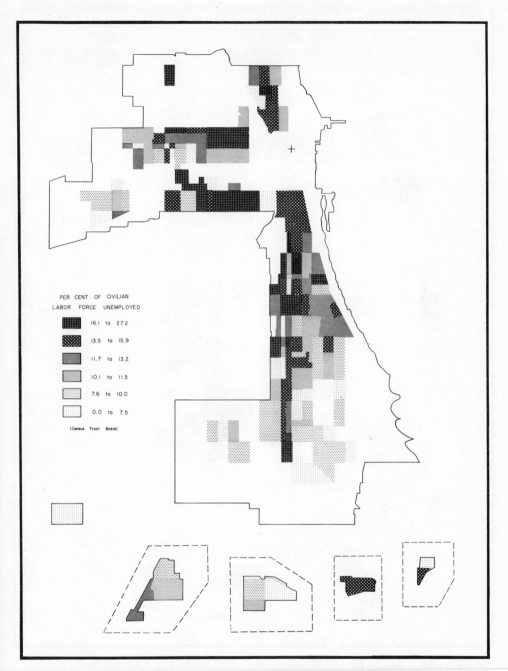

PER CENT OF CIVILIAN
LABOR FORCE UNEMPLOYED

16.1 to 27.2

13.5 to 15.9

11.7 to 13.2

10.1 to 11.5

7.6 to 10.0

0.0 to 7.5

(Census Tract Basis)

Fig. 29.—Unemployment, Non-white Males, Chicago, 1950

285

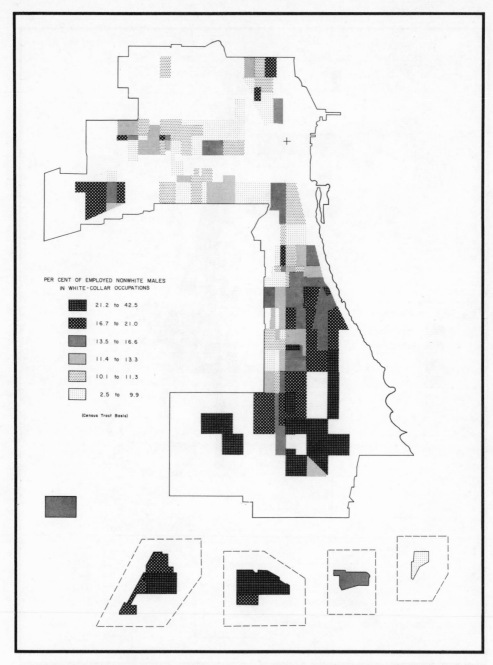

Fig. 30.—White-Collar Employment, Non-white Male Population, Chicago, 1950

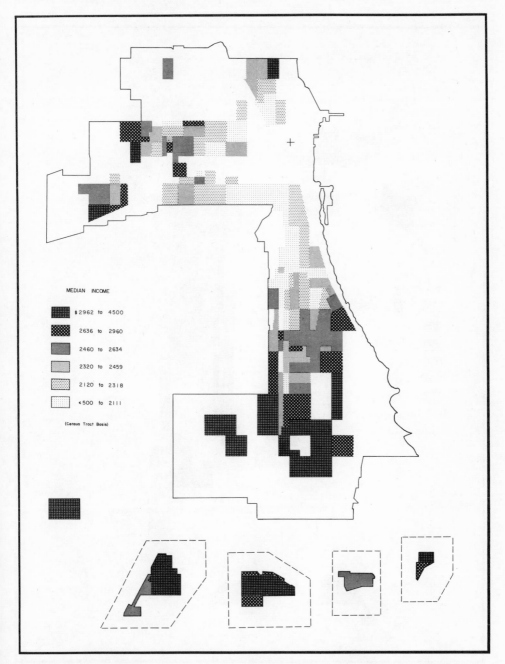

MEDIAN INCOME

$2962 to 4500

2636 to 2960

2460 to 2634

2320 to 2459

2120 to 2318

<500 to 2111

(Census Tract Basis)

Fig. 31.—Median Family Income in 1949, Non-white Population, Chicago, 1950.

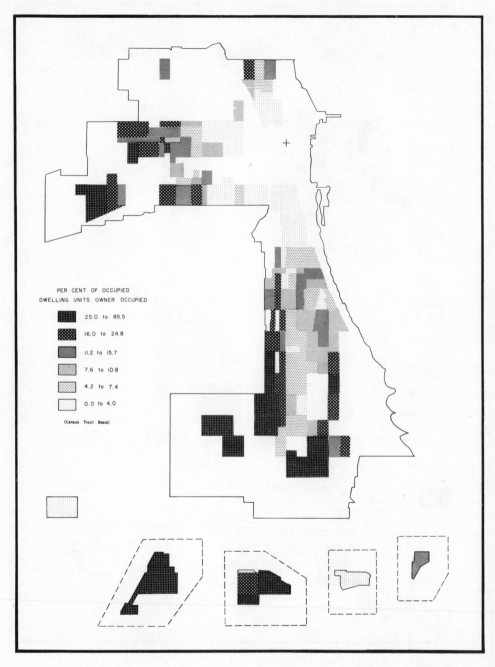

Fig. 32.—Homeownership, Non-white Population, Chicago, 1950

288

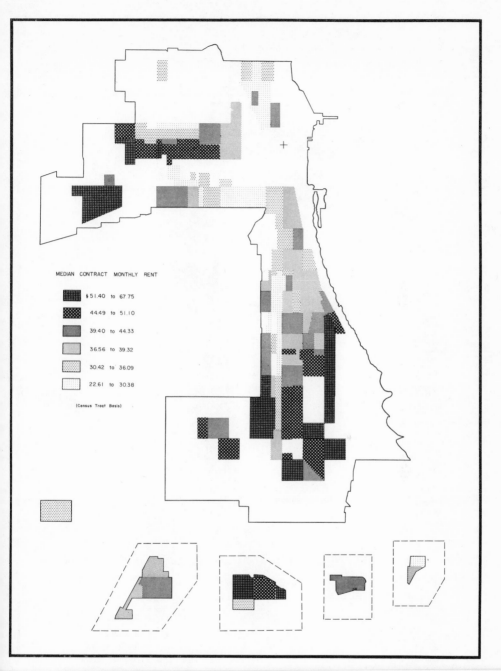

Fig. 33.—Median Rent, Non-white Population, Chicago, 1950

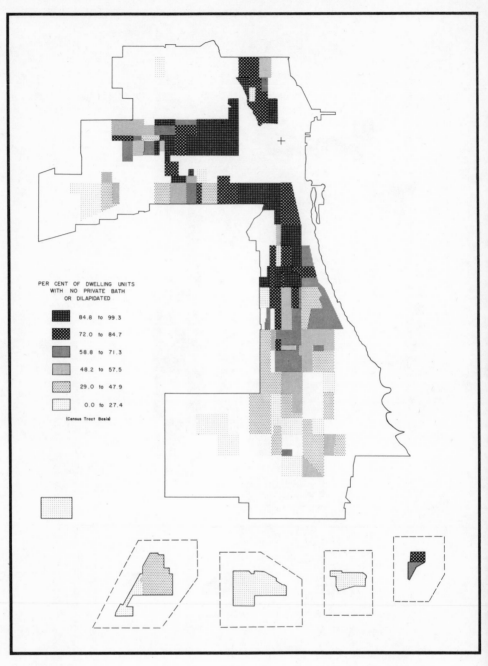

PER CENT OF DWELLING UNITS
WITH NO PRIVATE BATH
OR DILAPIDATED

84.8 to 99.3

72.0 to 84.7

58.8 to 71.3

48.2 to 57.5

29.0 to 47.9

0.0 to 27.4

(Census Tract Basis)

Fig. 34.—Substandard Housing, Non-white Dwelling Units, Chicago, 1950.

290

Table 68.—Percentage of Census Tracts with Indexes above the Median Tract, for Selected Characteristics of the Non-white Population, by Area, 1950

(See Text for Method of Computation)

Characteristic*	All Tracts	Direction and Distance (in Miles)									
		North	West			South					
		0-2	1-2	2-3	3-5	1-3	3-4	4-5	5-6	6-8	9-15
Crowding	50	22	80	62	33	60	78	67	47	18	15
Married couples w/o own household	51	56	30	48	39	60	39	81	87	36	31
Married females, spouse absent	50	22	70	62	39	80	78	57	40	9	46
Per cent unrelated individuals	50	33	40	38	22	90	74	76	73	36	8
Education (observed)	50	33	10	19	67	20	35	38	73	95	85
Unemployment	49	56	60	67	39	80	83	52	27	14	23
White-collar employment . .	50	33	10	10	33	30	52	52	73	95	85
Family income	50	11	0	43	61	0	9	67	67	95	100
Homeownership (observed) . .	50	22	0	48	100	10	30	43	53	73	77
Rent	50	22	20	43	78	10	17	52	73	91	54
Substandard dwelling units . .	50	78	100	71	28	80	83	52	20	5	15
Number of census tracts . . .	162	9	10	21	18	10	23	21	15	22	13

*See Appendix G for complete designations of characteristics.

the median tract, were tabulated and converted to a percentage of all tracts in the group.

The presence or absence of a zonal gradient with respect to the eleven characteristics can be ascertained for the 49 West Side tracts, located at distances of 1-5 miles from the city's center, and the 104 South Side tracts, located at distances of 1-15 miles from the center of Chicago. In general, the socioeconomic status of the population increases and the quality of housing improves as distance from the center increases, whereas congestion and family disorganization decrease with distance from the center.

The majority of exceptions to a zonal-gradient pattern occur in the outer zones of the South Side. The percentage of females with spouse absent, the unemployment rate, and the percentage of substandard dwelling units are higher in the zone 9-15 miles from the city's center than in the zone 6-8 miles from the center, whereas the educational level, the percentage of white-collar employment, and the rent level are lower. These differences are, of course, in the opposite direction from those anticipated on the basis of the zonal gradients. The five spatially distinct Negro settlements in the zone 9-15 miles from the center are not contiguous to the major Negro residential area; three of these peripheral settlements were established before 1920, and the other two were established between 1940 and 1950 through the construction of publicly financed housing projects. Although these isolated, peripheral Negro settlements do not conform perfectly with the zonal pattern existing within the major Negro settlement, differences between these peripheral settlements and the centralized parts of the major Negro residential area are in the direction expected on the basis of the zonal-gradient pattern.

One characteristic—the percentage of married couples without own household—manifests no consistent relationship to distance from the city's center. It may well be that the living arrangements of married couples without own household do vary with distance from the city's center, e.g., the percentage living with their parents or other relatives, the percentage living as lodgers, or the percentage residing in quasi-households; but this cannot be ascertained with the available data.

Systematic comparisons among North Side, West Side, and South Side tracts located at the same distance from the city's center are impossible, for all North Side tracts are located within 2 miles of the city's center, and South Side tracts are located at distances of 1-15 miles from the center of Chicago. But among highly centralized tracts, i.e., tracts located within 2 miles of the city's center, the North Side group of tracts ranks more favorably with respect to the selected indicators of socioeconomic status, quality of housing, and congestion than does the West Side group. And at distances of 3-5 miles from the center of Chicago, the West Side group of tracts ranks more favorably with respect to these indicators than does the South Side group.

The cartographic analysis indicates that areas within the Negro community in Chicago differ substantially with respect to one another in terms of socioeconomic status. The extent of this differentiation can be indicated quantitatively by measuring the degree of dissimilarity in residential distribution among major occupation groups comprising the Negro labor force.

The residential dissimilarity between pairs of occupation groups or the difference between the areal distributions of their residences is measured by the index of dissimilarity.[9] The index varies from 0, no residential dissimilarity, to 100, complete residential dissimilarity.

Indexes of dissimilarity in residential distribution among occupation groups in the Negro community are given in Table 69. The major occupation groups are listed in approximate order of their socioeconomic status. Few data are available which indicate the relative socioeconomic status of the major occupation groups in the Negro community. One indicator, educational level, is shown on p. 294 for non-white males twenty-five years old and over in each major occupation group residing in the North and West in 1950:

---

9.   For discussion of the computation and interpretation of the index see Otis Dudley Duncan and Beverly Duncan, "Residential Distribution and Occupational Stratification," American Journal of Sociology, LX (March, 1955), 493-503.

Major Occupation Group	Per Cent Having Some	
	High-School Education	College Education
Professional, technical, and kindred workers...................	86	62
Managers, officials, and proprietors, except farm.................	49	16
Clerical and kindred workers.........	74	22
Sales workers....................	62	20
Craftsmen, foremen, and kindred workers...................	45	7
Operatives and kindred workers.......	39	4
Service workers, except private household.......................	40	6
Laborers, except farm and mine.......	27	2

The educational level suggests only two reversals in order; managerial workers are less well educated than clerical and sales workers, and operatives are less well educated than service workers other than private household. Cross-tabulations of income by occupation for non-white males are not available; however, income by detailed occupation group is available for all employed males in the Chicago Standard Metropolitan Area, and the distribution of employed Negro males in the Chicago Standard Metropolitan Area by detailed occupation is available. On the basis of these two tabulations, it seems fairly certain that, in terms of income, managerial workers rank above clerical and sales workers and that service workers rank below operatives.

If it is assumed that the occupation groups are ordered in terms of socioeconomic status, then if, in fact, residential dissimilarity between groups increases as their difference in socioeconomic status increases, the indexes would increase reading up or to the right from any point on the diagonal in Table 69. In general this pattern is observed; dissimilarity in residential distribution between occupation groups in the Negro community does increase as their difference in socioeconomic status increases. Most exceptions to this pattern involve the dissimilarity between the residential distribution of service workers and those of workers in other occupation groups. Service

Table 69.—Indexes of Dissimilarity in Residential Distribution among Major Occupation Groups, for Non-white and White Employed Males in the City of Chicago, 1950

(Above Diagonal, Non-whites Based on Census Tracts; below Diagonal, Whites Based on Community Areas)

Major Occupation Group*	Major Occupation Group*							
	Prof., Tech., Kindred	Mgrs., Offs., Props.	Clerical, Kindred	Sales Wkrs.	Crafts-men, Foremen, Kindred	Operatives, Kindred	Service, except Private Household	Laborers, except Farm and Mine
Professional, technical, and kindred workers	...	19	15	22	23	27	22	33
Managers, officials, and proprietors, except farm	8	...	16	16	16	20	16	26
Clerical and kindred workers	21	20	...	16	15	19	15	26
Sales workers	9	6	21	...	15	17	13	23
Craftsmen, foremen, and kindred workers	28	27	10	29	...	9	13	16
Operatives and kindred workers	35	32	16	34	13	...	14	12
Service workers, except private household	24	23	12	25	19	20	...	20
Laborers, except farm and mine	42	40	25	42	24	16	24	...

*Does not include farmers and farm managers, private household workers, farm laborers, and occupation not reported.

workers, excluding private household workers, are most similar
to sales workers and to craftsmen in terms of their residential distribution, whereas they probably resemble operatives and laborers
more closely in terms of their socioeconomic status. In so far as 51
per cent of the non-white male service workers, other than private
household workers, in the Chicago Standard Metropolitan Area in
1950 were employed as janitors, sextons, or porters, a fair proportion of whom probably lived at their places of work, their residential
distribution reflects in part their workplace distribution.

Residential dissimilarity between occupation groups in the Negro
community in Chicago is compared with residential dissimilarity between occupation groups in the white community in Chicago in Table
69. The indexes of dissimilarity below the diagonal refer to white
employed males and are based on community areas, a rather gross
area unit; the indexes above the diagonal refer to non-white employed
males and are based on census tracts. Indexes of dissimilarity between occupation groups in the Negro community based on community areas are not shown; using the community area rather than the
census tract as the analytical unit lowers the value of the indexes,
but there is very little change in the relative positions of the occupation groups, as indicated by the correlation of .95 between indexes
of residential dissimilarity for non-whites based on community areas
and those for non-whites based on census tracts.

However, the indexes of residential dissimilarity in the Negro
community and the indexes of residential dissimilarity in the white
community are by no means perfectly correlated—a correlation coefficient of .59 is observed. Within the Negro community, the residential distribution of sales workers is most similar to the residential distributions of craftsmen and service workers, whereas the
residential distribution of sales workers in the white community is
most similar to the residential distributions of professional and
managerial workers. The correlation between the indexes of dissimilarity between sales workers and each of the other seven major occupation groups in the Negro community and the indexes in the white
community is only .14; the correlation between the indexes of dissimilarity between occupation groups other than sales workers in

the Negro community and the indexes in the white community is .76.

The composition of the sales group by detailed occupation differs markedly in the Negro and white communities. As compared
with whites, disproportionate numbers of the Negro male sales
workers are employed in relatively low-paying specific occupations,
especially as salesmen and sales clerks in the retail-trade industry.
Distributions of white and Negro male sales workers by detailed occupation and the median income of all male sales workers by detailed
occupation are shown below for the Chicago Standard Metropolitan
Area in 1950:

	White	Negro	Median 1949 Income for All Workers
All male sales workers	100.0	100.0	$3,698
Insurance agents and brokers .	11.7	17.1	4,130
Real estate agents and bro-			
kers	4.2	5.9	4,364
Other specified sales work-			
ers . . :	5.6	9.5	2,608
Salesmen and sales clerks:			
Manufacturing.	20.5	5.4	4,543
Wholesale trade	16.6	6.0	4,249
Retail trade	37.9	53.7	3,096
Other industries	3.5	2.4	4,000

One might speculate that salesmen and sales clerks in the retail-trade industry, who are engaged in serving the population directly, are identified with and do resemble other groups of service
workers, whereas salesmen and sales clerks in the manufacturing
and wholesale-trade industries are identified with and do resemble
managerial workers in these industries. In any case, there is strong
reason to suspect that differences in the composition of the sales
group in the Negro and white communities are related to differences
in their patterns of residential location.

On the basis of the foregoing analysis, it appears that the pattern
of differentiation with respect to socioeconomic status in the Negro
community resembles the pattern of differentiation in the white com-

munity. The Negro is segregated residentially from the white population in Chicago; but within both the Negro and the white community, high-status groups tend to share residential areas and to be residentially segregated from low-status groups. Apparently, the selective forces which produce differentiation of residential areas in the urban community operate in somewhat the same way upon the Negro and the white population. This is also in line with the finding that patterns of interarea differentiation with respect to physical characteristics of the area and social and economic characteristics of the residents tend to be maintained under the impact of succession from white to Negro occupancy.

Supplementary Tables on Population Changes

A-1.—Population by Race and Nativity, for the Chicago Standard
Metropolitan Area, 1900-1950

A-2.—Population by Color, for the City of Chicago, Chicago Metropolitan District, and Chicago Standard Metropolitan Area,
1950 and 1940

A-3.—Estimated Net Migration of White and Negro Population to the
City of Chicago, by Decade, 1910-50

A-4.—Estimated Net Migration per 100 Survivors, by Race and Age,
for the City of Chicago, by Decade, 1910-50

A-5.—Median Number of School Years Completed, for the Population
Twenty-five Years Old and Over, by Age and Color, for the
City of Chicago, 1950 and 1940

A-6.—Employment Status of Persons Fourteen Years Old and Over,
by Age, Sex, and Color, for the City of Chicago, 1950 and 1940

A-7.—Estimated Rate of Net In-movement, 1940-50, per 100 Survivors of the 1940 Population, by Age, for the Negro Population
in Census Tracts Grouped by Stage of Succession and Distance
from Center of City of Chicago

Table A-1.—Population by Race and Nativity, for the Chicago Standard Metropolitan Area, 1900-1950

Area and Year	Total Population	Race and Nativity			
		Native White	Foreign-born White	Negro	Other Races
Standard Metropolitan Area:					
1950	5,495,364	4,185,475	704,651	586,598	18,640
1940	4,825,527	3,625,010	865,652	329,726	5,139
1930*	4,675,877	3,297,416	1,094,074	278,333	6,054
1920	3,521,789	2,398,789	994,076	125,557	3,367
1910	2,752,820	1,763,465	937,336	49,676	2,343
1900	2,092,883	1,370,219	687,186	34,085	1,393
City of Chicago:					
1950	3,620,962	2,585,467	526,058	492,265	17,172
1940	3,396,808	2,441,859	672,705	277,731	4,513
1930*	3,376,438	2,281,316	855,777	233,903	5,442
1920	2,701,705	1,783,687	805,482	109,458	3,078
1910	2,185,283	1,357,840	781,217	44,103	2,123
1900	1,698,575	1,081,720	585,420	30,150	1,285
Outside Chicago:					
1950	1,874,402	1,600,008	178,593	94,333	1,468
1940	1,428,719	1,183,151	192,947	51,995	626
1930*	1,299,439	1,016,100	238,297	44,430	612
1920	820,084	615,102	188,594	16,099	289
1910	567,537	405,625	156,119	5,573	220
1900	394,308	288,499	101,766	3,935	108

*1930 figures revised to classify Mexicans as white, in conformity with procedures for other censuses.

Table A-2.—Population by Color, for the City of Chicago, Chicago Metropolitan District, and Chicago Standard Metropolitan Area, 1950 and 1940

Area and Year	Number			Per Cent		
	Total	White	Non-white	Total	White	Non-white
1950:						
City of Chicago..	3,620,962	3,111,525	509,437	100.0	85.9	14.1
Metropolitan District	5,072,401	4,476,399	596,002	100.0	88.3	11.7
Standard Metropolitan Area ..	5,495,364	4,890,126	605,238	100.0	89.0	11.0
1940:						
City of Chicago..	3,396,808	3,114,564	282,244	100.0	91.7	8.3
Metropolitan District.........	4,499,126	4,169,969	329,157	100.0	92.7	7.3
Standard Metropolitan Area ..	4,825,527	4,490,662	334,865	100.0	93.1	6.9

<u>Table A-3.</u>—Estimated Net Migration of White and Negro Population to the City of Chicago, by Decade, 1910-50

Race, Sex, and Decade	Population, Beginning of Decade (In 1,000's)	Estimated Survivors, End of Decade (In 1,000's)	Population Ten Years Old and Over, End of Decade (In 1,000's)	Estimated Net Migration* (In 1,000's)	Net Migration per 100 Survivors*
White, both sexes:					
1940-50	3,115	2,843	2,621	-221	- 8
1930-40	3,133	2,864	2,732	-132	- 5
1920-30	2,585	2,392	2,639	247	10
1910-20	2,131	1,894	2,067	173	9
White, male:					
1940-50	1,547	1,379	1,283	- 96	- 7
1930-40	1,588	1,441	1,352	- 90	- 6
1920-30	1,309	1,207	1,338	131	11
1910-20	1,095	971	1,048	77	8
White, female:					
1940-50	1,567	1,464	1,338	-126	- 9
1930-40	1,545	1,422	1,380	- 42	- 3
1920-30	1,276	1,185	1,301	116	10
1910-20	1,036	923	1,019	96	10
Negro, both sexes:					
1940-50	278	248	402	154	62
1930-40	234	201	238	37	18
1920-30	109	95	199	104	109
1910-20	44	35	97	61	174
Negro, male:					
1940-50	131	115	189	74	64
1930-40	115	99	111	12	12
1920-30	56	49	98	49	100
1910-20	22	19	50	31	164
Negro, female:					
1940-50	147	133	213	80	60
1930-40	118	102	127	25	24
1920-30	53	46	101	54	118
1910-20	21	17	47	31	185

*Minus sign denotes net out-migration; computed before rounding population to thousands.

Table A-4.—Estimated Net Migration per 100 Survivors, by Race and Age, for the City of Chicago, by Decade, 1910-50

Race and Age (Years)		Decade			
Beginning of Decade	End of Decade	1940-50	1930-40	1920-30	1910-20
White, total....		- 8	- 5	10	9
0-4 ...	10-14..	- 15	- 7	0	0
5-9 ...	15-19..	- 9	0	10	8
10-14...	20-24..	6	11	41	33
15-19...	25-29..	9	11	56	46
20-24...	30-34..	- 7	- 5	27	17
25-29...	35-39..	- 13	-13	7	3
30-34...	40-44..	- 12	-10	2	0
35-39...	45-49..	- 10	- 9	- 3	- 2
40-44...	50-54..	- 9	- 9	- 6	- 5
45 and over ..	55 and over .	- 11	-10	- 10	- 7
Negro, total....		62	18	109	174
0-4 ...	10-14..	54	14	101	153
5-9 ...	15-19..	52	25	152	273
10-14...	20-24..	119	54	314	552
15-19...	25-29..	163	85	370	596
20-24...	30-34..	137	34	169	304
25-29...	35-39..	75	4	78	146
30-34...	40-44..	43	0	42	86
35-39...	45-49..	26	- 2	33	58
40-44...	50-54..	19	- 1	10	29
45 and over ..	55 and over .	17	14	29	38

Table A-5.—Median Number of School Years Completed, for the Population Twenty-five Years Old and Over, by Age and Color, for the City of Chicago, 1950 and 1940

Age (Years)	1950*		1940	
	White	Non-white	White	Non-white
Total, 25 and over .	10.2	8.8	8.7	8.3
25-29...........	12.4	11.0	10.8	9.4
30-34...........	12.1	10.1	10.2	8.7
35-39...........	11.0	9.0	9.0	8.4
40-44...........	10.5	8.6	8.7	8.1
45-54...........	8.9	8.2	8.4	7.8
55-64...........	8.4	7.5	8.3	6.7
65-74........:....	8.3	6.5	8.3	5.3
75 and over	8.3	5.3	8.2	3.2

*Statistics based on 20 per cent sample.

Table A-6.—Employment Status of Persons Fourteen Years Old and Over, by Age, Sex, and Color, for the City of Chicago, 1950 and 1940

| Sex and Age (Years) | Per Cent in Labor Force | | | | Per Cent of Labor Force Unemployed | | | |
| | 1950* | | 1940 | | 1950*† | | 1940† | |
	White	Non-white	White	Non-white	White	Non-white	White	Non-white
MALE								
Total, 14 and over	82.4	79.1	82.4	78.1	4.1	11.3	14.4	35.2
14-15	8.5	3.7	1.6	1.3	10.1	28.6	25.2	54.7
16-17	28.2	23.8	19.0	17.1	14.5	39.0	53.3	76.4
18-19	66.6	58.7	65.9	55.2	9.4	30.3	36.2	69.9
20-24	83.7	81.4	90.4	85.8	5.9	18.4	19.5	50.8
25-34	92.9	88.8	97.1	92.1	3.3	11.3	10.5	34.6
35-44	95.5	90.4	96.9	91.1	2.7	9.2	10.6	29.8
45-54	94.0	89.2	94.2	86.6	3.5	8.1	13.9	32.5
55-59	90.5	82.5	88.6	79.5	4.3	7.6	17.5	35.0
60-64	84.3	76.1	77.6	66.3	5.2	9.3	18.2	33.1
65-74	54.2	43.9	43.4	28.0	6.9	8.8	13.6	24.1
75 and over	18.2	11.6	13.9	10.1	5.0	9.4	6.9	13.8
FEMALE								
Total, 14 and over	37.2	40.6	33.3	35.7	3.3	12.6	11.1	35.0
14-15	3.2	1.4	0.6	0.6	17.6	29.4	46.0	78.6
16-17	26.1	11.2	16.6	9.8	11.2	52.6	49.2	76.3
18-19	67.9	31.7	64.0	33.1	4.0	31.6	27.0	67.4
20-24	59.6	45.6	65.1	45.7	3.1	18.3	11.9	46.9
25-34	40.0	48.7	42.6	46.5	2.7	12.2	7.2	34.1
35-44	42.5	51.0	32.4	42.0	2.6	10.1	7.7	30.2
45-54	40.1	42.3	24.6	33.4	3.2	9.2	8.4	28.4
55-59	32.0	32.0	18.6	24.4	3.7	6.8	9.5	25.6
60-64	25.4	23.5	15.0	16.8	4.6	6.8	9.2	22.2
65-74	12.4	10.0	6.8	5.0	5.2	6.9	7.1	17.3
75 and over	3.0	1.2	2.0	1.2	2.4	0.0	5.2	5.9

*Statistics based on 20 per cent sample.

†Based on civilian labor force.

‡Unemployed includes persons on public emergency work and persons seeking work.

Table A-7.—Estimated Rate of Net In-movement, 1940-50, per 100 Survivors of the 1940 Population, by Age, for the Negro Population in Census Tracts Grouped by Stage of Succession and Distance from Center of City of Chicago

Age (Years)		City of Chicago	Piling-up Tracts			Late-Consolidation Tracts			Remainder of City
1940	1950		All	Within 5 Miles of Loop	5 Miles or More from Loop	All	Within 5 Miles of Loop	5 Miles or More from Loop	
All ages .	10 and over	62	11	41	4	31	35	28	274
0-4	10-14 . . .	54	- 3	53	-19	28	40	11	243
5-9 . . .	15-19 . . .	52	3	35	- 6	22	26	17	225
10-14 . . .	20-24 . . .	119	44	71	36	49	49	50	429
15-19 . . .	25-29 . . .	163	72	104	64	85	89	81	527
20-24 . . .	30-34 . . .	137	53	119	39	82	91	73	481
25-29 . . .	35-39 . . .	75	13	57	5	52	64	42	330
30-34 . . .	40-44 . . .	43	- 1	37	- 8	22	26	19	244
35-39 . . .	45-49 . . .	26	- 7	9	-11	14	14	13	172
40-44 . . .	50-54 . . .	19	-11	- 1	-14	4	1	6	152
45 and over . .	55 and over . . .	17	- 6	4	- 9	3	1	4	115

Estimation of Net Migration

The estimates of net migration by decade, 1910-50, in chapter iii were computed by the "survival ratio" technique. As used here, the term "survival ratio" refers to the proportion of persons of a given age at one time who are still alive ten years later. If the survival ratio is known, the net migration may be calculated as a residual. For example, there were 8,679 Negro males aged twenty to twenty-four enumerated in Chicago in 1940. If the survival ratio is .9287, then (.9287) (8,679) = 8,060 Negro males aged thirty to thirty-four would still be alive in 1950. Since the 1950 enumerated population was 21,165, it follows that there must have been a net in-migration of 13,105 (i.e., 21,165 minus 8,060) Negro males of this age group. It must be noted that this net migration was undoubtedly produced by a larger total volume of in-migration, counterbalanced by some out-migration. Thus care must be exercised not to confuse net and gross migration. Moreover, it is not possible to determine the timing of migration within the decade by this method.

A major problem with this technique is to secure appropriate survival ratios. Theoretically, the most accurate survival ratios would be those determined from a suitable life table. In practice, two difficulties are involved in using life-table survival ratios. First, life tables suitable for the population may not be available. Second, survival ratios computed from life tables do not take account of certain errors known to occur in census enumeration data. For example, it is quite regularly found that the national total of persons ten to fourteen years old at a given census period is larger than the number zero to four years old at the preceding one. Immigration can be ruled out as an explanation of this finding, the

306

most reasonable explanation of which is that children under the age
of five are incompletely enumerated. Thus, although the "true" survival ratio for this age group is less than unity (as any "true" survival ratio must be), to allow for the effect of underenumeration one
must use a "survival ratio" larger than 1.0. There are other errors
of underenumeration and misreporting of age which produce analogous effects. Hence, even if "true" survival ratios were available
from life tables, it would be necessary to "correct" them for application to census-enumerated populations.

For these reasons, many demographers now prefer to use
"census survival ratios." To illustrate, the number of Negro males
aged twenty to twenty-four enumerated in the United States in 1940
was 550,193, and the number thirty to thirty-four years old enumerated in 1950 was 510,970. Hence the survival ratio was .9287 (i.e.,
510,970 divided by 550,193). In applying this survival ratio to the
Chicago population, as in the example given earlier, one makes two
assumptions: first, that the "true" survival ratio of the Chicago
population was the same as that of the entire national population;
second, that errors of enumeration of the two censuses were present
in the same direction and degree in the local as in the national population. These assumptions can be no more than approximately correct, because both mortality and accuracy of census enumeration
vary from place to place. However, it is believed that the net error
of the two assumptions is less than that entailed by neglecting enumeration errors entirely, as would be done by using life-table survival ratios.

To form census survival ratios, one must work with a practically
"closed" national population, i.e., one not affected by immigration
and emigration. This condition is approximately met by the Negro
and the native white populations of the United States, but not for the
total white population, which increases by immigration. Hence the
survival ratios applied to the total white population of Chicago were
derived from the national enumerations of native-white population.

From the description of the technique it is clear that the survival ratio technique yields no more than approximate results at
best and may in some instances incur substantial errors. For this

reason cautious interpretation of variations between periods and population groups is required. If such variations are large and fall into a reasonable pattern and if the base populations are sizable, it is possible to draw judicious conclusions. All the computations of net migration for this study were carried out by five- or ten-year age intervals for each sex separately; but the results were often combined into more comprehensive groupings, to avoid presenting more details than are warranted by the accuracy of the estimates.

The estimates of net migration by number of school years completed in chapter iv were carried out in the way just described, except that the survival ratios were made specific for educational attainment. For example, in 1940 in the entire United States there were 115,758 non-white males aged thirty-five to forty-four who reported having completed eight years of school; in 1950 there were 91,350 non-white males aged forty-five to fifty-four who reported eight years of school completed. Hence the survival ratio for this group was .7891. In using survival ratios of this type, one automatically corrects for differential errors in the reporting of educational attainment in the two censuses, on the assumption that such errors were of the same relative magnitude in the local as in the national population.

The computations of net migration by school years completed are not comparable with those which do not involve this subdivision of the data. The survival ratio for the total age group is the weighted average of the school-year-specific survival ratios; but the appropriate set of weights is the national, not the local, distribution by school years completed. Hence, in applying the school-year-specific survival ratios to the local population, the total number of survivors over all school-year groups is not the same as the total survivors obtained by applying the survival ratio for the total age group to all persons in the age group. However, under ordinary circumstances the two results should not be greatly different.

In this study an additional reason for non-comparability is that the main migration calculations were carried out for Negroes, whereas the calculations by educational attainment were made for the entire non-white population.

Social Characteristics of Negroes Living in Census Tracts
Containing Less than 250 Non-whites

For a number of social characteristics, the only data available for
the non-white population in 1950 are those obtained by aggregating
census-tract distributions. These distributions are available only
for census tracts containing 250 or more non-white residents in 1950.
Since this study is focused on the Negro population, the data obtained
in this way are subject to two kinds of bias for the purposes of the
study: (1) the ratio of Negroes to total non-whites may be different
in census tracts containing 250 or more non-whites from that in
tracts with fewer than 250 non-whites; and (2) the social characteristics of Negroes living in the two groups of tracts may differ systematically.

On the first point, it is possible to compare directly the racial
composition of the two groups of tracts. The 1950 populations were as
follows:

	Negroes	Other Races
In tracts with 250 or more non-whites.........	481,364	10,225
In all other tracts......	10,901	6,947
City total...........	492,265	17,172

Thus, in tracts with 250 or more non-whites, Negroes made up 97.9
per cent of all non-whites, whereas in the remaining tracts Negroes accounted for only 61.1 per cent of the non-white population. Viewed
another way, the figures show that 97.8 per cent of the Negroes lived

in tracts containing 250 or more non-whites, but only 59.5 per cent of the population of other non-white races. It is therefore entirely possible that, if one wishes to approximate the characteristics of the total Negro population of the city, it is better to use the information for the non-whites in tracts containing 250 or more non-whites than to use data for the total non-white population. One thereby excludes from the universe nearly two-fifths of the other races, but only 2.2 per cent of the Negroes.

However, this assumption might be vitiated if it were true that Negroes living in tracts containing fewer than 250 non-whites were a highly select group in terms of their social characteristics. One can think of several reasons why this might be true, but there are no data available to test the point directly. Some indirect, but fairly conclusive, evidence is available for the statistics of educational attainment. Tabulations of the number of school years completed by the population twenty-five years old and over are given for all non-whites in the city and can be aggregated for the tracts containing 250 or more non-whites. The following comparison of the median number of school years completed is obtained:

In tracts with 250 or more non-whites .	8.6
In all other tracts	9.6
Total non-whites in city	8.8

These figures reveal a substantial difference between the two groups of tracts. But this difference may reflect only the difference in racial composition, since other races have a much higher educational attainment than Negroes. In the Chicago Standard Metropolitan Area in 1950 the median number of school years completed was 8.6 for Negroes and 12.4 for other races. One can calculate what would be the distribution of non-whites by years of school completed in the two groups of tracts if the Negroes and other races were distributed proportionally by educational attainment in each group of tracts as they were in the entire Standard Metropolitan Area and if the ratio of Negroes to all non-whites for the population twenty-five years old and over were the same as for the population of all ages. On these assumptions, one obtains the following "expected" medians:

In tracts with 250 or more non-whites . 8.6
In all other tracts 9.8
    Total non-whites in city 8.6

Thus nearly the same result is obtained when the race differences are statistically eliminated as when they are allowed to influence the comparison. In other words, the major explanation of the difference is that the two groups of tracts vary in the proportion of other races. There is no indication of any substantial difference in the educational attainment of Negroes in the two groups of tracts.

Of course, the foregoing computation is not precise, because the separate distributions for Negroes and other races are available only for the Standard Metropolitan Area and not the city proper, and the ratio of Negroes to all non-whites is somewhat different at ages twenty-five and over from that at all ages. Moreover, the evidence is indirect, at best. Still, allowing for some latitude of error, it seems safe to conclude that there was no pronounced difference in educational attainment of Negroes in the two groups of tracts in 1950. Since educational attainment is strongly associated with a number of other socioeconomic characteristics, it seems probable that a similar conclusion would be reached if the comparison could be made, say, for income or occupational status.

The conclusion, then, is that, for most purposes, data on characteristics of non-whites living in census tracts containing 250 or more non-whites can be accepted as a fair approximation to data on characteristics of all Negroes in the city. One caution is necessary, however. While this assumption has been partially checked for the city as a whole, it may not be equally satisfactory for subareas within the city. For any combination of census tracts, however, it is possible to determine what proportion of all Negroes live in tracts containing 250 or more non-whites and what is the ratio of Negroes to non-whites in these tracts.

It may be mentioned that for 1940 it is possible to estimate directly, with a small margin of error, the educational attainment of Negroes in the two groups of tracts. The results are as follows:

	Median School Years
Total Negroes.	<u>7.8</u>
Negroes in tracts with 250 or more non-whites	7.8
Negroes in tracts with fewer than 250 non-whites	7.7

Thus one reaches the same conclusion as before: there is no material difference in educational attainment between the two groups of Negroes.

Not only is this conclusion significant for its bearing on the validity of approximating data for all Negroes by aggregating selected census tracts (chap. iv); but it also suggests that the initial stage of Negro succession is not highly selective with respect to the socio-economic characteristics of Negroes involved in the penetration of white areas (see chap. vi). The data, however, by no means establish this point conclusively.

Estimation of Distribution of Negro Population in 1920

Special tabulations of the 1920 Census of Population were obtained
from the U.S. Bureau of the Census for the 499 census tracts then
comprising the census-tract system of the city of Chicago. The data
were published in Census Data for the City of Chicago, 1920, edited
by Ernest W. Burgess and Charles Newcomb (Chicago: University of
Chicago Press, 1931).

A census-tract system for the city of Chicago composed of 935
census tracts was developed for tabulating data of the 1930 Census
of Population; the 935-tract system was used for tabulation purposes
in 1940 and 1950 as well. In the discussion the 499-tract system will
be referred to as the "old" system and the 935-tract system as the
"new" system. Although in a very few cases a tract in the new system
represents a consolidation of two tracts in the old system, tracts in
the new census-tract system are generally subdivisions of one or
more tracts in the old system.

To show the spatial distribution of the city's Negro population
in 1920, 1930, 1940, and 1950 with a series of maps based on comparable area units, it was necessary to estimate the 1920 population,
by race, for a number of tracts in the new census-tract system. Although the estimates are crude, they are needed for any realistic
comparison of changes in the number and proportion of Negroes in
given census tracts through time.

For example, in 1920, 32.7 per cent of the population in tract
481 of the old system was Negro (205 Negroes in a total population
of 627). Tract 481 of the old census-tract system corresponds with
tracts 655, 683, 684, 685, and 686 of the new system. In 1910 the

entire area was devoted to non-residential land uses; tracts 655 and 684 have remained non-residential in character. Through 1940, the Negro population of the area resided in tracts 683 and 685; between 1940 and 1950 there was movement of Negro population into tract 686. It is unwarranted to assume that 32.7 per cent of the population in each of the five tracts of the new census-tract system was Negro in 1920.

The universe of 499 census tracts was dichotomized into (a) the 105 tracts in which Negroes constituted 1 per cent or more of the 1920 total population and (b) the 394 tracts in which Negroes constituted less than 1 per cent of the 1920 total population. More careful examination of the 105 tracts than of the 394 tracts was made.

a) Of the 105 tracts, about 40 per cent were directly comparable with tracts in the new census-tract system; the number and proportion of Negroes residing in these tracts could be obtained readily from the published materials by census tract. Estimates were prepared for the remaining 60 per cent of the tracts in the old census-tract system. Maps prepared from special tabulations of the 1910 and 1920 censuses for selected enumeration districts showing the distribution of Negroes in the city were examined,[1] as well as a map showing the distribution of Negro families in 1920.[2] Figures on total population in 1920 were available for "enumeration districts," subdivisions of tracts, for most tracts in the old system; the 1920 total population of census tracts in the new system could be reconstructed with fair accuracy from the data for "enumeration districts." Data on population, by race, for 1930 were examined for each tract. An arbitrary allocation of Negro population in each tract in the old system to tracts in the new system was made after a study of these materials.

---

1. Reproduced in Chicago Commission on Race Relations, The Negro in Chicago (Chicago: University of Chicago Press, 1922), pp. 106, 110, 116, 120.

2. Reproduced in Census Data for the City of Chicago, 1920, Appendix, Map 11.

Altogether, of the 105 tracts, 42 were directly comparable with tracts in the new system. For 30 tracts, the analysis indicated that there was little variation in proportion Negro among the tracts in the new system which comprised the original tract in the old system. For the remaining 33 tracts, the variation in proportion Negro among tracts in the new system which constituted the original tract in the old system was sufficient to result in components of the original tract being allocated to different intervals for mapping purposes.

The 33 tracts of the old census-tract system for which component tracts of the new system were allocated to different intervals are shown below, cross-classified by the proportion Negro in each component:

Estimated Per Cent Negro in Component B	Estimated Per Cent Negro in Component A					
	50.0-74.9	30.0-49.9	10.0-29.9	1.0-9.9	Under 1.0	No Negroes or Less than 100 Pop.
75.0-89.9	1	2	1	4	0	0
50.0-74.9	-	2	0	5	2	0
30.0-49.9	-	-	0	2	0	0
10.0-29.9	-	-	-	0	0	0
1.0-9.9	-	-	-	-	11	3

It may be seen that the estimating procedure involved separating the two components of the old tract by one interval in 14 of the 33 cases and by more than one interval in 19 cases.

b) The procedure by which tracts in the new system comprising the 394 tracts in the old system in which Negroes constituted less than 1 per cent of the total population in 1920 were allocated to intervals for mapping was as follows: If a tract in the old system had no Negro population in 1920, it was, of course, assumed that each component tract in the new system had no Negro population in 1920. If a tract in the old system had one or more Negro residents in 1920, the 1930 population, by race, of each component tract in the new system was examined. Any component tract in the new system which had no Negro population in 1930 was assumed to have had none in 1920;

similarly, any tract with less than 100 total population in 1930 was assumed to have had less than 100 total population in 1920. In either case the tract was assigned to the interval "No Negroes or total population under 100" for 1920. Any component tract in the new system which had one or more Negro residents in 1930 was allocated to the interval "Under 1.0 per cent" for 1920. The probable bias in these procedures is to make the 1920 and 1930 spatial distributions resemble each other more than they actually did. This bias seemed preferable to that of exaggerating the changes in distribution between the two dates.

Finally, in 1920 as in 1930, 1940, and 1950, census tracts 159 and 493 of the new census-tract system were allocated for mapping purposes to the interval "No Negroes or total population under 100." The Negro population in these two tracts is wholly institutional.

Census-Tract Classification for Succession Analysis

Table E-1 shows the classification of each census tract having 250 or more non-white inhabitants in 1950 according to the scheme of succession stages developed in chapter vi. The table shows, as well, the basis of each tract's classification, i.e., the percentage of the population non-white in 1940 and in 1950. The reasons for excluding 21 tracts from the succession analysis are given, for each tract individually, in Appendix F.

Table E-1.—Classification of Census Tracts According to Stage of Succession, for 175 Census Tracts with 250 or More Non-white Population, Chicago, 1950

Piling Up			Late Consolidation			Consolidation		
Census Tract	Per Cent of Population Non-white		Census Tract	Per Cent of Population Non-white		Census Tract	Per Cent of Population Non-white	
	1940	1950		1940	1950		1940	1950
386	99.8	99.1	360	80.1	94.8	122	4.3	12.0
540	98.4	99.0	376	94.2	99.4	123	5.7	16.3
542	98.5	99.8	377	84.0	97.1	127	32.6	80.0
545	99.4	99.9	385	94.7	96.3	128	36.1	83.0
547	99.2	99.6	434	81.5	97.3	133	21.7	34.0
550	98.6	99.9	440	91.9	97.8	134	33.5	63.9
551	99.5	100.0	521	90.5	98.5	359	16.6	59.8
552	99.4	99.8	522	82.3	94.6	361	27.7	83.9
553	99.1	99.7	537	90.7	99.6	378	73.8	92.2
556	98.2	99.8	538	94.3	99.1	379	66.0	88.5
557	99.8	99.7	541	97.0	99.0	380	56.4	88.0
573	98.1	99.9	543	85.1	96.9	397	8.8	13.2
576	98.1	99.5	548	82.3	97.5	402	44.7	72.1
577	99.8	99.4	554	96.7	98.8	415	13.7	42.7
578	99.1	99.1	555	85.2	98.0	431	26.8	61.6
579	99.6	99.1	559	86.1	99.5	432	9.7	87.0
580	98.9	99.6	574	89.0	98.9	433	43.5	91.2
581	98.7	99.3	575	96.8	99.0	435	11.5	30.8
582	99.6	99.7	589	97.2	97.7	441	47.0	83.8
583	99.4	99.6	590	97.4	98.7	442	66.5	93.1
584	98.7	99.4	591	96.0	98.1	520	38.9	89.9
585	99.5	98.8	601	95.7	97.0	534	16.5	96.9
586	99.6	99.5	607	91.4	99.1	535	64.2	92.8
587	97.7	98.9	625	92.4	97.7	536	75.1	96.0
588	99.4	99.5	634	89.3	98.4	549	77.2	88.2
592	99.6	98.4	683	97.1	99.3	560	22.7	94.1
600	99.6	99.6	685	96.6	99.8	566	31.2	70.9
602	97.9	98.7	935	94.7	92.2	570	58.7	92.7
603	99.2	99.3				623	15.9	99.4
604	98.9	99.7				670	24.6	50.0
605	98.7	99.8				681	55.6	99.4
606	98.2	98.9				861	65.6	93.6
						872	26.0	61.5
						877	3.1	24.1
						933	20.1	27.9

Table E-1 (continued)

Early Consolidation			Invasion			Census Tracts Excluded from Analysis
Census Tract	Per Cent of Population Non-white		Census Tract	Per Cent of Population Non-white		
	1940	1950		1940	1950	
121	4.5	38.4	299	1.4	4.5	23
126	27.3	54.1	319	0.6	19.9	24
135	4.0	20.5	362	0.9	32.5	27
381	9.5	80.7	370	0.1	24.6	124
382	2.1	30.3	371	0.4	72.1	129
384	2.3	37.1	373	0.5	12.7	159
403	4.2	61.6	383	1.0	24.4	493
412	15.5	79.7	395	0.9	65.8	523
413	4.5	46.3	410	1.7	40.3	524
416	2.6	18.3	414	1.5	39.3	539
426	4.8	38.9	418	0.5	7.1	544
428	2.7	9.1	419	1.0	9.0	546
443	59.5	92.4	450	0.3	12.4	594
448	3.5	21.7	451	0.4	21.7	595
517	4.2	32.1	452	1.0	50.0	620
519	7.0	83.6	453	0.3	47.2	630
533	21.0	48.4	454	1.7	39.9	653
558	3.5	88.4	562	0.4	65.4	686
561	5.3	67.3	565	0.3	19.2	717
564	12.5	46.6	569	0.5	61.2	901
567	5.4	39.4	593	1.8	26.2	934
572	21.1	89.0	596	0.9	20.4	
617	3.2	16.5	608	1.2	30.5	
858	4.2	7.6	616	1.2	6.1	
895	6.9	16.9	624	0.2	98.4	
897	3.2	93.6	627	0.3	48.5	
			629	0.1	24.7	
			671	0.9	11.6	
			695	0.0	28.2	
			878	0.3	79.6	
			881	1.9	7.0	
			885	0.0	29.5	
			886	0.1	9.8	

Appendix F

Census Tracts Excluded from Succession Analysis

Census Tracts Excluded from Succession Analysis because Other
Races Outnumbered Negroes

Census-tract data on population characteristics are not available
separately for Negroes and non-whites of other races (Japanese,
Chinese, and others). Since the population of other races is known
to have a higher average socioeconomic status than the Negro population and to differ in other respects from Negroes, data for all non-
whites combined are not representative of Negroes if they include
a large proportion of other non-whites. For this reason the eleven
census tracts with 250 or more non-white population in 1950 in which
other races outnumbered Negroes were excluded from the analysis
of Negro succession patterns. The available data on the composition
of the non-white population, by race, in these tracts are summarized below. Since the breakdown of other races into Japanese, Chinese, and others is available only for community areas (in Philip
M. Hauser and Evelyn M. Kitagawa, Local Community Fact Book
for Chicago, 1950), it is sometimes possible to make only rough inferences as to the race composition of individual tracts. Another
problem, encountered in tracing population changes back to 1920, is
that the system of census tracts for 1920 is different from that employed in later censuses. Certain tracts have identical boundaries
in the old and new systems, while others have such different boundaries that only rough estimates or no estimates at all are warranted
for 1920. Table F-1 summarizes the census-tract data on non-white
population by race in the eleven tracts for 1920, 1930, 1940, and 1950.
The inferences that may be drawn with some confidence from this
material are discussed below.

320

Table F-1.—Population and Per Cent Negro and Other Races, for Eleven Census Tracts with 250 or More Non-white Population in 1950 in Which Other Races Outnumbered Negroes, Chicago, 1920-50

Census Tract	1920			1930		1940			1950		
	Population	Per Cent Negro	Per Cent Other Races	Population	Per Cent Negro*	Population	Per Cent Negro	Per Cent Other Races	Population	Per Cent Negro	Per Cent Other Races
23	...†	2.4†	...†	4,521	5.2	5,775	4.6	1.1	6,184	3.9	4.0
24	...†	Under 1‡	...†	9,009	0.4	11,288	0.3	0.6	13,162	0.3	1.9
27	...†	Under 1	...†	6,335	1.0	7,928	0.4	0.1	9,064	0.5	3.3
124	6,122‡	0.7	0.2	7,291	0.8	7,823	0.4	0.6	8,881	0.7	4.3
129	6,343	0.4	0.2	6,901	0.5	7,614	0.3	2.3	8,178	10.5	10.9
523	...†	...†	4.9§	7,443‖	3.6	5,353	2.9	16.5	6,172	10.0	20.5
524	8,009	0.9									
594	7,905	1.0	0.1	4,622	0.3	5,103	0.2	0.1	6,577	8.2	13.3
595				4,832	0.2	4,726	0.1	0.1	6,224	3.4	10.4
620	...†	1 to 10‡	...†	4,182	3.3	4,275	3.4	1.1	4,903	3.3	5.6
630	...†	Under 1†	...†	6,295	0.2	7,240	0.0+	0.2	8,022	2.1	2.5

*Census figures on population of other races are not comparable with figures for other years, owing to the classification of Mexicans as non-white in 1930.

†Not available; census tract shown in combination with other area in 1920 Census.

‡Estimated.

§Tract known to have a significant proportion of other races, but a numerical estimate is not warranted.

‖Census tracts 523 and 524 combined because of the small population of 523 after 1920.

Source: Ernest W. Burgess and Charles Newcomb, Census Data of the City of Chicago, 1920 (Chicago: University of Chicago Press, 1931); Ernest W. Burgess and Charles Newcomb, Census Data of the City of Chicago, 1930 (Chicago: University of Chicago Press, 1933); Sixteenth Census of the United States, 1940, Population and Housing, Statistics for Census Tracts and Community Areas, Chicago, Ill. (Washington: Government Printing Office, 1943); 1950 United States Census of Population (Bull. P-D10) (Washington: Government Printing Office, 1952).

Tracts 23, 24, and 27, in community area 3, Uptown. — There was a small nucleus of Negro settlement in tract 23 in 1920, which expanded somewhat between 1920 and 1930 to 5.2 per cent of the total population but declined to 4.6 per cent in 1940 and 3.9 per cent in 1950. Tracts 24 and 27 have had no more than 1 per cent of their population classified as Negro from 1930 through 1950. Between 1940 and 1950 all three tracts were invaded by Japanese (who comprise 75 per cent of all other races in this community area). In 1950 other races (predominantly Japanese, presumably) comprised 4.0 per cent of the population in tract 23, 1.9 per cent in tract 24, and 3.3 per cent in tract 27.

Tracts 124 and 129, in community area 8, Near North Side. — There have been small numbers of Negroes in these tracts since 1920, but in both tracts the proportion of Negroes was less than 1 per cent at each census, 1920-40. During 1940-50 tract 124 was invaded by other races, and tract 129 by both Negroes and other races. Presumably, the bulk of the other-races population was Japanese, since 70 per cent of the other races in the entire community area are Japanese.

Tracts 523 and 524, in community area 34, Armour Square. — This is a historical locale of Chinese settlement in Chicago. Almost all—98 per cent—of the non-whites other than Negroes in this community area are Chinese, and the community area contains 35 per cent of all the Chinese in the city (1950). However, the area made up by these two tracts has contained small numbers of Negroes since 1920, and there was a considerable increase in the proportion of Negroes between 1940 and 1950, amounting to an "early consolidation" of Negro settlement during the decade. At the same time, there was an increase in absolute number and percentage of other races, who composed 20.5 per cent of the population of the combined tracts in 1950, as compared to 10.0 per cent for Negroes.

Tracts 594 and 595, in community area 39, Kenwood. — In 1920, 1 per cent of the combined population of these two tracts were Negroes, but in 1930 and 1940 there was only a trace of Negro population. The proportion of other races was negligible throughout the period 1920-40. The two tracts were invaded between 1940 and 1950 by both Negroes and other races, the latter predominantly Japanese, presumably, since 95 per cent of the community area's population of other races was Japanese in 1950. However, the Japanese invasion was stronger than the Negro, since Japanese well outnumbered Negroes in 1950.

Tract 620, in community area 41, Hyde Park.—The tract had a small proportion of Negroes, around 3 per cent, in 1930, 1940, 1950; the proportion was probably somewhat larger in 1920 and 1910. Between 1940 and 1950 the proportion of other races increased from 1.1 to 5.6 per cent. This increase is difficult to interpret. There was no increase in the number or proportion of dwelling units occupied by all non-whites between 1940 and 1950. Since the tract contains International House, where a number of University of Chicago students reside, and since the enumeration procedure for college students was changed between 1940 and 1950, the population data for the two years are not comparable.

Tract 630, in community area 42, Woodlawn.—This tract was scarcely penetrated by either Negroes or other non-whites until after 1940. By 1950 its population was 2.1 per cent Negro and 2.5 per cent other races. Since in the entire community area 75 per cent of the other-races population are Japanese, probably the increase in the proportion of other races in the tract represents an invasion of Japanese, along with Negroes.

Summary.—There are, then, five distinct areas represented by the ten tracts whose population changes can be interpreted. These may be classified into four types as follows:

a) Invasion by Japanese in and near an old, but small and isolated, Negro settlement (in community area 3, Uptown)

b) Invasion by Japanese and Negroes near an area of earlier Negro settlement (in community area 8, Near North Side)

c) Invasion by Japanese and Negroes near other areas experiencing invasion by Negroes (in community area 39, Kenwood, and community area 42, Woodlawn)

d) Early consolidation of Negro penetration in an area near older areas of Negro settlement, coupled with growth of the established Chinese settlement in the same area (in community area 34, Armour Square)

Thus it appears that there were four instances of major invasions by Japanese during the decade, all of which were associated with Negro succession patterns, and one case of Negro succession occurring along with Chinese succession. Unfortunately, census-tract data on population characteristics are not available separately for Negroes and other non-whites. Hence the succession analysis must neglect the few instances where succession involves both Negroes and other non-whites and confine itself to the more typical case of white-to-Negro succession.

Census Tracts Excluded from Analysis because of Unusual Changes

Seven census tracts whose population changes deviated from those exhibited by a majority of tracts undergoing succession were excluded from the analysis of tract characteristics by stage of succession. The circumstances which suggested the advisability of such exclusions are outlined below.

Census tract 539.—This tract includes the site of the Chicago Housing Authority Dearborn Homes housing project, occupied in 1949. During the 1940-50 decade a number of old structures were removed to make room for the project, as is indicated by the following data on age of dwelling units:

Number of Dwelling Units, by Year Built

	1940	1950
1940 or later:	. . .	420
1920-39	1	. . .
1919 or earlier	544	300
Total reporting.	545	720

Between 1940 and 1950 the white population of the tract increased from 191 to 338, and the non-white from 1,334 to 2,335. Changes in number of dwellings by color of occupant were as follows:

Occupied Dwelling Units, by Color of Occupant

	1940	1950
White	102	172
Non-white	362	568
Total occupied units . .	464	740
Vacant	82	2
Total units	546	742

It appears that the demolition of old structures and construction of
a public housing project interrupted the process of succession from
white to non-white occupancy in the tract. The proportion of non-
whites in the tract population showed no change over the decade,
being 87.5 per cent in 1940 and 87.4 per cent in 1950.

Census tract 544.—During the decade the number of dwelling
units in this tract increased from two sources—conversion of units
in old structures and construction of a new apartment-house development, the latter being built as housing for staff members of the Illinois Institute of Technology. The census-tract statistics indicate
these changes as follows:

Number of Dwelling Units, by Year Built

	1940	1950
1940 or later	. . .	115
1920-39	9	5
1919 or earlier	395	495
Total reporting	404	615

The effect of the Institute's housing development was to interrupt
the succession sequence, so that the proportion of non-whites in the
tract's population decreased from 97.6 per cent in 1940 to 85.5 per
cent in 1950.

Census tract 546.—This tract is the site of several residence
halls of the Illinois Institute of Technology. Because of the change in

procedure for enumerating college students introduced in the 1950 Census, many residents of these halls would have been counted as residents of the tract in 1950 but not in 1940. The differences between the 1940 and 1950 figures shown below result, therefore, both from actual changes in the area and from changes in definitions.

Population and Occupied Dwelling Units, by Color

	1940	1950
Population:		
White	64	372
Non-white	1,923	2,728
Total	1,987	3,100
Dwelling units:		
White	13	14
Non-white	620	1,042
Total	633	1,056

It will be noted that the large increase in number of white residents was not paralleled by an increase in white dwelling units, indicating that most of the white residents were members of quasi-households. There was an increase in both non-white population and dwelling units, but the latter must have resulted from conversion, since no new dwelling units were constructed in the area between 1940 and 1950.

Because of the lack of comparability in the 1940 and 1950 figures, the change in the non-white proportion, from 96.8 to 88.0 per cent of the population, is misleading.

Census tracts 653 and 686.—Neither of these tracts had any non-white population in 1940, but, by 1950, tract 653 was 28.9 per cent and tract 686 was 65.6 per cent non-white. From study of these figures alone, the tracts would be classified as "invasion" tracts. However, in each case, only the southern part of the tract is involved. Here there was a strip of vacant land south of the Rock Island Railroad tracks in 1940 which had been built up with non-white residences by

1950. The white residences in the northern part of each tract are separated from the non-white residences in the southern part not only by the railroad tracks but also by vacant land and land used for commercial and industrial purposes. The building-up of the southern parts of tracts 653 and 686 represents an extension of the Negro community of "Lilydale" (the northern tip of community area 49, Roseland), composed of tracts 681, 683, and 685, which has grown largely through original settlement by Negroes rather than invasion by Negroes of former white-occupied areas. The changes between 1940 and 1950 in tracts 653 and 686 are not, therefore, representative of the white-to-non-white succession pattern, but rather they reflect a succession from non-residential to residential land use.

Census tract 717.—This tract increased from 0.4 per cent non-white in 1940 to 84.3 per cent in 1950. At the same time, the total population increased from 1,509 to 9,782. Both changes are primarily accounted for by the construction of the large Chicago Housing Authority Altgeld Gardens housing project on hitherto vacant land in one part of the tract. The population changes in this tract, therefore, represent succession from non-residential to residential use rather than from white to non-white occupancy.

Census tract 934.—In 1940, 91.6 per cent of the population in this tract was non-white, but in 1950, the proportion was only 67.9 per cent. The change was brought about by an increase in white population rather than a decline in non-white, as is indicated by the following statistics:

Population, by Color

	1940	1950
White	207	1,403
Non-white	2,252	2,973
Total	2,459	4,376

An examination of block statistics shows that the increase in white residents is largely explained by the construction of new dwelling units in the eastern portion of the tract, which was hitherto vacant. The new dwelling units were occupied very largely by white owners in 1950, and the area in which they were constructed was separated from the remainder of the tract (where non-whites predominated) by non-residential land. The population changes in this tract do not, therefore, represent a reversal of the white-to-non-white succession pattern but rather result from a succession of non-residential to residential land use.

Summary.—The seven census tracts whose population changes have just been reviewed are unusual, as compared to the majority of tracts undergoing succession, in the following ways:

Two areas (tracts 539 and 544) where succession was interrupted by housing projects, one public and one institutional.

Three areas (tracts 653 and 686, 717, and 934) where apparent residential succession is found actually to be succession from non-residential to residential uses. In one area there was occupancy of hitherto vacant land by white population, and in two areas occupancy by non-whites. One of the cases of non-white occupancy involved a public housing project; the other two cases involved private developments.

One area where population changes reflected changes in census definitions primarily. The area would otherwise probably have been classified as undergoing consolidation of Negro occupancy.

This review shows that it is important to distinguish between population changes resulting from replacement of non-residential by residential land uses and those produced by white-to-non-white succession. It also suggests that in some cases the usual sequence of succession can be interrupted by public or private programs of urban redevelopment, although the evidence is too meager to permit the assessment of the long-term effects of such programs.

It may be noted that not all tracts were excluded from the analysis where public housing projects were constructed. The exclusions were made only where such construction appeared to be associated with a departure from the typical pattern of succession.

Census Tracts Excluded for Other Reasons

These include one census tract (901) whose total population was under 100 in 1940, and two tracts (159 and 493) in which the non-white inhabitants were almost entirely residents of institutions, i.e., the city of Chicago House of Correction (in 493) and the Municipal Tuberculosis Sanitarium (in 159). It is evident that these three tracts do not belong in an analysis of white-to-non-white residential succession.

Definition of Census-Tract Characteristics

Gross Population Density

The total population of each census tract in 1940 and 1950 is available from the 1940 and 1950 census-tract bulletins. The gross land area of each census tract in 1940 and 1950 is given in a release of the Chicago Community Inventory, University of Chicago, entitled Gross Land Area and Gross Population Density of Census Tracts and Community Areas for the City of Chicago, 1950. Details of the technique of measurement of gross land area are available in the release cited.

Density figures in hundreds of persons per square mile were employed in the analysis. The density figures used are gross rather than net population densities. Net residential densities are ordinarily higher, and the difference is quite important for census tracts including substantial areas of non-residential use (commercial, industrial, park, institutional, vacant, etc.).

Room Crowding

The number of households with 1.51 persons per room or more in 1940 was obtained from the 1940 census-tract bulletin for each census tract; the number of households with 1.51 persons per room or more in 1950 was obtained from photoprints of unpublished tabulations of the 1950 Census obtained from the U.S. Bureau of the Census. Data by color for both 1940 and 1950 are available for census tracts with 250 non-whites or more.

The number of households with 1.51 persons per room or more was divided by the estimated number of households with 2 members or more which reported persons per room in each census tract, to obtain the proportion of "crowded" households in the tract. The estimated number of households with 2 members or more which reported persons per room in each census tract was obtained by subtracting the number of 1-person households from the total number of households reporting persons per room.

This procedure of obtaining the proportion of "crowded" households differs somewhat from that generally employed. It is customary to use as the numerator the number of households with 1.51 persons per room or more; but total households rather than households with 2 members or more are generally used as the denominator. However, 1-person households cannot, by definition, have more than 1 person per room; hence they are not exposed to the risk of crowding if crowding is defined in terms of households with 1.51 persons per room or more.

Per Cent White-Collar Workers

Distributions of the employed labor force, by sex and major occupation group, are available for census tracts in the 1940 and 1950 census-tract bulletins. Data are available only for total population in 1940; in 1950, data by color are available for census tracts with 250 non-whites or more.

The number of males in occupations usually termed "white-collar" (professional, managerial, clerical, and sales) was divided by the number of employed males who reported their occupation in each census tract, to obtain the proportion of males engaged in white-collar occupations. This proportion, termed "per cent white-collar workers" for convenience, is employed in the analysis as an indicator of the socioeconomic level of the census tract.

Per Cent with Some High-School Education

Distributions of the population twenty-five years of age or older, by years of school completed, are available for census tracts in the 1940 and 1950 census-tract bulletins. Data by color are available for census tracts with 250 non-whites or more in both 1940 and 1950.

The number of persons who had completed one or more years of high school (including those with college training) was divided by the number of persons reporting school years completed in the census tract, to obtain the proportion of the population twenty-five years of age or older with at least one year's training at the secondary level.

Per Cent with Some High-School Education, Standardized for Age

To permit intertract and white-non-white comparisons with respect to educational attainment freed of the influence of age composition, indirect standardization was employed. The following table shows age-specific proportions of the population, by color, having completed one year of high school or more for 1940 and 1950:

Age (Years)	White Population		Non-white Population	
	1950	1940	1950	1940
25 and over	54.62	40.62	43.59	30.92
25-29	85.74	69.57	67.25	53.26
30-34	78.92	59.33	57.73	40.99
35-39	69.39	48.21	47.87	32.00
40-44	60.47	37.94	39.23	26.26
45-54	45.88	27.21	31.12	22.19
55-64	30.05	22.54	24.90	17.60
65-74	24.51	19.17	19.28	11.16
75 and over	22.72	16.04	15.58	7.74

The indirect standardization for age was carried out as follows:

1. Distributions of population, by age and color, for each census tract were obtained from the 1940 and 1950 census-tract bulletins (see col. 1 of example).

2. The age-specific proportions of the population twenty-five years old and over having completed one year or more of high school for the white population of the city of Chicago in 1940 were chosen as a "standard" set of proportions or rates (see col. 2 of example).

3. The expected number of persons twenty-five years of age and over having completed one year or more of high school, assuming that the "standard" age-specific proportion of the population in each age group has completed at least one year of high school, was computed for each color group in each census tract (see col. 3 of example).

Example of computational procedure for non-white population, 1940, in a hypothetical census tract:

Age (Years)	Non-white Population, 1940 (1)	"Standard" Percentages (Whites, 1940, City of Chicago) (2)	(1) x (2) Expected Non-whites with One Year High School or More, 1940 (3)
25-29	1,000	69.57	696
30-34	1,000	59.33	593
35-39	1,000	48.21	482
.	.	.	.
.	.	.	.
.	.	.	.
75 and over . .	500	16.04	80
25 and over . .	. . .	. . .	1,851 (sum col. 3)

4. The actual (enumerated) number of persons twenty-five years old and over having completed one year or more of high school for the specified color group in the specified tract was divided by the expected number of persons twenty-five years old and over having completed one year or more of high school for the same color group in the same census tract.

5. The proportion of "actual to expected" (step 4) was multiplied by the proportion of the white population twenty-five years old and over having completed one year or more of high school in the city of Chicago, 1940 (40.62 per cent), to obtain the "per cent with some high school, standardized for age."

Per Cent Homeowners

Distributions of occupied dwelling units or households, by color and tenure, are available for each census tract in the 1940 and 1950 census-tract bulletins.

The number of occupied dwelling units which were owner-occupied or the number of households who owned the dwelling unit in which they resided was divided by the number of occupied dwelling units or households in the specified color group to obtain the percentage of homeowners in the given group.

Per Cent Homeowners, Standardized for Type of Structure

Owner-occupied dwelling units as a percentage of all dwelling units, by type of structure in which the unit is located, are shown below for the city of Chicago in 1950:

Type of Structure	Owner-occupied as Per Cent of All Dwelling Units
All types.	29.8
1-unit, detached.	84.2
1-unit, attached	38.7
1- or 2-unit, semidetached. .	44.8
2-unit, other	41.4
3- and 4-unit.	20.6
5- to 9-unit.	8.9
10-unit or more.	2.8

Source: 1950 Census of Housing, Table 17, Bull. HA-13.

1. Distributions of all dwelling units (occupied or unoccupied) and of dwelling units occupied by non-whites, by type of structure in which the unit is located, for each census tract were obtained from photoprints of unpublished tabulations of the 1950 Census of Housing. By subtracting the distribution of units occupied by non-whites from the distribution of all units, the distribution of all dwelling units not occupied by non-whites, by type of structure, can be obtained; because the number of vacant units was negligible in 1950, the distribution of all units not occupied by non-whites closely approximates that of units occupied by whites. Because of the high vacancy rate in 1940, it was impossible to standardize homeownership for type of structure by this technique of indirect standardization for that year.

2. The type of structure-specific proportions of all dwelling units owned by their occupants in the city of Chicago in 1950 was chosen as a "standard" set of proportions or rates.

3. The expected number of dwelling units owned by their occupants, assuming that the "standard" type of structure-specific proportion of units in each type of structure group are owned by their occupants, was computed for each group of units, classified by color of occupants, in each census tract.

4. The actual (enumerated) number of dwelling units owned by

their occupants for units with occupants of the specified color in the specified tract was divided by the expected number of dwelling units owned by their occupants for units with occupants of the given color in the given tract.

5. The proportion of "actual to expected" (step 4) was multiplied by the proportion of all dwelling units owned by their occupants in the city of Chicago in 1950 (29.8 per cent) to obtain the "per cent of homeowners, standardized for type of structure."

Median Contract Rent

Distributions of tenant-occupied or renter-occupied dwelling units, by contract monthly rent, are available for census tracts in the 1940 census-tract bulletins; similar distributions, by color of occupants, are available for census tracts with 250 or more non-whites in 1940. Distributions of renter-occupied and vacant non-seasonal not dilapidated dwelling units for rent, by contract monthly rent, are available for census tracts in the 1950 census-tract bulletins; distributions of dwelling units rented by non-whites, by contract monthly rent (with slightly different intervals), are available for census tracts with 250 non-whites or more in 1950. By subtracting the distribution of units rented by non-whites from the distribution of renter-occupied and vacant non-seasonal not dilapidated dwelling units for rent, the distribution of dwelling units rented by whites and vacant non-seasonal not dilapidated dwelling units for rent can be obtained; because the number of vacant units was negligible in 1950, the distribution of dwelling units rented by whites and vacant non-seasonal not dilapidated dwelling units for rent closely approximates that of dwelling units rented by whites.

Medians were computed from the published distributions of renter-occupied units, by contract monthly rent. Rents were reported to the nearest dollar; in computing the medians, the limits of the class intervals were taken as the mid-point of the $1.00 interval between the end of one of the rent groups shown in the distribution and the beginning of the next. For example, the limits of the interval designated in round dollars $30-$39 were assumed to be $29.50-$39.49.

Per Cent with Mechanical Refrigeration

Data on type of refrigeration equipment are available for all occupied dwelling units from the census-tract bulletins for 1940 and
1950. (The 1950 statistics are based on a 20 per cent sample.)

The number of households or occupied units with mechanical refrigeration (operated by electricity, gas, kerosene, gasoline, or other
source of power) was divided by the number of households or occupied
units reporting refrigeration equipment to obtain the proportion of
households with mechanical refrigeration.

Per Cent with Central Heating

Data on type of heating equipment are available for all occupied
dwelling units from the census-tract bulletins for 1940 and 1950.
(The 1950 statistics are based on a 20 per cent sample.)

The number of households or occupied units with central heating
(piped-steam or hot-water or warm-air furnace) was divided by the
number of households or occupied units reporting equipment to obtain the proportion of households with central heating.

Median Family Income

Distributions of families by 1949 income are available from special
tabulations of the 1950 census-tract summary cards; the cards were
obtained from the U.S. Bureau of the Census by the Chicago Community Inventory, University of Chicago. Distributions by income
are available for white and non-white families separately for those
census tracts with 250 or more non-white residents in 1950. No comparable income data are available from the 1940 Census.

Each family is classified by the family income, i.e., the combined income of all members of the family. Income is defined as the
sum of money received from wages or salary, net income from the
operation of a farm, business, or profession, net income from rents
or lodgers, royalties, periodic income from trust funds or insurance
policies, and governmental payments. The figures represent the
amount of income received before deductions for personal income
taxes, social security, etc. The composition of the family is as of

April, 1950; however, the time period covered by the income statistics is the calendar year 1949. The income data are based on a 20
per cent sample.

Per Cent Substandard Dwellings

The number of occupied dwelling units which have no private
bath or which are dilapidated was obtained from the 1950 census-
tract bulletin; data are available for units occupied by whites and
those occupied by non-whites separately for census tracts with 250
or more non-white residents in 1950. No comparable data are available from the 1940 Census.

Units classified as having no private bath are those which lack
a private flush toilet or a private bathtub or shower, as well as units
which have no running water; units classified as dilapidated had serious deficiencies (weathertightness, safety hazards, etc.), were run-
down or neglected, or were of inadequate original construction. For
convenience, these units are referred to as "substandard units."

The number of substandard units, i.e., units lacking private bath
or dilapidated, was divided by the number of occupied units reporting condition and plumbing facilities, to obtain the percentage of substandard dwellings.

Per Cent of Married Couples without Own Household

The number of married couples without their own household was
obtained from the 1950 census-tract bulletin. Data by color are available for census tracts with 250 or more non-white residents in 1950.
No comparable data are available from the 1940 Census.

A married couple is defined as a husband and his wife enumerated as members of the same household or quasi-household. If the
husband is not the head of the household, the couple is classified as
"without own household." Data on married couples are based on a
20 per cent sample.

The percentage of married couples without own household was
obtained by dividing the number of married couples without own
household by the total number of married couples.

Per Cent of Married Females with Spouse Absent

The number of married females and the number of married couples were obtained from the 1950 census-tract bulletin. Data by color are available for census tracts with 250 or more non-white residents in 1950.

Married females include those who have been married only once, those who have remarried after being widowed or divorced, and those who are separated; the data relate to marital status as of April, 1950. The number of married females minus the number of married couples equals the number of married females who were not members of the same household or quasi-household as their spouse, i.e., the number of married females with spouse absent. The spouse is not necessarily absent because of marital discord or legal separation. Data on marital status are based on a complete count, whereas those on married couples are based on a 20 per cent sample.

The percentage of married females with spouse absent was obtained by dividing the number of married females who were not members of the same household or quasi-household as their spouse by the total number of married females.

Per Cent Unrelated Individuals

The number of families and unrelated individuals and the population fourteen years of age and over were obtained from the 1950 census-tract bulletin; the number of families was obtained from special tabulations of the 1950 census-tract summary cards. The three sets of data are available by color for census tracts with 250 or more non-whites in 1950.

The number of unrelated individuals was obtained by subtracting the number of families from the number of families and unrelated individuals. Unrelated individuals are persons (other than inmates of institutions) who are not living with any relatives. If the unrelated individual is a household head, living alone or with only non-relatives, he is classified as a primary individual; if the unrelated individual is not a household head, he is classified as a secondary individual. The statistics on unrelated individuals used in the analysis are limited to those fourteen years old and over. The number of unrelated individuals is based on a 20 per cent sample; the population fourteen years old and over is based on a complete count.

The percentage of unrelated individuals was obtained by dividing the number of unrelated individuals fourteen years old and over by the total population fourteen years old and over.

Per Cent of Males Unemployed

Persons fourteen years old and over were classified as unemployed if they were not at work during the census week but were seeking work or would have been seeking work except for reasons of temporary illness, expectation of returning to jobs from which they were laid off, or the belief that no work was available. In computing unemployment for 1940, the number of persons on public emergency work (WPA, NYA, etc.), shown separately in the census-tract bulletin, was added to the number of persons seeking work. Data are available for total males in the labor force in 1940 and 1950 and for non-white males in the labor force who resided in census tracts with 250 or more non-white residents in the respective years. The percentage of unemployment was obtained by dividing the number of unemployed males by the number of males in the labor force; for 1950, the base of the percentage was taken as the civilian labor force (excluding members of the Armed Forces).

Appendix H

Problems of Statistical Inference in Regression Analysis

In the regression analyses of chapter vii the typical procedure was
to compute, for a small number of census tracts, the regression of
the 1950 values of some index (e.g., per cent with one year or more
of high-school education) on the corresponding 1940 values of the
same index. There are two problems in interpreting such regressions
for which no mathematical solution appears to be available and which,
accordingly, preclude the use of the conventional tests of statistical
significance for regression analysis and analysis of covariance.

The first problem is that the size of the unit of observation—in
this case, the census tract—has been found to affect the size of the
obtained correlation coefficient and would presumably affect the constants of the regression equation as well.[1] Thus one would not expect
to get the same results by using a larger (e.g., square mile) or smaller (e.g., block) unit than the average census tract. On the one hand, the
smaller unit would probably be more homogeneous, on the average, than
the tract, and the range of variation among units should increase with
decreasing size. This would tend to increase the size of the correlation coefficient. On the other hand, the larger unit would often be more
stable over time, because less markedly affected by "chance" changes,
than the small one. How these and other effects of area-unit size
would balance out cannot be predicted.

Some mathematical work has been done on the problem of interpreting so-called "ecological correlations" and "ecological regres-

---

1.   C. E. Gehlke and Katherine Biehl, "Certain Effects of Grouping upon the Size of the Correlation Coefficient in Census Tract Material," Journal of the American Statistical Association, XXIX (March,
1934, suppl.), 169-70.

sions" from the standpoint of their bearing on the association between characteristics of individuals living in areas such as tracts.[2] However, this work is not pertinent for the present problem, where the concern is with changes in the composition of the aggregate populations of the areas taken as units.

The problem of size of unit is exacerbated by the fact that Chicago's census tracts vary greatly among themselves both in area size and in population size. It sometimes seems obvious, in examining the raw data, that a wide deviation from the regression relationship evidenced by some small tracts is due to the sheer statistical instability of an index computed for small populations. However, the correction of all the regressions by weighting for tract size was too formidable a computation to undertake.

It seems plausible that the difficulty with area-unit size in this study is somewhat mitigated by confining most interpretations to relative comparisons, either for the same tracts or for groups of tracts somewhat similar in average size and size variability. In such a comparison each term of the comparison is affected in somewhat the same way, and the bias, if any, is a more or less constant one. Clearly, one would not be justified in making close comparisons of the present results with those of a study using, say, wards as the unit of observation.

The second problem, that of independence, is perhaps even more serious in its implications for the application of statistical criteria of significance. According to statistical theory the sampling error of a correlation coefficient is, roughly, inversely proportional to the square root of the number of pairs of observations on which it is computed. But this criterion is appropriate only for the case where

2. W. S. Robinson, "Ecological Correlations and the Behavior of Individuals," _American Sociological Review_, XV (June, 1950), 351-57; Herbert Menzel, "Comment on Robinson's 'Ecological Correlations and the Behavior of Individuals,'" _American Sociological Review_, XV (October, 1950), 674; Leo A. Goodman, "Ecological Regressions and Behavior of Individuals," _American Sociological Review_, XVIII (December, 1953), 663-64; Otis Dudley Duncan and Beverly Davis, "An Alternative to Ecological Correlation," _American Sociological Review_, XVIII (December, 1953), 665-66.

the X-values are mutually independent and the Y-values likewise. In terms of the present problem this means that knowing the index value for a given tract would not enable one to make a better-than-chance prediction of the value for another tract in the set. It is easy to see why this requirement is essential for application of the conventional error formula. Suppose that the analysis were based on five census tracts, each of them being internally homogeneous. Then suppose that each tract were divided into four new tracts, each having, by hypothesis, the same index value as its parent tract. Then in the first case one would test the obtained correlation for significance on the basis of five observations, but in the second, where an identical correlation would be obtained, on the basis of twenty observations. Clearly, the apparent difference in sampling reliability between the two cases is a mere artifact of the areal classification of the data. While no such simple, extreme case would arise in practice, there is undoubtedly a "space correlation" among neighboring tracts that has an analogous effect. Some empirical evidence on this follows.

For experimental purposes, an analysis was made of the figures on educational attainment for the piling-up tracts. For each tract in the piling-up set (except 386, which is located by itself on the Near West Side) a list was made of all other tracts in the set contiguous to it, including under the definition of "contiguity" contact at but one point. There were then 2 tracts with only 1 contiguous tract each, 3 with 2 contiguous tracts, 5 with 3 contiguous tracts, 10 with 4 contiguous tracts, 5 with 5 contiguous tracts, 1 with 6 contiguous tracts, 2 with 7 contiguous tracts, 2 with 8 contiguous tracts, and 1 with 9 contiguous tracts. Regression analyses were then carried out, comparing the index value in the given tract (Y) with the mean index value (X) for the tracts contiguous to it. In the first regression analysis both Y and X referred to 1950 data, and a correlation of .71 was obtained. Thus, approximately half (.71 squared) of the variance in tract values is accounted for by the mean value for contiguous tracts. This is indeed a considerable departure from strict independence. In the second regression analysis, Y referred to the year 1950 and X to the year 1940, and again a correlation of .71 was obtained. Thus, in this example at least, tract indexes in a given year were as closely related to indexes for surrounding tracts of a decade earlier as to the contemporaneous indexes of neighboring tracts. It will be recalled from chapter vii that the standardized index of educational attainment in 1950 was correlated with the 1940 index for the same tract to the extent of .80, not a great deal higher than the correlation, .71, based on 1940 indexes for surrounding tracts. To put the matter another way, one could infer the 1950 index of educational attainment for a given tract about as well from a knowledge of the educational attainment in contiguous tracts in 1940 as from information on the tract's own level of educational attainment in 1940.

The third regression analysis was directed to the hypothesis that a substantial proportion of the "space correlation" could be attributed to the fact that a given tract and its contiguous tracts have a similar zonal location. From chapter vii, one can ascertain that the 1950 mean percentage (standardized) with one year or more of high school was 5.9 points higher for Zone 5 than for Zone 3-4, and 13.6 points higher for Zone 6-7 than for Zone 3-4. A crude way of eliminating zonal variation, therefore, was to subtract 5.9 from the percentages for all tracts in Zone 5 and from the corresponding means of their contiguous tracts (not all of which, however, were necessarily in the same zone), and similarly to subtract 13.6 from the figures for tracts falling in Zone 6-7. With this translation of the three zonal sets of tracts to a common mean, the regression was computed with Y the "adjusted" 1950 value for a given tract and X the "adjusted" 1950 value for its contiguous tracts. The correlation between Y and X was found to be .42, materially lower than the correlation of .71 obtained before adjusting for zonal mean. Thus much of the "space correlation" is due to variation in level of educational attainment by zone. This suggests that the within-zone analyses carried through in chapter vii come closer to meeting the requirement of independence than do those for the entire set of tracts classified in a given stage of succession. Nevertheless, despite the crudeness of the zonal adjustment in this experimental calculation, it seems improbable that the "space correlation," or lack of independence among neighboring tracts, is wholly attributable to any simple gradient pattern, in view of the .42 correlation remaining after zonal adjustment.

A summary of the three regression analyses just described is as follows:

	M_Y	M_X	a	b	r
1. Y—1950 value, given tract X—1950 mean, contiguous tracts	37.6	38.0	0.9	0.97	.71
2. Y—1950 value, given tract X—1940 mean, contiguous tracts	37.6	26.7	12.6	0.94	.71
3. X and Y adjusted for zonal means: Y—1950 value, given tract X—1950 mean, contiguous tracts	31.1	31.5	7.8	0.74	.42

These results have both substantive and methodological implications. Substantively, they force one to recognize that the characteristic of "stability," which is emphasized throughout chapter vii, pertains not solely to the individual tract but depends to a significant degree upon its similarity to tracts in its general vicinity. The nature of this dependence is obscure, but one could hypothesize tentatively that a tract located in a generally homogeneous area would be more likely to manifest stability than one located in the midst of widely dissimilar and heterogeneous tracts. An effective means for testing this hypothesis remains to be found.

Methodologically, the foregoing results imply, of course, that the conventional tests of statistical significance are inapplicable to the kind of regression analyses employed in this study. Other procedures that assume independence, such as analysis of covariance, are, of course, likewise inapplicable. It should be pointed out that this technical obstacle to the use and interpretation of refined statistical procedures is not unique to the present study. It is, in fact, a generic problem of all studies employing areas as units of observation—despite the fact that many research workers have ignored the problem. To the writers' knowledge, mathematical statisticians have not produced a general solution to this problem that can be adapted to research designs based on census-tract data. The problem was, however, called to the statisticians' attention more than two decades ago.[3] Meanwhile, the somewhat analogous problem of lack of independence in the successive observations in a time series has received much attention, and there are well-known techniques, such as serial correlation, for coping with it. It is hoped that some fundamental work on the interpretation of "ecological regression" will be forthcoming to the aid of research workers whose materials seem to suggest a regression approach.

Some final remarks on the effect of the "space correlation" phenomenon on the conclusions and interpretations of this study: tests of significance were avoided, because of their evident inapplicability. The within-zone results seemingly are less subject to qualification on grounds of non-independence than those for complete sets of tracts. The problem of independence may be less important for sets of tracts, like those in the invasion or early-consolidation stages, which have a wider spatial scatter than the piling-up tracts do. In interpreting correlation and regression results, more attention was given to the patterning and consistency of findings for a considerable number of characteristics than to the absolute level of regression and correlation coefficients. Finally, all interpretations of possible causal relationships were cautious and tentative, in view of the limitations imposed on the statistical techniques by the nature of the problem. Because of all these considerations, the authors of this study have some degree of confidence in the validity and reliability of the conclusions stated. But two warnings are in order. First, the reader should be extremely cautious in pushing the interpretation of the study's data further than its authors have seen fit to do. Second, lacking the appropriate refined and powerful statistical tools suitable for a problem of the kind encountered here, one must content one's self with rather generalized, approximate, and sometimes vague conclusions. The study will prove to be eminently worthwhile if it serves

3.   Frederick F. Stephan, "Sampling Errors and the Interpretation of Social Data Ordered in Time and Space," Journal of the American Statistical Association, XXIX (March, 1934, suppl.), 165-66.

to stimulate some fundamental methodological research designed
to overcome the limitations imposed on investigations like this one.

Summary Statistics on Census-Tract
Characteristics, 1940 and 1950

List of Tables

Note

The following abbreviations are used in these tables:

wtd.: weighted mean
unwtd.: unweighted mean
obs.: observed
std.: standardized
wh-col. empl.: white-collar employment
home own: homeownership
mech. refrig.: mechanical refrigeration

Table I-1.—Means of Census-Tract Characteristics, by Stage of Succession, 1950 and 1940

Characteristic* and Year	Piling Up	Late Consolidation	Consolidation	Early Consolidation	Invasion
1950:					
Density, wtd.†. . .	540	332	236	213	385
Density, unwtd.† .	615	374	378	336	410
Crowding	31.2	24.8	21.7	26.4	16.6
Education, obs. . .	38.8	38.9	38.9	38.7	48.7
Education, std. . .	37.4	36.3	35.2	35.4	46.3
Unemployment . .	12.5	12.3	11.4	9.0	8.1
Wh-col. empl. . .	15.5	15.6	19.2	20.8	29.0
Home own, obs. .	9.6	14.0	16.6	16.6	17.9
Home own, std. . .	16.1	17.1	17.7	20.6	24.0
Rent (dollars) . . .	37.23	36.84	34.17	36.76	44.53
Central heating . .	73.1	63.3	50.3	61.8	80.0
Mech. refrig. . . .	64.3	68.5	69.0	66.8	83.9
1940:					
Density, wtd.† . .	467	248	193	169	342
Density, unwtd.† .	523	287	301	252	357
Crowding	25.3	14.4	8.2	12.0	8.9
Education, obs. . .	28.1	26.9	25.1	27.5	36.7
Education, std. . .	26.6	26.6	25.2	27.7	37.2
Unemployment . .	40.0	39.3	33.1	27.9	20.0
Wh-col. empl. . .	15.5	17.8	24.9	27.4	37.8
Home own, obs. .	5.9	13.8	15.3	15.2	14.4
Rent (dollars) . . .	24.79	22.57	18.90	20.35	28.30
Central heating . .	67.2	51.2	38.1	56.6	75.7
Mech. refrig. . . .	29.7	29.6	30.6	32.6	53.6

*See Appendix G for complete designations of characteristics.

†In hundreds of persons per square mile of gross land area; all other characteristics, except rent, are in percentage form.

Table I-2.—Means of Census-Tract Characteristics, by Color and Stage of Succession, 1950 and 1940

Characteristic* and Year	White				Non-white				
	Late Consolidation	Consolidation	Early Consolidation	Invasion	Piling Up	Late Consolidation	Consolidation	Early Consolidation	Invasion
1950:									
Crowding	18.8	12.5	16.6	12.0	31.2	25.0	25.6	33.6	25.7
Education, obs.	44.9	40.9	40.4	49.1	38.8	38.7	36.6	36.9	46.4
Education, std.	45.1	40.3	42.5	49.7	37.4	36.0	31.7	31.0	38.2
Unemployment	4.5	7.8	6.7	7.0	12.5	12.5	13.1	11.4	10.2
Wh-col. empl.	33.1	28.1	27.2	33.9	15.5	15.1	13.4	13.4	17.4
Home own, obs.	22.4	20.8	19.2	16.9	9.6	13.7	14.8	15.4	22.2
Home own, std.	15.1	17.4	19.3	20.8	16.1	17.3	16.4	20.4	31.4
Rent (dollars)	34.20	30.43	33.56	41.84	37.23	36.95	35.66	40.59	51.85
1940:									
Crowding	9.9	7.3	...	8.9	25.3	14.8	9.5	...	...
Education, obs.	31.8	27.4	...	36.7	28.1	25.9	22.3	...	...
Education, std.	35.4	27.8	...	37.2	26.6	25.3	21.6	...	...
Unemployment	20.7	26.4	...	20.0	40.0	41.4	44.4	...	...
Home own, obs.	33.1	20.3	17.1	14.4	5.9	12.1	7.9	7.6	...
Rent (dollars)	21.25	19.77	...	28.30	24.79	22.70	17.67	...	...

*See Appendix G for complete designations of characteristics.

Table I-3.—Means of Census-Tract Characteristics, by Stage of Succession and Area, 1950 and 1940

Characteristic* and Year	Piling Up			Late Consolidation			Consolidation			Early Consolidation		Invasion	
	Zone 3-4	Zone 5	Zone 6-7	Zone 2-3	Zone 4-5	Zone 6-14	North Side	West Side	South Side	North and West Side	South Side	West Side	South Side
1950:													
Density, wtd.†	650	636	447	275	453	308	426	324	209	277	161	412	358
Density, unwtd.†	597	642	606	296	437	374	553	390	296	404	257	444	374
Crowding	35.4	30.5	27.1	34.0	24.9	17.4	14.3	23.6	22.9	28.4	24.0	20.9	12.0
Education, obs.	32.6	37.8	46.6	29.0	34.4	51.4	41.0	32.8	43.7	31.5	47.0	41.0	47.0
Education, std.	31.1	37.0	44.7	25.9	32.4	48.7	37.0	28.6	40.7	29.0	42.8	38.7	54.5
Unemployment	14.8	11.9	10.5	15.2	12.4	9.8	10.2	13.0	10.4	9.1	8.8	9.2	7.0
Wh-col. empl.	14.4	14.7	17.8	12.3	12.4	21.6	23.6	15.6	20.8	17.7	24.6	22.9	35.4
Home own, obs.	10.3	9.5	9.0	5.7	12.2	22.5	7.9	11.8	24.6	13.8	19.8	14.0	22.0
Home own, std.	15.1	16.7	16.5	11.3	16.4	22.6	12.7	15.7	21.5	19.1	22.5	22.1	26.0
Rent (dollars)	33.08	36.40	42.74	31.72	34.07	43.72	29.18	31.54	38.61	34.92	38.90	40.64	48.67
Central heating	60.6	73.6	86.2	49.0	59.6	78.4	38.2	42.9	62.1	55.9	68.7	76.7	83.4
Mech. refrig.	47.7	67.7	78.8	54.5	66.2	82.1	73.9	62.0	73.7	63.1	71.1	77.4	90.9
1940:													
Density, wtd.†	398	584	427	186	340	240	354	276	163	217	131	373	312
Density, unwtd.†	418	581	575	197	344	303	443	330	218	294	203	387	326
Crowding	23.2	25.7	27.1	13.2	15.7	14.2	5.0	8.8	8.8	12.8	11.1	10.7	7.1
Education, obs.	23.3	25.5	36.2	18.7	22.4	38.0	22.5	20.1	30.8	21.7	34.3	28.4	45.4
Education, std.	23.1	24.0	33.3	18.6	22.5	37.2	22.4	19.8	31.4	21.7	34.7	29.0	45.9
Unemployment	50.0	38.9	30.0	46.0	44.4	28.8	33.8	37.4	28.9	33.2	21.6	24.5	15.2
Wh-col. empl.	15.5	15.1	15.9	13.7	18.2	20.8	26.9	22.4	26.4	24.9	30.4	32.9	43.1
Home own, obs.	5.9	5.3	6.5	5.0	8.4	26.2	10.5	11.1	21.1	12.9	18.0	10.9	18.2
Rent (dollars)	19.64	24.39	30.88	17.66	21.03	28.04	15.58	16.46	22.49	17.75	23.37	22.55	34.40
Central heating	53.2	66.8	82.9	31.8	48.6	69.4	19.1	34.5	49.0	49.8	64.4	72.1	79.5
Mech. refrig.	14.3	28.1	48.4	12.6	22.0	50.8	25.3	23.4	39.5	24.5	42.1	37.1	71.2

*See Appendix G for complete designations of characteristics.

†Hundreds of persons per square mile of gross land area; all other characteristics, except rent, are in percentage form.

350

Table I-4.—Means of Census-Tract Characteristics, by Color, Stage of Succession, and Area, 1950 and 1940

Characteristic,* Year, and Color	Piling Up			Late Consolidation			Consolidation			Early Consolidation		Invasion	
	Zone 3-4	Zone 5	Zone 6-7	Zone 2-3	Zone 4-5	Zone 6-14	North Side	West Side	South Side	North and West Side	South Side	West Side	South Side
1950													
White:													
Crowding	.....	.....	.....	.....	.....	.....	8.6	14.6	12.0	21.5	11.0	15.3	8.4
Education, obs.	.....	.....	.....	.....	.....	.....	42.2	33.5	47.2	32.5	49.6	42.0	56.6
Education, std.	.....	.....	.....	.....	.....	.....	40.6	31.3	48.7	32.6	54.1	42.6	57.2
Unemployment	.....	.....	.....	.....	.....	.....	7.0	9.4	6.8	7.1	6.3	8.1	5.9
Wh-col. empl.	.....	.....	.....	.....	.....	.....	29.6	25.2	30.3	23.6	31.4	27.1	41.3
Home own, obs.	.....	.....	.....	.....	.....	.....	10.4	15.6	29.7	16.9	22.0	12.9	21.2
Home own, std.	.....	.....	.....	.....	.....	.....	15.5	16.7	18.8	19.1	19.5	19.2	22.6
Rent (dollars)	.....	.....	.....	.....	.....	.....	26.90	27.45	34.63	33.70	33.39	37.83	46.12
Non-white:													
Crowding	35.4	30.5	27.1	34.2	25.0	17.7	19.0	29.1	25.0	36.0	30.8	32.5	18.6
Education, obs.	32.6	37.8	46.6	22.7	34.4	51.2	38.0	29.8	42.5	30.4	44.4	38.9	54.4
Education, std.	31.1	37.0	44.7	25.3	32.2	48.6	31.6	24.8	38.2	25.5	37.4	30.6	46.3
Unemployment	14.8	11.9	10.5	15.7	12.5	9.9	13.1	14.7	11.7	10.6	12.3	11.4	9.0
Wh-col. empl.	14.4	14.7	17.8	11.2	12.1	21.3	13.4	10.4	16.2	10.5	16.9	12.7	22.5
Home own, obs.	10.3	14.7	9.0	5.4	12.0	22.0	5.8	9.6	23.3	12.2	19.1	17.0	27.8
Home own, std.	15.1	16.7	16.5	8.1	16.5	22.8	10.5	13.7	21.3	18.7	22.5	28.7	34.2
Rent (dollars)	33.08	36.40	42.74	32.21	34.00	43.69	30.06	33.92	39.53	38.87	42.59	48.92	54.96
1940													
White:													
Crowding, obs.	.....	.....	.....	8.8	12.8	7.7	4.6	10.0	5.8	.....	.....	10.7	7.1
Education, obs.	.....	.....	.....	29.6	31.4	28.0	22.6	23.3	33.2	.....	.....	28.4	45.4
Education, std.	.....	.....	.....	37.9	35.8	33.0	23.3	23.7	33.5	.....	.....	29.0	45.9
Unemployment	.....	.....	.....	24.3	24.4	14.1	31.0	31.7	19.5	.....	.....	24.5	15.2
Home own, obs.	.....	.....	.....	28.4	30.4	39.5	13.3	16.3	26.8	15.4	19.0	10.9	18.2
Rent (dollars)	.....	.....	.....	18.97	23.14	22.78	15.82	17.33	23.63	.....	.....	22.55	34.40
Non-white:													
Crowding, obs.	23.4	25.7	27.1	13.7	16.2	14.4	6.2	7.2	13.0	.....	.....	.....	.....
Education, obs.	23.3	25.5	36.2	12.5	21.3	38.6	17.8	16.9	29.1	.....	.....	.....	.....
Education, std.	23.1	24.0	33.3	15.3	21.1	37.5	16.7	15.8	29.0	.....	.....	.....	.....
Unemployment	50.0	38.9	30.0	50.1	46.4	25.5	48.1	48.2	39.4	.....	.....	.....	.....
Home own, obs.	5.9	5.3	6.5	2.6	6.4	25.5	1.0	2.0	16.1	3.4	12.4	.....	.....
Rent (dollars)	19.64	24.39	30.88	17.72	20.87	28.50	14.69	17.15	19.36	.....	.....	.....	.....

*See Appendix G for complete designations of characteristics.

351

Table I-5.—Within-Stage Regression Coefficients for 1950 on 1940 Census-Tract Characteristics, by Stage of Succession and Color

Characteristic* and Color	Average Within-Stage Coefficient	Piling Up	Late Consolidation	Consolidation	Early Consolidation	Invasion
Total population:						
Density	1.04	0.96	0.99	1.08	1.34	1.03
Crowding	1.07	0.56	0.92	2.74	1.22	1.26
Education, std.	0.83	0.75	1.05	0.93	0.73	0.75
Unemployment	0.21	0.15	0.17	0.29	0.17	0.31
Wh-col. empl.	0.82	0.79	0.53	0.78	0.95	0.86
Home own, obs.	0.93	1.03	0.65	1.21	0.95	1.11
Rent (dollars)	0.85	0.93	0.81	1.01	0.97	0.74
Central heating	0.85	0.88	0.80	0.87	0.90	0.80
Mech. refrig.	0.63	0.90	0.66	0.67	0.69	0.44
White:						
Crowding	1.20	...	...	1.34	...	1.14
Education, std.	0.81	...	...	0.83	...	0.79
Unemployment	0.22	...	...	0.18	...	0.30
Home own, obs.	1.19	...	...	1.36	1.06	1.09
Rent	0.97	...	...	1.09	...	0.92
Non-white:						
Crowding	0.74	0.56	0.93	0.99	...	...
Education, std.	0.90	0.75	1.02	0.88	...	...
Unemployment	0.19	0.15	0.17	0.21	...	...
Home own, obs.	0.71	1.03	0.60	0.99	0.48	...
Rent	1.01	0.93	0.86	1.49	...	...

*See Appendix G for complete designations of characteristics.

Table I-6.—Correlations between 1950 and 1940 Census-Tract Characteristics, by Color and Stage of Succession

Characteristic* and Color	Piling Up†	Late Consolidation	Consolidation	Early Consolidation	Invasion‡
Total:					
Density	.92	.92	.88	.89	.96
Crowding	.64	.58	.84	.75	.86
Education, obs. .	.83	.89	.75	.88	.94
Education, std. .	.80	.92	.82	.80	.89
Unemployment .	.48	.60	.70	.42	.76
Wh-col. empl. .	.73	.53	.73	.92	.92
Home own, obs..	.73	.86	.94	.93	.97
Rent	.89	.71	.78	.78	.86
Central heating .	.98	.94	.88	.97	.93
Mech. refrig. . .	.75	.75	.74	.69	.80
White:					
Crowding	. . .	.12	.64	. . .	.89
Education, obs..	. . .	.12	.57	. . .	.95
Education, std. .	. . .	.26	.55	. . .	.90
Unemployment .	. . .	.27	.36	. . .	.72
Home own, obs..	. . .	.48	.83	.91	.93
Rent	. . .	.38	.82	. . .	.90
Non-white:					
Crowding	.64	.61	.42	. . .	. . .
Education, obs. .	.83	.90	.71	. . .	. . .
Education, std. .	.80	.94	.77	. . .	. . .
Unemployment .	.48	.62	.65	. . .	. . .
Home own, obs..	.73	.84	.95	.61	. . .
Rent	.89	.76	.75	. . .	. . .

*See Appendix G for complete designations of characteristics.

†Correlations assumed to be essentially the same for non-white and total, since population was essentially non-white in both years.

‡Correlations for whites are between 1950 white population and 1940 total (essentially white) population.

Table I-7.—Correlations between 1950 and 1940 Census-Tract Characteristics, by Stage of Succession and Area

Characteristic*	Piling Up			Late Consolidation			Consolidation			Early Consolidation		Invasion	
	Zone 3-4	Zone 5	Zone 6-7	Zone 2-3	Zone 4-5	Zone 6-14	North Side	West Side	South Side	North and West Side	South Side	West Side	South Side
Density........	.93	.99	.98	.92	.84	.99	.94	.68	.92	.88	.90	.95	.96
Crowding......	.55	.91	.93	.70	.61	.94	.55	.89	.83	.75	.81	.88	.78
Education, obs. .	.66	.81	.90	.61	.92	.76	.43	.62	.82	.85	.84	.82	.93
Education, std. .	.63	.79	.90	.55	.91	.90	.63	.63	.87	.78	.72	.63	.87
Unemployment .	-.23	.57	.80	.49	.22	.80	.69	.64	.75	.34	.72	.72	.79
Wh-col. empl. .	.70	.88	.64	.48	-.34	.92	.87	.34	.74	.81	.89	.89	.93
Home own, obs. .	.32	.44	.95	.86	.86	.82	.01	.85	.97	.83	.96	.90	.98
Rent........	.72	.97	.86	.53	.86	.44	-.16	.76	.85	.71	.85	.70	.89
Central heating .	.97	.99	.99	.85	.98	.92	.18	.92	.91	.98	.95	.92	.95
Mech. refrig. .	.71	.84	.38	.49	.83	.60	.34	.89	.76	.61	.75	.77	.89

*See Appendix G for complete designations of characteristics.

354

Bogue, Donald J. An Estimate of Metropolitan Chicago's Future Population, 1955 to 1965. Chicago: Chicago Community Inventory, and Scripps Foundation for Research in Population Problems, 1955.

Bogue, Donald J., and Duncan, Beverly. "A Composite Method for Estimating Postcensal Population of Small Areas by Age, Sex, and Color" (hectographed document, Population Research and Training Center, University of Chicago). Chicago, 1956.

Burgess, Ernest W. "The Growth of the City," in R. E. Park, E. W. Burgess, and R. D. McKenzie, The City. Chicago: University of Chicago Press, 1925.

---. "Residential Segregation in American Cities," Annals of the American Academy of Political and Social Science, CXL (November, 1928), 105-15.

Chicago Commission on Race Relations. The Negro in Chicago. Chicago: University of Chicago Press, 1922.

Cressey, Paul F. "Population Succession in Chicago, 1898-1930," American Journal of Sociology, XLIV (July, 1938), 59-69.

Drake, St. Clair, and Cayton, Horace R. Black Metropolis. New York: Harcourt, Brace & Co., 1945.

Duncan, Beverly. Growth and Redistribution of the Resident Population in the Chicago Standard Metropolitan Area. Chicago: Chicago Plan Commission, 1954.

Duncan, Otis Dudley, and Davis, Beverly. "An Alternative to Ecological Correlation," American Sociological Review, XVIII (December, 1953), 665-66.

---. Contributions to the Theory of Segregation Indexes. ("Urban Analysis Series," No. 14.) Chicago: Chicago Community Inventory, University of Chicago, 1953.

355

356 / The Negro Population of Chicago

Duncan, Otis Dudley, and Duncan, Beverly. "A Methodological Analysis of Segregation Indexes," American Sociological Review, XX (April, 1955), 210-17.

---. "Residential Distribution and Occupational Stratification," American Journal of Sociology, LX (March, 1955), 493-503.

---. Chicago's Negro Population: Characteristics and Trends (a report by the Chicago Community Inventory to the Chicago Plan Commission and the Office of the Housing and Redevelopment Coordinator). Chicago, 1956.

Ford, Richard G. "Population Succession in Chicago," American Journal of Sociology, LVI (September, 1950), 156-60.

Frazier, E. Franklin. The Negro Family in Chicago. Chicago: University of Chicago Press, 1932.

---. "Negro Harlem: An Ecological Study," American Journal of Sociology, XLIII (July, 1937), 72-88.

Freedman, Ronald. Recent Migration to Chicago. Chicago: University of Chicago Press, 1950.

Gehlke, C. E., and Biehl, Katherine. "Certain Effects of Grouping upon the Size of the Correlation Coefficient in Census Tract Material," Journal of the American Statistical Association, XXIX (March, 1934, suppl.), 169-70.

Gibbard, Harold A. "The Status Factor in Residential Successions," American Journal of Sociology, XLVI (May, 1941), 835-42.

Goodman, Leo A. "Ecological Regressions and Behavior of Individuals," American Sociological Review, XVIII (December, 1953), 663-64.

Hauser, Philip M. "Differential Fertility, Mortality, and Net Reproduction in Chicago, 1930." Unpublished Ph.D. dissertation, University of Chicago, 1938.

Hauser, Philip M., and Kitagawa, Evelyn M. Local Community Fact Book for Chicago, 1950. Chicago: Chicago Community Inventory, 1953.

Hawley, Amos H. "Dispersion versus Segregation: Apropos of a Solution of Race Problems," Papers of the Michigan Academy of Science, Arts, and Letters, XXX (1944), 667-74.

Kennedy, Louise V. The Negro Peasant Turns Cityward. New York: Columbia University Press, 1930.

Kitagawa, Evelyn M. "Differential Fertility in Chicago, 1920-40." Unpublished Ph.D. dissertation, University of Chicago, 1951.

---. "Differential Fertility in Chicago, 1920-40," American Journal of Sociology, LVIII (March, 1953), 481-92.

Lindstrom, Frederick B. "The Negro Invasion of the Washington Park Subdivision." Unpublished M.A. thesis, University of Chicago, 1941.

Mayer, Albert J. "Differentials in Length of Life, City of Chicago, 1880 to 1940." Unpublished Ph.D. dissertation, University of Chicago, 1950.

Mayer, Albert J., and Hauser, Philip M. "Class Differentials in Expectation of Life at Birth," Revue de l'Institut International de Statistique, Vol. XVIII (1950).

Menzel, Herbert. "Comment on Robinson's 'Ecological Correlations and the Behavior of Individuals,'" American Sociological Review, XV (October, 1950), 674.

Nesbitt, George B. "Relocating Negroes from Urban Slum Clearance Sites," Land Economics, XXV (August, 1949), 275-88.

Ogden, Mary Elaine. The Chicago Negro Community: A Statistical Description. Chicago: U.S. Work Projects Administration, Illinois, 1939.

Redick, Richard W. "Population Growth and Distribution in Central Cities, 1940-1950," American Sociological Review, XXI (February, 1956), 38-43.

Robinson, Corienne K. "Relationship between Condition of Dwellings and Rentals, by Race," Journal of Land and Public Utility Economics, XXII (August, 1946), 296-300.

Robinson, W. S. "Ecological Correlations and the Behavior of Individuals," American Sociological Review, XV (June, 1950), 351-57.

Ross, Frank A., and Kennedy, Louise V. A Bibliography of Negro Migration. New York: Columbia University Press, 1934.

Schietinger, E. F. "Race and Residential Market Values in Chicago," Land Economics, XXX (November, 1954), 301-8.

Scott, Estelle Hill. Occupational Changes among Negroes in Chicago. Chicago: U.S. Work Projects Administration, Illinois, 1939.

Star, Shirley A. "Interracial Tension in Two Areas of Chicago: An Exploratory Approach to the Measurement of Interracial Tension." Unpublished Ph.D. dissertation, University of Chicago, 1950.

Stephan, Frederick F. "Sampling Errors and the Interpretation of Social Data Ordered in Time and Space," Journal of the American Statistical Association, XXIX (March, 1934, suppl.), 165-66.

Thompson, Charles H. (ed.). The Relative Status of the Negro Population in the United States. Yearbook Number, Journal of Negro Education, Vol. XXII (Summer, 1953).

U.S. Bureau of the Census. Negro Population of the United States, 1790-1915. Washington: Government Printing Office, 1918.

---. Negroes in the United States, 1920-1932. Washington: Government Printing Office, 1935.

U.S. Housing and Home Finance Agency. Housing of the Nonwhite Population, 1940 to 1950. Washington: Government Printing Office, 1952.

Wallace, David A. "Residential Concentration of Negroes in Chicago." Unpublished Ph.D. dissertation, Harvard University, 1953 (available on microfilm at University of Chicago Library).

Weaver, Robert C. The Negro Ghetto. New York: Harcourt, Brace & Co., 1948.

Woofter, T. J., Jr. Negro Problems in Cities. New York: Doubleday, Doran & Co., 1928.

[Printed in U.S.A.]